Tales from a Grandfather

—from the joys of a small country town to the rewards of world-wide engineering.

William B. Ball

First published by Dog Ear Publishing
4010 W. 86th Street, Ste H
Indianapolis, IN 46268
www.dogearpublishing.net

ISBN: 978-159858-537-7

This book is printed on acid-free paper.

Printed in the United States of America

Table of Contents

List of Illustrations

1 Chalmette Aluminum Plant, Louisiana on the banks of the Mississippi
2 Valco Aluminum Plant, Ghana, Africa
3 Akosombo Hydro Project, Ghana, providing power for Valco
4 Nordberg gas generators erected to power Chalmette Aluminum
5 National Southwire Smelter, Kentucky
6 P.T. Semen Cibinong, Cement plant, Indonesia
7 El Sobrante Outlet Works, San Pablo Reservoir, California, built for EBMUD
8 Industrias Kaiser Argentina (IKA) integrated automobile plant, Cordoba, Argentina

Epilogue
60th Anniversary – Helen & Bill

<h1 style="text-align:center">Prologue</h1>

Dear Vanessa and Ariel,

In 1972, your grandmother Helen suggested that I write a brief story of my life and leave for our grandchildren a trail in the dust of the past, to give you an idea of what those times were like and what they meant to me. The result has been that one memory has led to another in greater detail than I would have expected. It has been a nostalgic trip filled with joy, a little pride in what I have accomplished, and, of course, tears.

KANSAS AND MICHIGAN

As a part of this prologue I include what I know and some of what I can imagine of my antecedents and yours.

In 1887, Nicholas and Priscilla Rich, having sold their home and farm in Kansas, packed a few precious belongings into the covered wagon Nicholas had built and joined a wagon train headed for the promised land of California, where the fertile soil and the plentitude of sun and water made year-round crops a reality.

It is not hard to imagine the serious expressions on the faces of your great-great-grandparents as they faced the long journey ahead, contrasted with the excitement and joy of their three young children as they readied for the big adventure.

Mindful of the terrible ordeal of the ill-fated Donner Party in 1847, departure was scheduled so that the crossing of the formidable Sierra Nevada Mountains would be accomplished in summer. The trip probably was uneventful, and as the train split up in the foothills the Rich family may have passed what was later known as Camp Far West. Today there is a stone memorial e to the segment of the Donner Party that survived. From that point it was only a few miles to the farm Nicholas either bought or homesteaded, just outside the small town of Wheatland, founded in 1847, forty miles north of Sacramento. The family grew to include seven children (see illustrations), and all worked hard on the farm to contribute to its success. Each of these offspring had successful lives as adults, with the exception of Rosetta, who died at age thirty. Jim, the oldest, opened a paint company in Oakland and, upon retirement, farmed in Woodland. Bill became a lawyer and later was elected to the California Senate, where he was a highly respected member and speaker for eighteen years. Liberta, or Bee as she was known, became head bookkeeper for a large truck manufacturer in Oakland. She was later to be my mother, and still later your great-grandmother. Jesse and Etta, known as Mimi, were twins. Jesse did well as an insurance salesman, and Mimi married Ralph Waldo, who was the San Francisco representative of a New York chemical and dye company. Henry, the youngest, secured a position with the Sacramento District of the Corps of Engineers after a course in engineering. He later rose to the position of manager of that division and, after retirement, became a farmer near Sacramento. During World War II he instituted innovations in the planting and growing of rice.

Ten years after Nicholas and Priscilla had packed to leave Kansas, there was a stirring in a family home near Lansing, Michigan. Cary, Bert, and Bob Ball, attracted by news of the fast-growing lumber business in Oregon, set off to seek their fortunes. There is no record of the journey, but it is not hard to imagine their long and arduous trip with no more than a few dollars in their pockets and one old suitcase among the three. In the winter of 1896 they arrived in Salem, Oregon, and almost immediately found jobs in a big lumber mill near that city.

By 1905, the brothers had gone their separate ways, with Cary remaining at the mill; Bert (William Bertran Ball), who was to be my dad, moving to San Francisco to take a job as precision machinist with Risdon Iron Works; and Bob leaving the lumber business to open a barber shop near Sonora in the California gold country. I still use a pair of barber scissors Bob gave my dad in 1925.

Cary rose to become manager of the mill where he got his first job and, in 1922, he spent two years in Japan supervising the building and start of operations of that country's first major lumber mill. He later married the widow Evenson, who had two children, Shirley and Franklin, from her former marriage. I liked Cary and his new family, especially the attractive, blond Shirley. I thought she was the cat's meow until I met your grand-mother. After that Shirley became only a distant memory.

The 1906 San Francisco earthquake destroyed both the Risdon Iron Works and Bert's boarding house. All my dad salvaged from that cata-strophic day were the clothes he was wearing, two ten-dollar gold coins half melted together in some blaze and found lying in a gutter of flowing water, and a violin and bow, undamaged amidst some abandoned debris. The lat-ter two items are family heirlooms.

Homeless and jobless, Bert took a ferry to Oakland, where he found work as a chauffeur. Although there is no real evidence, the vehicle he drove may have been one from a Buick dealer who made his autos available to people in the terrible days after the quake. That dealer was the man who later became the owner of Seabiscuit, the famous racehorse.

How and when Bert met Lib is not known, but you can see how the unrelated movements of two different families and the vagaries of chance led to your creation. In any event, Bert and Lib were married on June 17, 1906. I was born June 21, 1915. Early in 1916, our little family moved to Wheatland to assist Lib's parents in the transition from farming to retire-ment. It was a move made necessary because no other members of the Rich family wanted to take on that responsibility. However difficult the move was for my parents, it was the first step in a wonderful childhood for me. The small town and the nearby river were my kingdom, and I ruled there for eighteen years.

I begin this story at the age of four, a time in my life that today allows me only brief snippets of memory. I liken it to a puzzle with numbered dots. When you connect the dots in numerical sequence there appears a picture. The dots are my memories and the lines are what my parents later told me. In the first chapters there will be much of the dot-line picture, but after that the story will be from my memory only, with no research except to use my old resume to check chronology.

It is now, with much love, that I give you the Ball, Rich, Hederman, and Buffum saga in *Tales from a Grandfather*.

Rich Family Reunion 1953
Siblings standing left to right: William P. Rich (2nd oldest),
Henry M. Rich (5th), Etta (Mimi) Waldo (4th twin), Liberta C. Ball (3rd),
James M. Rich (oldest), Jesse Rich (4th twin)

Rich Family Montage Assembled 1953 for Reunion
Pictures circa 1903: Nickolas & Priscilla Rich, James, unknown, William
& Rosetta, Liberta, Henry, Etta & Jesse

Chapter One

The Drowning

*I*t was a hot summer morning. All the hands had been fed and the day's work begun. The big old farmhouse stood in the midst of some ancient oaks, their limbs bent like arthritic fingers, and, around back, the apple trees were loaded with growing fruit. Off to the right ran the county road, fenced with weather-beaten wood posts and rusty barbed wire. Back a ways was the wooden bridge over the dry wash, where water ran only during winter. I will always remember that old bridge for its music. It had one tune for autos and another for steel-wheeled wagons, and both were lovely to hear. The rattle and rumble was an announcement of someone's arrival, either headed for the ranch or on down the road, but in either case it was worth a quick dash to a window or other vantage point to see who was coming or going. Speeds on the dusty graveled roads in those days were twenty-five to forty miles per hour in an auto and, contrary to what you may think, that was fast. In a wagon, five or six miles per hour was tops. Those old roads were made by excavating two ditches and piling the resulting material between. The roadbed was crowned to drain rainwater, and a layer of gravel was placed to hold the mud in winter and reduce the dust in summer. Needless to say, many an unwary driver wound up in the ditch. (See illustration.)

This was the setting for the frightening adventure I was to experience before I had my fourth birthday. One morning, I was out with my best friend looking for something to do. We were just wandering down from the house toward the fields thinking about nothing, and suddenly it happened! She fell in! The water was muddy and looked syrupy as it swirled swiftly along and, try as I might, I couldn't reach her. I looked for a stick or something to hold out to her, but there was nothing. I ran along the bank, nearly slipped and fell, got my shoes muddy . . . what to do? I stood back from the bank. There was not a sound as I stood paralyzed, looking at my poor friend. Then, somewhere, a dog barked, insects buzzed, out in the field the tractor and harvester clanked along. The bridge rumbled as a car came down the road and brought me back to reality.

Almost as if in a dream, with my feet weighing a hundred pounds each, I ran back to the house, burst through the screen door and shouted for help. Mother came running from the kitchen, and after my frantic explanation we went out to the scene of the tragedy where, with a rake, we pulled my friend from the water where she had caught on a diversion gate in the irrigation ditch. Being a rag doll, it took my friend only a few hours to dry out after being hung out on the clothesline in the hot sun. It took me a little longer to get over the scolding I got from Mother.

The events you just read are real, and I do believe I have that memory even though I was not quite four years old at the time. It may be that my parents told me of the affair when I was older. In any case, it all took place on a rice farm where Dad harvested and Mother cooked for the harvest hands. We actually lived in a wagon-trailer, which I will tell you about in the next chapter.

1918 Road

Chapter Two

The Wheat Farm

*I*n The Drowning, I mentioned the harvesting and cooking for harvest hands. Now I'll tell you about what my parents were doing at the farm and how harvesting was done in 1918. A few other details of our life at that time may also be of interest.

Harvesting wheat then was not as simple as it is now, and more equipment and help were needed to get the job done. There was a tractor, a harvester, a wagon or truck, and a raker (see illustration). To manage all of this required a tractor driver, a swamper (oiler), a header tender, a sack sewer, a wagon or truck driver, two loaders, and a rake driver, for a total of eight men. Often there were two harvesters working, and this allowed a single truck and rake to do the job for both. Some of the crew slept at home and some in the bunk house, but all ate in the kitchen—all twelve of them!

Dad was boss of the crews and got a percentage of the harvest from the elderly couple who owned the farm. He had a partner, and between them they worked several farms. This arrangement worked well for a few years until the partner cashed in one year's crop and took off for parts unknown. When finally found, the culprit had spent nearly all the money, leaving Dad holding a large empty bag. Facing financial restrictions and the feeling that farming was not his greatest love, Dad looked elsewhere for gainful employment, which will lead to the next part of this tale. For now, however, we'll go on with wheat, tractors, trailers, and cooking.

We began our day in the early morning before the rooster crowed. For Mother that meant about three a.m. The big old woodstove, with coals banked the night before, came to life with fresh wood and breakfast preparations got underway. Pies had been baked the day before, and it took at least four to start the day. Biscuits were a must, and three dozen was just about right. Not just little ones, mind you, but good man-sized ones, three or four inches across. Mother used to say to the hands, "Anyone who opens my biscuits with a knife won't get another one. Break them open with your fingers so they won't be tough." Three dozen eggs were fried, sunny side up, accompanied by mounds of hand-sliced bacon or ham, and all were washed down with milk and boiled-on-the-stove coffee. I must tell you about the milk; it was kept in a five-gallon can in the gunnysack drip cooler out on the back screen porch. For meals, it was poured into half-gallon pitchers. It had to be stirred frequently as it sat or the cream would start to rise. And this was even after some cream had been separated out to make butter!

Dinner was at noon, give or take a little, for the noon stop depended upon the harvester being near the house. Supper was around nine p.m., and after a short gabfest everyone "hit the hay." The working day started when it got light and ceased when it got dark. A long day of hard work, and it didn't stop for a weekend of skiing or other recreation until the season was over. After that, there was equipment maintenance, hunting, fishing, Saturday night dances, and other homemade entertainment.

My first memory of the harvest days is of living in a trailer. This was not a fancy aluminum affair with a butane heater stove, an oven, and all those other goodies. Rather, it was quite primitive; perhaps a forerunner of the modern vacation trailer, but built for moving around with a team of horses. A sketch of this trailer as I remember it is included at the end of this tale (see illustration). It was a wooden box with a curved, corrugated iron roof. There was a door at the rear and it had a couple of small windows, while inside was a tiny woodstove, a double bed, a small bunk, and a washstand with a basin and water pitcher.

Two things only do I recall with any clarity about life in the trailer. One was a big book that Mother read to me. It was the story of a big red automobile, a very fast one capable of climbing the steepest of hills with ease. I knew it was fast because it was an open car and the passengers' hair blew back in the wind. As I write this now, there is the faint, fleeting memory of the two of us sitting on the double bed, propped up on pillows and reading that book for the umpteenth time. The other thing I recall was the wasps' nest under the roof near the door. The paper-like cone hanging by a small cord lingers in memory to this day.

Cchuffff-wheeezzz-pluuunnk-bang!-punchel-punchel-punchel-punchel at around four a.m. announced that the recalcitrant old beast of a tractor had, indeed, been coaxed to face another day of work. You can see a sketch of it along with the trailer, and I'll tell you how to start it in case it may be necessary one day. First, take a small can of gasoline and fill the little cup at each cylinder with about half an ounce. When they are all full, open the petcocks to drain the fluid into the cylinders. Don't forget to close them! Quickly move to the flywheel (which is just behind the engine and in front of the seat and steering wheel). Insert the steel bar into one of the holes in the wheel and give it a big tug to turn the engine. I should warn you to retard the spark before turning the wheel—because if you don't, the engine may backfire and jerk the bar violently from your hands and jam it into the well beneath the wheel. This can cause ordinarily nice men to say terrible things about all machinery in general and about that tractor in particular. That is where I learned to say some things not said in mixed company. Now you can start a tractor, 1918 vintage!

When I think back to those times, I cannot but be amazed at the amount of work everyone did each day—all without dishwashers, microwave ovens, clothes washers and dryers, refrigerators, and other conveniences. Women got up before the men, worked all day, and finally hit the hay after everyone else was asleep! No movies, no television, no radio, no supermarket, no diaper service, no air-conditioning, and no telephone to call someone to share your cares. In spite of these things, people were happy. They created their own amusement and lived in a different way than we do today, and, just perhaps, their way might have been better. Anyway, that's how it was circa 1919 or 1920 on a farm.

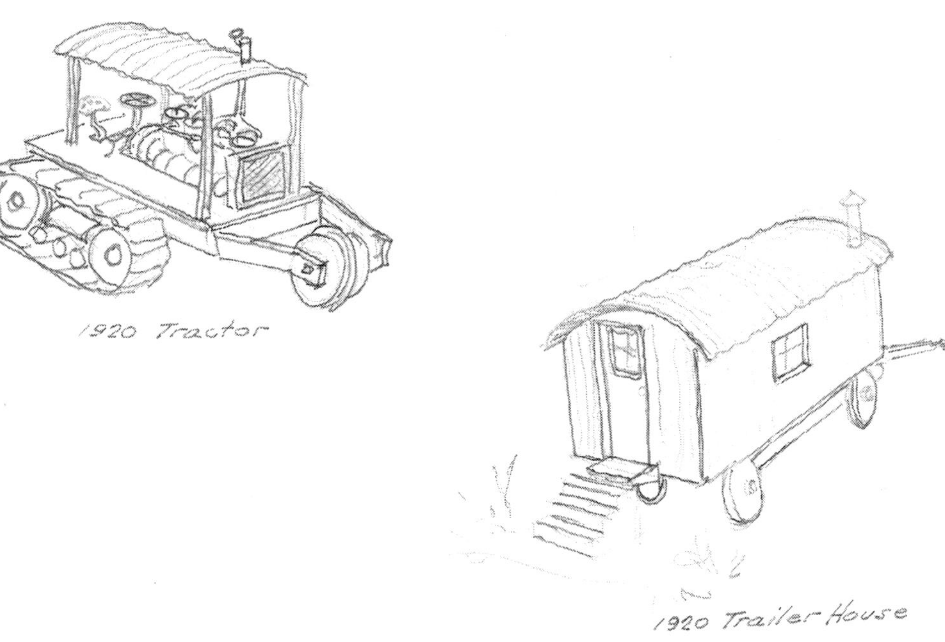

1920 Tractor & Trailer House

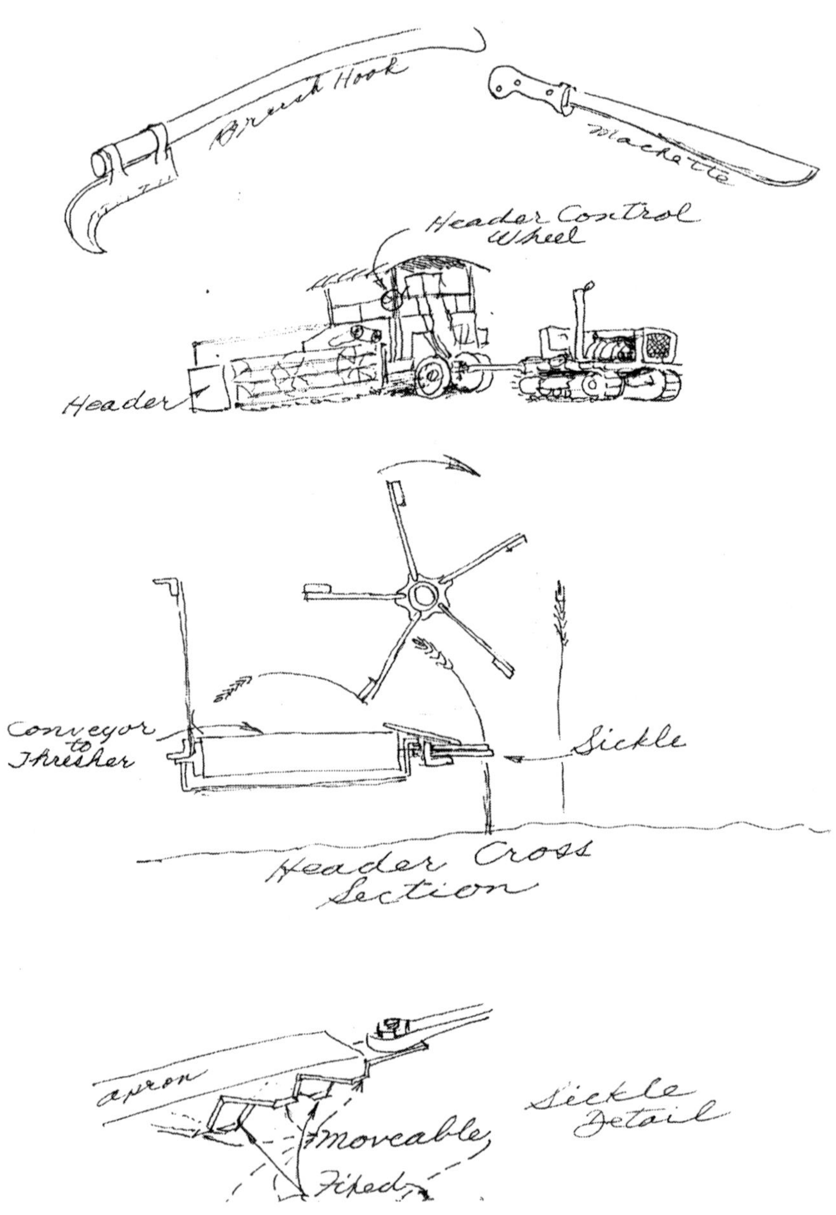

Harvesting Tools

Chapter Three

The Big House

After the house on Dry Creek, we moved to the Big House in Wheatland. This was a three story edifice right on the edge of town (see illustration). There was nothing beyond it except for fields and, about a mile away, Bear River. The town of Wheatland, a small community of five hundred souls, surrounded by farmland and sitting at an elevation of fifty feet above sea level, was to be my home for the next fourteen years. We were to have three houses during that time, all of them now remembered with much love. I was five years old when we moved to the Big House, so only a few things stand out as recalled events for me to tell you about in this tale.

The move was prompted by the need to be with my grandparents, who had lived in the Big House for ten years, and the need for Dad to look into a new activity. Grandfather still did a bit of farming, including taking care of two cows, two horses, maybe twelve chickens, and four pigs. He was beginning to lose his eyesight and was having cardiac difficulties. Grandmother's health was frail, though she did not have any specific problems. Nicholas and Priscilla were both made of stern stuff, she being the one who always had cookies in the jar, and he being the lean, tough autocrat. As I said, Grandfather still farmed a bit, but only with a team of horses, and he did no heavy work like plowing. For Grandmother, the big old house was too much of a chore even though the two of them had once come out of Kansas by wagon train.

To clarify the location of the house, I must point out that about two hundred feet to the south, toward Bear River, the land dropped off steeply to a slough, through which there was a flow of water until early summer. A roughly graded road ran from the back of the barn down the slope to a bridge that spanned the stream and led to the fields where, one sunny morning, Grandfather was headed to bring in some hay. I had helped a bit as the team was hitched up, and Grandfather and I walked along with the team as the wagon rattled on down the road to the bridge. I don't know how old that patched-up structure was, but the wood was weathered and wheel-worn. Two planks on either side formed a path for wagon wheels, and the cross-planks that supported them made up the deck. The deck had been patched and repatched, and it needed work that Grandfather hadn't gotten around to.

I dallied behind the wagon, and out in the field there was a mead-owlark announcing his pleasure in the warm sun. Have you ever heard a meadowlark? To me, theirs is a nostalgic song always reminding me of country, the fields, and my boyhood. In later years I put the song to words, and it goes like this: "There's weeds in your wheat, there's weeds in your wheat." (Bad grammar, but it goes better with the song.) Next time you hear that lark, see if I'm not right. Anyway, listening and daydreaming, I forgot the oft-given warning about the perils of the bridge until suddenly there I was, hanging by my arms with the rest of me through a splintered hole, feet a couple of inches above the water. I shouted to Grandfather, afraid I would slip down into that awful chasm below. Finally, after what seemed an eter-nity, I was pulled out. The water, only six inches deep, and the bridge, only three feet above, seemed at that moment like the bridge below Niagara Falls. Much chastened, I rejoined Grandfather with the team at the head of the wagon as we resumed our walk to load up some hay. The meadowlarks were still singing!

We must have been at the Big House for at least one Christmas, because that is where I got the magnificent Irish Mail scooter. I haven't seen one of those machines for years and years, but mine was a beautiful red one with gold trim and black rubber tires (see illustration). I sat on a leather seat affixed to a wooden frame and steered with stirrups connected to the single front wheel. I was the engine, supplying power to the two rear wheels by way of a pair of handlebars pivoting on the frame and extending below to rods connected to cranks on the rear axle. Uncle Bill and Aunt Jinx were the Santa Clauses, and what a present that was! To gain any speed on the gravel driveway required great effort, but on the street by Grandma Alexander's I could really zing along. Since street-running required parental supervision, that was an infrequent pleasure. That vehicle lasted until I got a bike many years later, and during those times it got a regular service and an occasional paint job from Dad. Ultimately, my brother, Dick, who showed up about a year after our move to the Big House, inherited the machine.

Now we come to the event that shook up the family and left a mark on me for many years. The Big House on the bluff was a three-story affair with two upper rooms, each with a dormer window; one looked north and the other south. When up that high I almost felt like I was flying, particularly when looking south over the bluff toward Bear River, and this made a good spot for quiet play. On this fateful occasion, Mother had decided to do a general cleanup that included taking down the window curtains for washing. The curtain rods were pretty impressive devices, made of solid brass with large spherical ends. Where I got the idea I'll never know, for I can't recall having seen an orchestra or band, but Mother said she heard me making a noise, maybe like a trombone, and then silence. I remember having the rod in my mouth, bulb end down, and marching around the room. As I walked through the doorway it happened. The bulb caught on the doorsill between the room and hall, causing the other end to jam into the roof of my mouth, ripping a large flap nearly the size of my tongue. There was much blood, great panic, and a mad rush to the local sawbones. After a temporary patch job, Dad arrived and we drove to Sacramento, forty miles away, for a more professional repair.

For about three months after that, meals consisted of milkshakes and soup. For at least a month I couldn't talk, which must have been a relief to everyone but me. For some years after, neither milkshakes nor soup were a part of my diet, and when I finally tried a shake again at the local ice cream parlor, I asked that they make it using half soda water and half milk. That took away the more cloying feel of a regular shake. I'm back on regular shakes now, although at my age I shouldn't be. I can still feel the scar and remember the stitches, and I don't play trombone with curtain rods anymore.

Some time after the affair of the curtain rod we moved to our third house, and my grandparents moved at the same time to a place that ultimately became our fourth and final home in Wheatland. The third house was two blocks east of Main Street and again on the south side of town. Bill Alexander's house was on the other side of the street and down a half block, so, over a little garden and through about a mile of hop fields, we had a view of Bear River. Incidentally, Wheatland was, at one time, the largest supplier of hops in the country.

From this time on, I became more involved with kids my own age and began to learn what a town was all about. As I look back now, I realize what a wonderful thing a small town can be, and, in the case of ours, what the countryside can offer to anyone who is willing to get out on foot and explore. Sitting here at the computer today, all kinds of adventures fill my mind, and I am anxious to tell you about the house, trains through town at night, Damm's warehouse fire, salmon fishing in the Bear River, goose hunting in the mud and rain, and so much more. I didn't realize what a beautiful trail to the past this would be for me, and I hope I can convey just a little bit of it to you.

THE BIG HOUSE

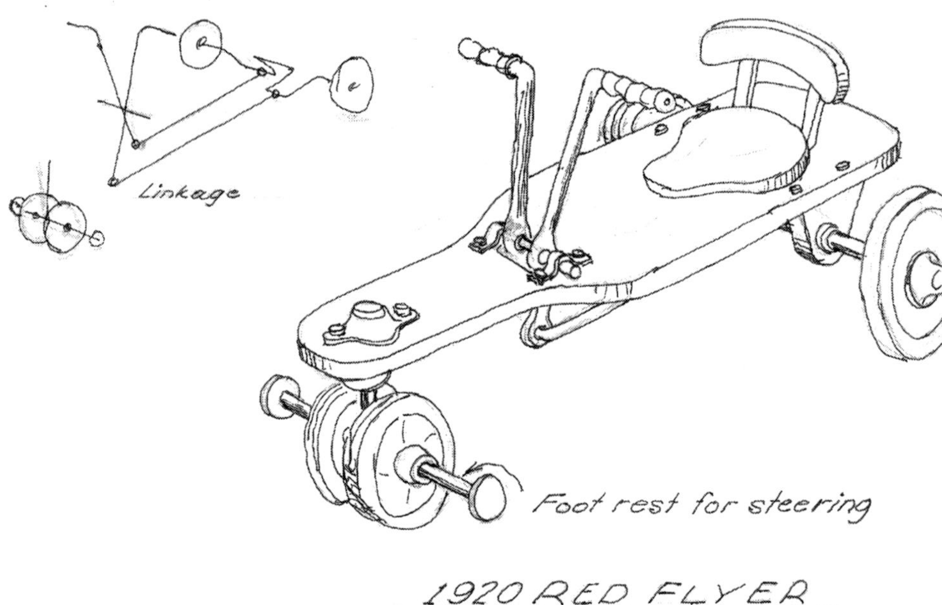
Linkage
Foot rest for steering
1920 RED FLYER

Chapter Four

The House on Dry Creek

After the wheat farm and the trailer, we moved to a small house near Dry Creek, about a mile from the town of Wheatland. This was a rental arrangement, and included a garden and 160 acres of good farmland in wheat and sorghum, which we called gyp corn. A good part of the area was river bottom. As a result, it was very productive. For harvest, Dad rented the equipment and did the work himself, except when the gyp corn was ready, and then he and I were a two-hand crew. More about that later, and about the tragedy on 99 E.

Dry Creek, as you no doubt have guessed, had no water in the summer, but in a good winter it would overflow its banks and raise all kinds of hob. Our house was four hundred feet from the stream, and the ground sloped gradually up so it seemed safe enough, but I do recall watching with trepidation as water once rose to within fifty feet of the house. The real problem was with traffic on the highway. The road was 99 E between Marysville and Wheatland, and it would regularly be under a couple of feet of flowing water in those wet periods. Most of the people around the area knew how to navigate the flood using the bridge over the creek as a landmark, but often someone would come along and get swept into the ditch, where water came in over the floorboards of the car. We could see all this from our house, and Dad would crank up the tractor and rescue the car and driver. A charge of $2.00 seemed like a lot in those days, but to the guy who sat with his feet on the dashboard of the stalled auto it was cheap.

While we are still in the winter season of this tale, I'll tell you about Gyp, my dog. He was a small black Cocker Spaniel and my absolute pride and joy. Adventuresome, curious, friendly, and tireless, he was always ready for a walk, a swim, a run, or a rabbit chase. One time, when the water was still high in the creek but within its banks, I whistled up my friend for a walk. No dog! Not a sound save for the gurgle of water! I ran upstream and called. Then I heard a welcome bark. Out from under the bridge floated some old steps from a house or barn, and riding majestically downstream on them was my dog. I say majestically, but I'm not sure if he was scared stiff or having a good time because I couldn't entice him ashore. The problem was solved by finding a long broken tree branch, with which dog and flotsam were pulled ashore together. Much jumping and shaking resulted in muddy and wet clothes, about which Mother was very stern.

And then there was the rabbit chase. We had a sizeable garden with corn, potatoes, squash, tomatoes, lettuce, and a few other things, and of course such goodies attracted rabbits. Mr. McGregor's garden was a famous target. Gyp helped patrol the plot and did a pretty good job, but he was defeated one day. I swear it went like this: dog chased rabbit up and down a couple of rows, only to have second rabbit step in as in a relay, whereupon after a few circuits dog repaired to sidelines with tongue hanging out. I can't swear to this clever planning by a team of stupid rabbits, but it hangs there as a persistent memory, so you be the judge.

Now the tragedy. This I remember as if it were yesterday. It was a warm spring day. I was out back bouncing a ball on the concrete pad at the foot of the back stairs. In the distance, I vaguely heard the drone of a car on the way from Marysville. Sounds fast, I thought, but sometimes they drove fast along that stretch of 99 E just before slowing down for Wheatland. Then I heard a yelp of mortal pain, the receding roar of the car, and then silence. I knew but didn't want to accept it. Running around the house and out to the gate, I saw my little black dog, dusty and quivering beside the highway. I picked him up and carried him back to the house, trying not to hurt him, but he died as I sat in the gravel of the driveway. Mother said some years later that I sat, rocking Gyp and saying after the departed car, "You son of a bitch, you killed my dog." Gyp was buried with honors near the corner of the fence between the house and garden, and there, I presume, he still lies. I never had another dog; who could, after Gyp?

But now to more pleasant things, like harvesting gyp corn. The plant grows about three feet tall, with a head about the size of my fist. We harvested the stuff by hand, using a finger knife and tossing the heads into a horse-pulled wagon (see illustration). The wagon had steel wheels and a bed with two-foot high sideboards. The old horse was sort of an automatic transmission and seemed to know when we got behind, because he would stop and wait until we caught up. The work was a good time for me. Dad and I wouldn't talk much; the silence seeming to be as good as talk. The plodding horse, the creak of the wagon, the snap of cutting, and the thud as heads of corn hit the bed made a rhythmic, hypnotic song. The corn was sold for hog food, and some people made sorghum molasses from it.

The garden mentioned above provided us with much good food, both fresh and canned, but of all of it I recall best the tomatoes, corn, and potatoes. Dad and I would go out with a salt shaker and pick a ripe tomato, wet a spot by tongue, sprinkle a little salt, and enjoy those delicious, firm, red fruits. The routine for corn was to have the water boiling in the pot, go out and pick and husk, hurry back to the house and pop the corn into the boiling water. There was nothing quite so tasty, and I often ate as many as six ears. I can't believe that later, when I was older, I ate twelve ears for dinner, but this is an authentic family record. Ah, now the potatoes. Of course, I liked them just about any old way except raw. Have you ever had a bite of a raw spud? Well, I tell you, it isn't worth trying, and I know that from bitter experience. I was watching Mother peeling some freshly dug up potatoes, and the crisp, moist slices she was preparing for frying looked so good I had to have a bite or two. Even after Mother said, "You won't like it," I persisted and bit off a big chunk. Surprise! Oh surprise! What a terrible taste! I tried to put on a bold face and get the bite down, but it wouldn't go, so I was forced to lean over the sink and spit out the chewed-up mess. No one said a word, no one smiled, and that's how I can tell you not to try raw potatoes.

That little house is still there beside Dry Creek and 99 E, and it still brings back fond memories when I pass by on a rare trip back to Wheatland. Someday, I may stop and ask whoever is living there if I could just step in for a minute to stand in the kitchen and imagine my mother before the stove, apron on, frying potatoes for dinner. Maybe she would smile a bit now about raw potatoes. Maybe, too, Dad and I could salt a tomato or two.

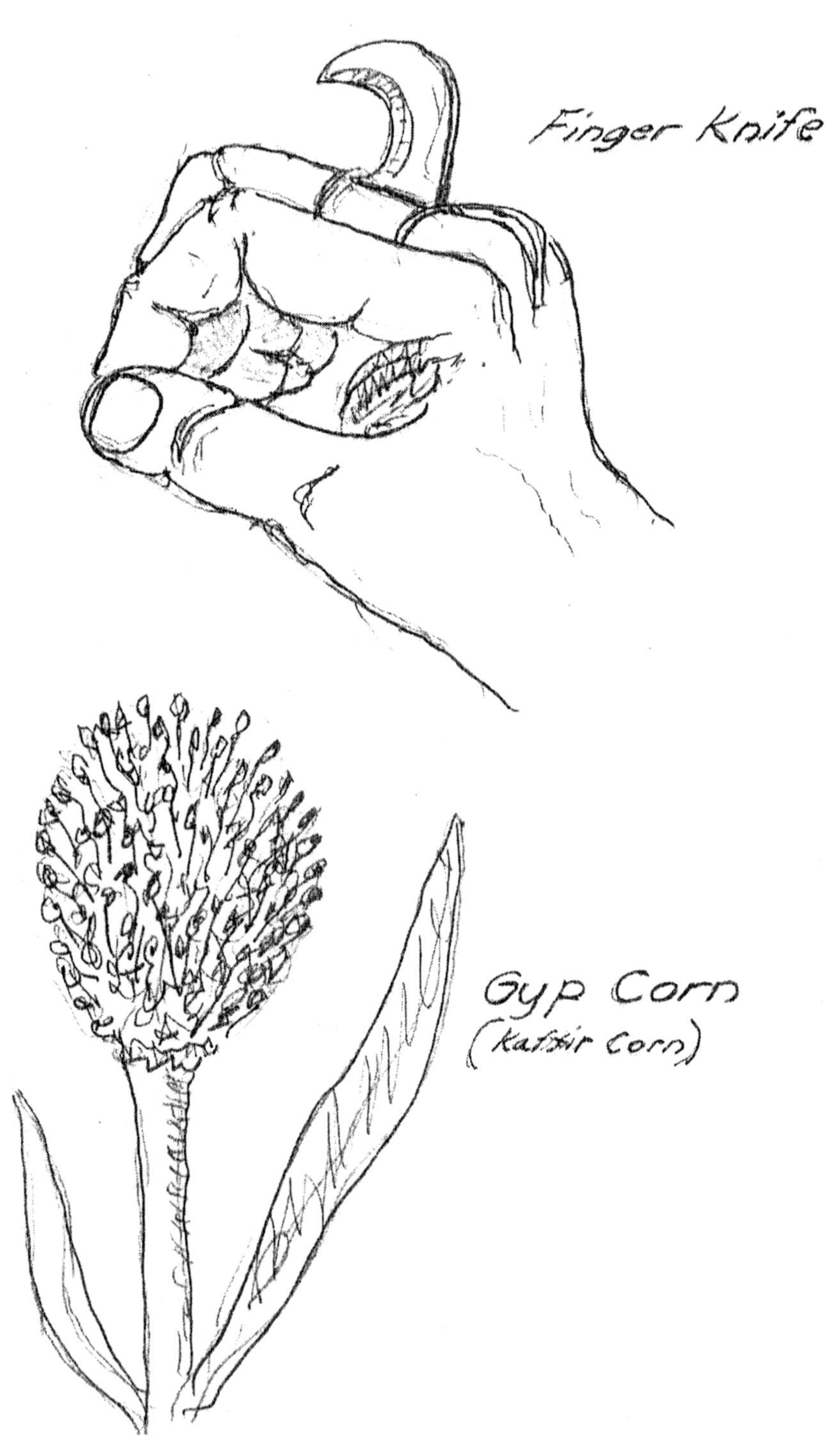
Finger Knife
Gyp Corn
(Kaffir Corn)

Chapter Five

House at the Foot of the Hill

As you read in Chapter Four, Dad had found a house in town, and we were going to move again. I began to have a feeling that my life was just one move after another. Not only that, but it would mean leaving Gyp when we left Dry Creek. Somehow I felt moving would take away from the place where I imagined his happy bark when we played and the vision of him as he chased rabbits out of our garden. When I told Mother that I was sad about it, she said it didn't matter where I went; I could always remember those times, and I knew she was right.

Moving day began as a big truck came crunching up the driveway. Dad and the driver loaded the first truck full and Mother, my brother, and I held down the fort. It took a second load to empty the house, and then we were on our way to a new home. It must have been a sad moment to hear the front door close and the lock click for the last time.

I have no memory of first meeting my new neighbor, but I can imagine the occasion. Two kids approaching each other, a bit warily, hands in pockets, maybe one of us kicking a stone in the graveled road. One of us might have said, "My name's Bill, what's yours?" The ice breaking answer was, "Mine's Bill, too." And we both would have laughed. However it happened, it was the beginning of the most treasured friendship of my life, enduring for eighty-four years to date. We went through school together, played on the tennis, basketball, baseball, and track teams together, and graduated from Wheatland High School together. We went to Sacramento College, and after that he transferred to Oregon State and I to Cal. We both had long careers in engineering. We met infrequently over the years, but it was always an emotional event. Our last get-together was on June 28, 2005. We had lunch and I admit to a misty-eyed greeting. When last I heard, Bill's son and wife were driving him up to Wheatland for a visit to the old home town and as I write I await a report on the visit.

The street to our house was steep. Going up in an auto, Dad had to shift gears. I could make it with a one-speed bike if I pumped real hard. Going down on a bike had its thrills because a fair amount of speed was generated, and at the bottom of the street there were three options: sharp right turn, sharp left turn, or bang into Bill Alexander's fence. A right turn took the rider into a grove of quince trees after about a hundred feet; a left took you up the street to the east where there was plenty of room to bleed off that blinding speed. The third alternate wasn't desirable, but sometimes sloppy riding left no choice.

The east-going street climbed up a slope a couple of blocks past our house, and at the crest was the old quarry with its forbidden rafting pool. The bluff made a sharp bend at this point, and it may be assumed that the old river had eddied around the rock ten thousand or so years earlier. Across the bike-run street was a big old faded red livery stable. When we arrived, the stable was still being used, but only partly for horses, with the rest as miscellaneous storage.

On the other side of the stable, a corrugated steel building had, in the past, been a blacksmith and wagon repair shop. Here, Dad finally found the opportunity he was looking for, and set up an auto repair shop. A small beginning, it was to continue and expand all the years of my time in Wheatland. As business in the little shop grew, Dad developed a reputation for honesty and quality work that was to follow him throughout his life. The main business was auto repair, but it included repair of all sorts of farm equipment such as tractors, wagons, harvesters, and ploughs. In those days you didn't go to Sears and buy a new battery. Dad took an old one and rebuilt it so it looked like new. I remember the big tube glowing blue as it recharged one or more batteries. Finally a service station was added and Dad sold Mobil gas (see illustration). Gas was 15 cents a gallon, but I recall a gas war where the price got down to a nickel. Dad's pride and joy was a big thirty-foot South Bend lathe, something no doubt reminding him of his days as a machinist in San Francisco before the great quake.

Downtown on Main Street we had two groceries, one called Nightingale's. Then came the pool hall, post office, ice cream parlor, phone switchboard, Guy Glazier's butcher shop, Burchell's hardware, and the Eastern Star Hall. The railroad ran north and south a half a block west of Main

Street, with a station between. That old station was a classic, painted railroad yellow with brown trim. A big loading platform with a long ramp for freight handling, a ticket and telegraph room, a waiting room, a restroom, and a baggage room made up that lovely old structure. Many years later on a trip back, it distressed me to see that it had been torn down. What a shame!

I liked the stationmaster, and on one occasion he put me on board an engine while they were switching cars onto the sidings. Needless to say, this was a dream come true as I sat in the engineer's seat with my elbow on the padded windowsill and looked ahead over that steel monster. Moving the throttle sent chills down my spine, and as we began to move I imagined that we were rolling down the tracks at high speed delivering an important load of freight. I got to blow the whistle and ring the bell too! That experience was the most exciting thing that had ever happened to me, and I can still remember the details of the engine and see the steam coming from the whistle.

Before we had radio, communication with a moving train was by the semaphore, or the loop. Now and then a fusee, a little pad attached to the rail with metal straps, signaled an emergency with a loud bang when a locomotive wheel ran over it, but the loop was the one to watch. It was made of a wicker rod about one-quarter inch thick, shaped in the form of the letter P. A written message would be attached to the stem, and as the train came thundering through town, the stationmaster would stand near the tracks holding the loop. A conductor or brakeman leaned from the train with arm bent at the elbow so that he could pick up the loop. He would grab the message and toss the loop to the ground further down the tracks. I never saw them miss a pickup and was always fascinated by the procedure which, sadly, is now a part of the past.

Back to the house now, and I'll tell you what it was like not having a bathroom in the house. No bathtub, shower, or toilet. All those amenities were out back, and you got to them by a wooden walkway. Washroom and bath were on a wooden platform in the woodshed, and the toilet was at the end of the walkway. During the summer, it was fine, but in winter it was cold as blitzen. For baths, we used a galvanized tub: one of those round affairs about thirty inches across and eighteen inches deep. Hot water was hauled out in a teakettle and mixed with cold from the garden hose. Heat came from a portable kerosene device standing maybe thirty inches high and having a shutter-like damper on top and another a third of the way up.

(See illustration.) This arrangement gave one a lot of control, and I still think those kerosene heaters were one of the best little gadgets ever invented, but I must admit there were certain perils attendant to their use. I found out about one, much to my chagrin. On a cold winter day, with the heater going full blast and the top damper open, I stepped out of the tub and stumbled on something. I tried to catch myself and Mother grabbed me, but not before the heater caught me and I sat hard on the top. Sizzle and smoke and the smell of burning flesh, and I was branded! The damper opening was neatly imprinted on my backside. No sitting for a couple of weeks, and the tattoo mark lasted for years; maybe, on close inspection, the faded design might still be visible, but I'm not going to look.

Light for the kitchen came from a bare bulb in a socket suspended from the ceiling by the cord. A hanging string operated the switch, and to get to the bulb one had to stand on a stool. One evening, Mother had just removed a burned-out bulb and gone to get a new one. Wanting to help, I climbed up on the stool so Mother could hand me the new bulb. It turned out to be a pretty high perch and sort of unstable, so I reached for the cord and socket to steady myself. That was a grave mistake because I carelessly let a thumb slip into the socket. With the switch on, I got a terrible jolt and thought I was going to lose my whole hand. Nursing the injured member, I climbed off the stool and left the room so Mother wouldn't find out about my foolish accident.

As time went by, there were opportunities to meet and make friends with many of my contemporaries, including Artie Lewis, who was deaf and dumb. With Artie, dumb didn't mean stupid, and several of us spent many enjoyable hours with him. On an occasion when we were involved in some strenuous activity, Artie called a halt and made it known that he had to return home by five p.m., but that it would be more enjoyable if we sat around for the next few minutes and just talked, which for him, of course, meant signing. He made it clear to us that time would go by more slowly that way, and thus more pleasantly. A great philosophical lesson, and we could use the reverse system—if we were bored, we could get busy and the time would fly by.

Approach of the winter season meant that the days got shorter and it got dark earlier. This often gave us playtime in the evening after the street lights came on, and led to one of our favorite games. Soon after the lights went on, all kinds of moths, bugs, and flying insects gathered around. Across the street, the livery stable hosted a small colony of bats that would come flying out after those bugs, and this was the game we invented: gathering beneath our street light, we tossed hats or caps into the air in hopes of capturing a bat. The first guy to catch one won an aggie (an agate marble, a prized possession, particularly when it was a "taw" or shooter). This business didn't seem to bother the little winged mice much, but on rare occasions one would be entangled and drop to the ground in a cap. We would then carefully disentangle him and inspect the little wonder, being careful to avoid the tooth end. From that experience, I learned to respect the flying skill, cleanliness, and benefits of bats.

We were still at the little house with about two years of school gone by and a brother beginning to act like he wanted to grow up. He had been through a bout of whooping cough, and it was a worrisome time. Several remedies were tried, but the most effective seemed to be a sugar cube with a couple of drops of kerosene. The liquid was allowed to soak in for a while, and then the cube was popped into his mouth and sucked on until dissolved. Upon reflection, I suppose this was a sort of kill or cure method, and since Dick is still with us I guess it was not the former. It is frightening to reflect upon the state of medicine so many years ago, and to recall the seasonal plagues we lived through. Each year brought its anxieties and quarantines as polio, smallpox, mumps, chicken pox, or other diseases swept through the community. Sometimes, as the tide of trouble receded, it took with it one or more members of our town, and because we were only five hundred the gaps were like missing teeth.

THE SHOTGUN INCIDENT

There was to be a visitor! Dad received a letter from his brother Clarence, telling us that he would arrive in about two weeks with his wife Annie. Things would be a bit crowded, but the visit was looked forward to with eager anticipation. Sleeping quarters were rearranged and other plans were made to welcome them. Finally the big day arrived, and I will never forget the first sight of Uncle Clarence! He stood six foot six, weighted 250 pounds, and my first thought was, "Here comes the giant from the story of Jack and the Beanstalk." As he walked up the stairs and onto the porch, the house shook. My Dad was six one and weighed around 190 pounds, but the contrast between the brothers could not have been greater. Clarence roared when he talked, and to Mother's disgust he addressed his wife as "WOMAN." And he could eat! I still remember watching with awe as great quantities of food disappeared into that maw.

After a time the visit began to pale a bit on all of us, and it ended abruptly with a blast. Everyone was sitting on the screen porch while Dad and Clarence talked hunting. The subject of guns came up and Clarence asked what Dad used for ducks and geese, whereupon Dad brought out his pride and joy, a Browning 12-gauge automatic shotgun, and explained that it might be a little more difficult to bring down a duck with the #6 shot he used, but it didn't tear up the bird as much as the #4 some people used. While listening, Clarence put the gun stock on the floor and slipped a few shells into the magazine. He then proceeded to cycle the loading and ejecting system to see how it worked. Unfortunately, as the last shell entered the firing chamber, a clumsy finger hit the trigger, and with a terrifying blast the gun went off. There was a stunned silence, and then we all looked skyward through the gaping hole in the porch roof. After a few seconds a shingle or two fell back to earth, followed by some of the shot. More silence . . . then Mother said, "Clarence, it was good of you to come see us. You can catch the noon train tomorrow, and it will take you and Annie to Roseville where you can catch the Eastbound over the mountains." So Clarence and Annie did just that, and I never saw them again, nor wanted to, I guess.

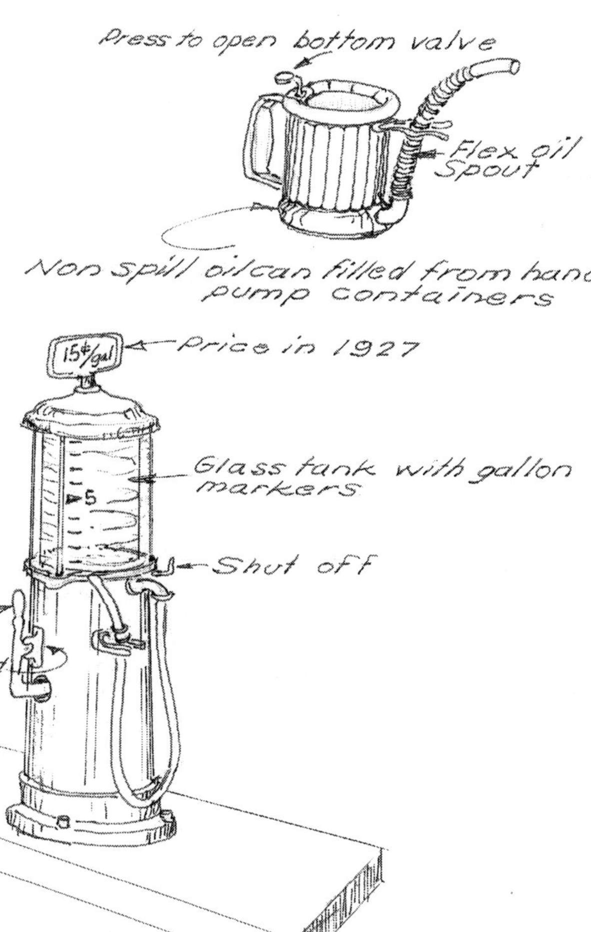

GASOLINE PUMP — 1927

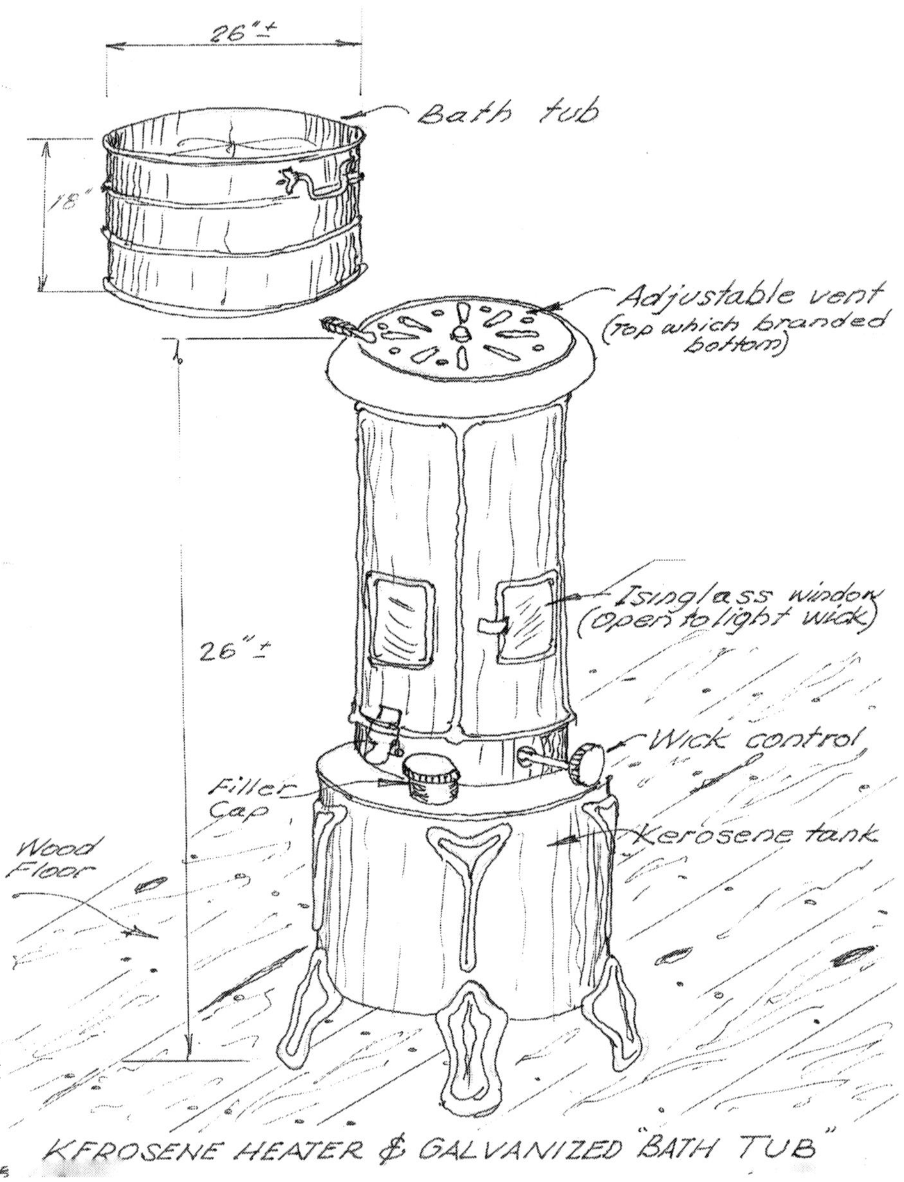

KEROSENE HEATER & GALVANIZED "BATH TUB"

Chapter Six

School Days

Our school at the east end of town was a three-story building housing both high school and grammar school. When Dad took me by it for the first time I thought it was the biggest thing I had ever seen. In those days the lower grades, first through eighth, were in the south side with their own separate entrance. High school classes—freshman through senior—were in the north side with their separate entrance. The upper grades for both high school and grammar school occupied the third floor, and both lower grades were on the second floor. There was a basement or ground floor for rainy-day play that also had storage space, a janitor's room with a furnace, and restrooms. Classes and recesses were announced by the ringing of a bell operated by the janitor. The principal, Cocky Cunningham, so named because of a gimpy leg, presided over all grades. Our first- and second-grade teacher, Miss Sheets, represented the best of the profession, and I know of no one who didn't like her. She was strict, caring, and made learning a joyous adventure.

The school was located in a triangle formed by two streets and an alley, with an outdoor playground at the base for high school kids and another at the apex for us younger ones. Across the street to the south we had our baseball diamond, and beyond center field you could see the quarry. Back toward town at the northwest corner of the triangle loomed the water tower (we had the sweetest water of any place I have ever lived). This tower constituted the basic challenge for all the town's macho kids. If you could climb the ninety-foot tower ladder and then the twenty-five-foot ladder on the tank without chickening out and, even more important, without getting caught, you became a hero first class. Not everyone made it, but when you did the view was spellbinding. In later years, the ladder entrance was put under lock and key, thus depriving the next generation but maybe saving a life or two.

One sunny spring day everyone took advantage of a school recess to get out into the playgrounds, the upper class in their yard and we in ours. Somehow, either chasing a ball or not paying attention, I strayed into the big guys' territory. Next thing I knew, there was a terrific thud and I found myself trying to get up, only to realize that one arm wouldn't work. I had difficulty focusing my eyes, and when I looked down I saw a curve in my left arm. As a matter of fact, it looked a little like the letter S. Looking further, there appeared a big pair of boots, in which, it turned out, was George Muck, a six-foot, 190-pound senior. Neither of us had been looking where we were going and so we ended up at the same place at the same time. George helped me up and walked me in to the school nurse. Mother was summoned and off we went to Marysville, where I had my first experience with ether. Arm straightened and in a cast, I was brought back home where I received solace for my wounds.

One has to make concessions while wearing a cast, but during that time I had an opportunity to wreak vengeance on an archenemy. In our town we had a family by the name of Dalton. There were three boys in the family, whose first names are long forgotten. The two younger were twins, and they had a dog named Pujer. They were mean, nasty stinkers, and would pick a fight at the drop of a hat. Even two guys couldn't stand them off because Pujer always entered the fray, snapping and biting. One person didn't stand a chance, as I learned from bitter experience, but if there were several of us, we could manage to beat them and Pujer. To get them primed for a fight when we had sufficient numbers, we would taunt them with the cry "Pujer Dujer!" repeated over and over until the boiling point was reached and the fun began.

One afternoon while still wearing the cast, I was riding my bike. Suddenly accosted by the twins, I was pushed off the bike to the ground, hitting the cast in the process. It hurt like hell and, throwing caution to the winds, I got up and whacked one twin along side the head with the cast. While he was clutching a bleeding ear, the other moved in and I clobbered him. Pujer appeared to have a healthy respect for the cast, and the trio left for safer grounds. After the cast was gone, I felt some concern over the chance of another meeting; however, not long after that the Daltons moved from town. This engendered no regret from us kids, and even the grown-ups seemed to join us in our relief.

Time passed smoothly as I made my way through the grades at school. We were in scouting and other activities, but one game met with some resistance from the mothers. As summer approached, the black walnut trees became loaded with nuts. While the nuts were still in their husks, we had a game called War. Each combatant picked up a load of husk-covered nuts and sought cover, venturing out only to fire at an exposed enemy. Kills were easily recorded because the husk would break, leaving a stain wherever the missile landed. Face or arm hits left you spotted for a few days. The stain resisted ordinary efforts in the laundry, and mothers were always happy to have summer heat dry the projectiles so the husks would either fall off in flight or be too dry to leave a mark.

Sometime near the end of the fourth grade, Grandmother passed away. Only a few days earlier I had paid one of my usual visits, and I could not believe she would no longer be there. This was my first experience with death, and it was hard for me to understand the finality of it. The photo you see in the Prologue is of a very stern person, but she was a warm, loving grandmother who always had a full cookie jar when I came to visit. She still churned her own butter (see illustration) and would let me shape the pats after the moisture had been wrung out in the cheesecloth bags. Out on the back pantry were jars of jam, jelly, and canned fruit. I always returned home with butter and jam. She was of good, tough pioneer stock and I remember her fondly. Grandfather was left alone in the house where he and Grandmother had moved after leaving the Big House. Grandfather had, by this time, become quite blind, and, although Mother spent much time with both him and Grandmother, it was too much of a chore to run back and forth so we moved one more time. In that house with the barn, I was to live until I went off to college in 1933.

I wish to pay homage to my grandfather. He, too, was a pioneer with the courage to move his family to California, begin a new life, raise a remarkable group of children, and create a successful farm while being a respected member of the community of Wheatland. He bore his blindness with equanimity and, although I was not his favorite—my brother was—I respected him. One evening he drank his usual glass of hot salt water before retiring. The next morning he was gone.

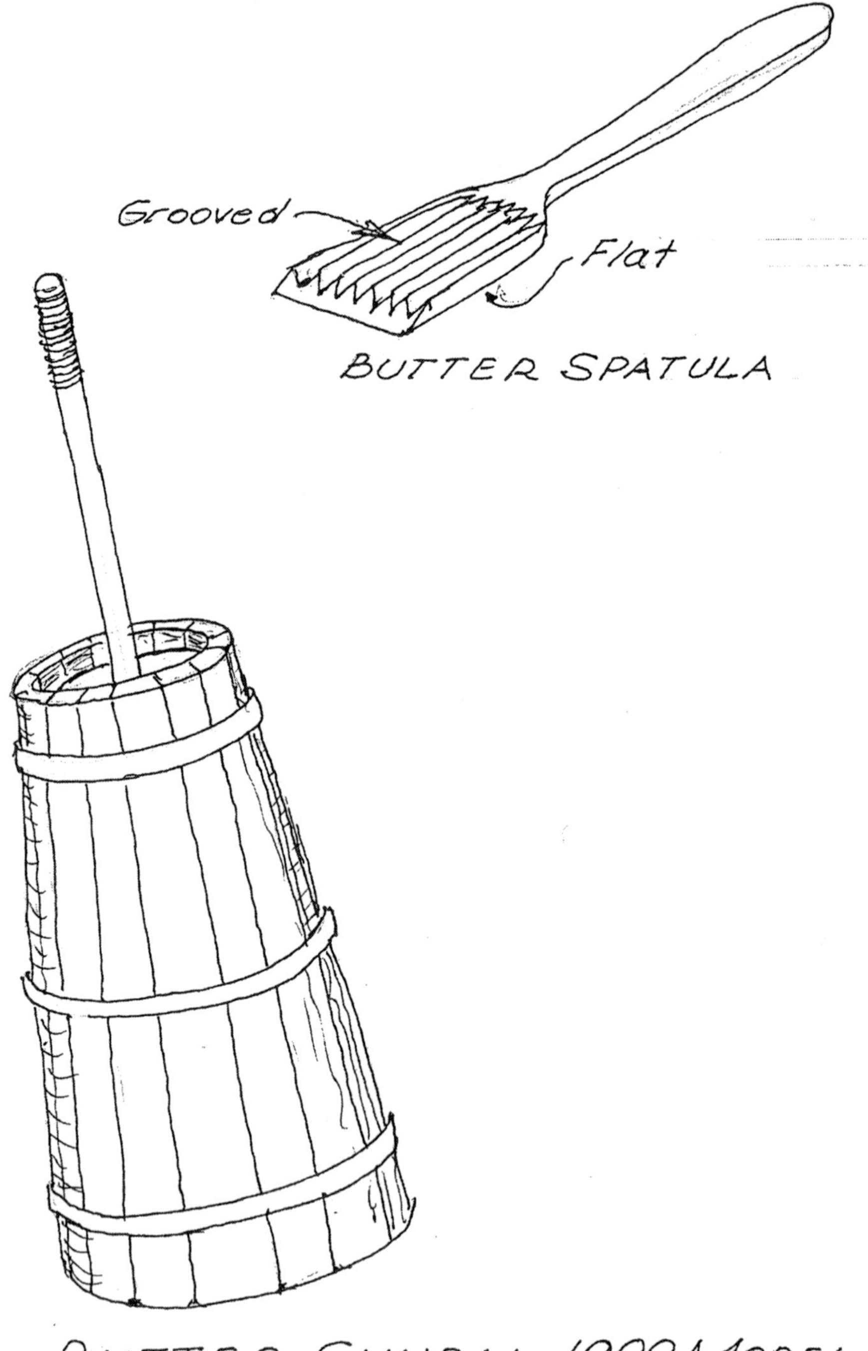
Grooved
Flat
BUTTER SPATULA
BUTTER CHURN, 1900 MODEL

Chapter Seven

House with the Barn

We moved to this house to be with Grandfather after Grandmother died because by now, being quite blind, Grandfather could not do all the housekeeping by himself, and because our own house was small and without much in the way of conveniences. Taking up half of a city block was the house, a big barn, an even bigger barnyard, a fenced-off chicken yard, a woodshed, and a large area of lawn around the house. (See illustration.) When I asked Mother why my grandparents wanted such a big place, she said it was because Grandfather had been a farmer all his life, and while he could still see he liked to stand on the screen porch and look out at the big red barn even if there were no animals out there. I understood and felt a twinge of sadness for my grandfather.

From the screen porch door, down three steps and along a gravel walk and through a gate, you entered the chicken yard. A woodshed served as storage for firewood, and as a nesting place for the fowl. This was where my loving, cookie-baking, butter-churning, gentle grandmother turned into a Frankensteinian witch, and why, to this day, I do not find chicken to be one of my favorite dishes. The first act of bestiality was to go into the shed and rudely hoist the hens off the nests to gather eggs so painfully laid and so patiently sat on. I hadn't given much thought to where eggs came from, but once I saw that it didn't seem fair.

The terrible act to follow, however, was the one I shall always remember. Grandmother would emerge from the house with a long apron on and march down the walk and through the gate with a cruel gleam in her eye, a ghoulish smirk on her mouth, and fingers curled like claws. Unsuspecting chickens gathered, hoping for an extra tidbit of grain and then, with a sudden malevolent swoop, the poor victim would wind up in those unforgiving claws. A couple of expert twists and a flip, and it was all over. Once a head-less chicken got loose, and by reflex action staggered across the yard, blood spurting from the severed neck. Each execution caused panic as hens fled in all directions from the scene, but they never learned, and each time was a new event for them. So you see why I'm not a lover of chicken. Inciden-tally, on the property there was a piece of tree trunk about eighteen inches in diameter and twenty-four inches high, complete with hatchet, for those unfortunate Thanksgiving turkeys! I don't like turkey either.

The house we were moving into had two bedrooms, and after Grand-mother passed away it became obvious that more space would be needed for Dick and me. The solution lay in access to the attic, but at the moment that was by a ladder at one end of a closet. Obviously a stairway was needed, but Dad worked long hours in his shop and Mother felt he shouldn't have to be a carpenter in the evenings. So what to do? Well, that left Mother and my blind grandfather, and between the two of them it got done. Mother did the measuring and marked with the point of a nail. Grandfather could feel the marks. He sawed, fitted, and nailed a very professional-looking set of stairs enclosed by a wall and entered through a door. That attic served Dick and me for many years, and although it was hot in the summer the feather beds and comforters were welcome in winter.

I must tell you a little more about Grandfather. He was never one to sit around and fuss over his blindness, and to the day of his death he arose at the crack of dawn and started the day by building a fire in the big old cook stove in the kitchen. When the teakettle was on the boil, Grandfather poured a glass of hot water and added a couple of teaspoons of salt. After a stirring, the whole glassful would go down the hatch, and I wondered how he could do it. After that, breakfast consisted of rolled-oat mush with brown sugar and two cups of coffee. The rest of the day, Grandfather kept busy at little repair jobs, drying dishes, mopping the kitchen floor, and gardening. We had a great expanse of lawn, and I can see him to this day as he care-fully felt his way over the sod until he came to a piece of Bermuda grass, which he pulled out and put in a trash bucket. His death was sudden, and I have wondered since how much that daily glass of salt water had to do with the stroke and heart failure that felled him at age seventy-three. As I said, he and I never got along that well (Dick was his favorite), but I respected him for his stern, uncompromising way of life.

As time went by, we added a glassed-in porch, which served as a bed-room and sewing room. Along the outside, a huge Cecile Bruner rose climbed nearly to the top of the window and filtered the autumn sun through blossoms and leaves. Another screen porch replaced the front stoop and was often used to cool off in the evening after a hot day. This one faced Highway 99 E, which ran right through the middle of town, but the traffic had not yet reached the point of being a bother. Dad added a swamp cooler, an oil fire system in the living room stove, and concrete walkways around the house. That was the end of house construction.

About six months after we moved in, Dad finally began transferring equipment from the tin shed by the livery stable to the barn on our property. This was quite a task, and I watched with fascination as the big old motor was hoisted into position on the prepared platform in the barn rafters. A long overhead shaft installed above all the machinery supplied power to each unit by way of a clutch and belt system. One exciting aspect of those belts was the generation of static electricity. If I stood on a ladder and held my extended fingers to within four inches of the belt while it was running, sparks would jump from fingers to belt with a sharp crackle, and, I might add, some sensation. Finally, workbenches were added and some new windows were cut in the walls. The floor remained the original dirt, which had been compacted over the years by animal hooves. With a coating of road oil to hold down the dust, the Ball General Garage and Machine Shop had been created.

Ultimately the woodshed came down, the chickens were gone, and some new structures went up to provide garage, storage, and shelter for our family car. I also got a spot of my own for model making and to set up my tennis racket stringing business. The fences came down, hedges were planted, and Mother and Grandfather put in a vegetable garden, including a couple of rows of a new berry called boysenberry. The huge old eucalyptus by the corner of the house bit the dust after a big limb fell and hit a corner of the roof. Mother hated the thing because it always created a mess mo matter how often you cleaned the area. Also, the owls who roosted there were forever dropping their little fur balls containing tiny bones and other unappetizing detritus.

An appendage to the barn was built to house an office, oil tanks, battery rebuilding area, gas pump, air compressor, and other miscellaneous things. This time, we got a concrete floor! Gasoline at 15 cents a gallon and oil at 10 cents a quart were the norm, but at times, when a little price war erupted, both were a nickel. I worked in the shop in my free time, and over the years I learned to love things mechanical, which is the reason I finally decided to be an engineer, I guess.

There is one incident I should relate while I think of it. My after-school job was to man the gas pumps so Dad wouldn't have to drop what he was doing and rush out to pump gas. One afternoon, a monster of a vehicle drove up to the pumps. It was the biggest thing I had ever seen, and it seemed as long as two ordinary autos. The top, having been folded, offered plenty of fresh air, but both front- and rear-seat occupants were protected by large windshields. The driver asked if I would please check the oil and water levels, and volunteered the information that the gauges were just behind the front wheel beneath the fender. I spotted the gauge glasses, which showed about half full, and then, to my dismay, something else caught my eye; a small flame flickering in a sort of housing! I shouted, "Mister, your car's on fire, you better get out and I'll get a fire extinguisher." He responded, "Don't worry, son, that's okay, this is a Stanley Steamer, and that's the pilot light for the boiler firebox." Terribly embarrassed, I poured a quart of oil, added some water, got paid 15 cents plus a nickel tip, and watched as that magnificent machine pulled away with hardly a sound save for the scrunching of the tires in the gravel. It used to be said that the factory would give you one of those vehicles free if you dared to hold the throttle wide open for five minutes, but I can't vouch for the veracity of that statement. I do know that car was very fast and very expensive. They were the rage for a few years, but lost favor as the internal combustion engine improved and cost became a factor.

Many wonderful years went by, with that house and garage looming large in my memory as places where new things were always happening and where I always had an anchor in the storms of growing up. Events are jumbled in memory, but seem to get sorted out into categories and priorities, so, for a while, we'll just pick the ones that bubble to the top.

OUR FIRST SELF CONTAINED REFRIGERATOR
Maybe 1927

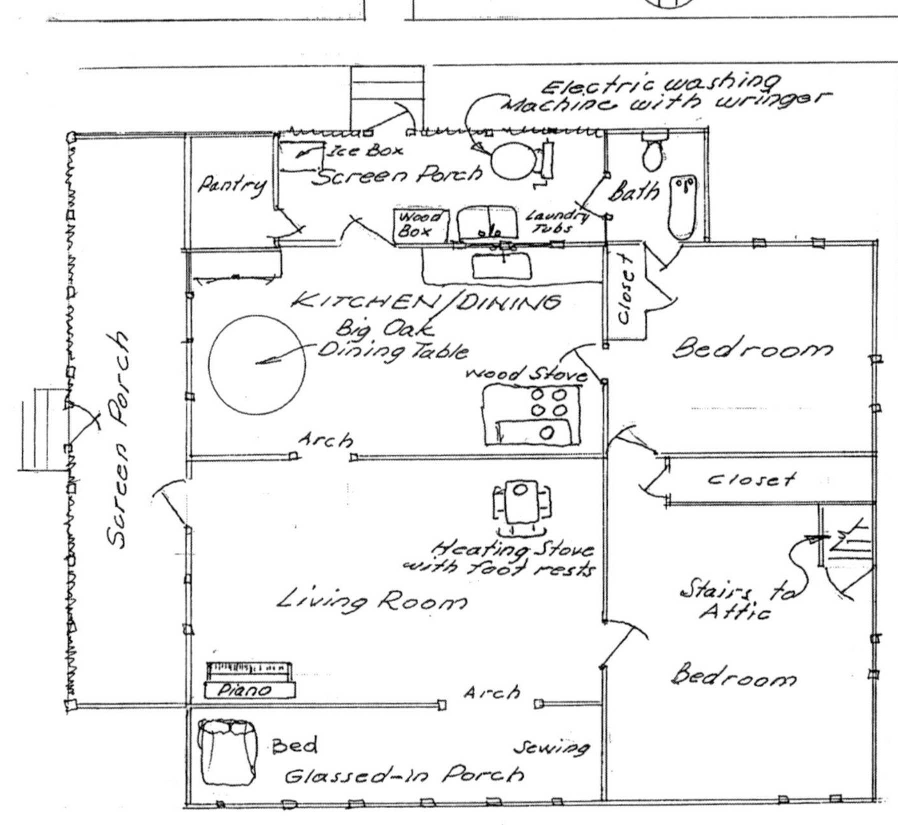

HOUSE BY THE BARN CIRCA 1928

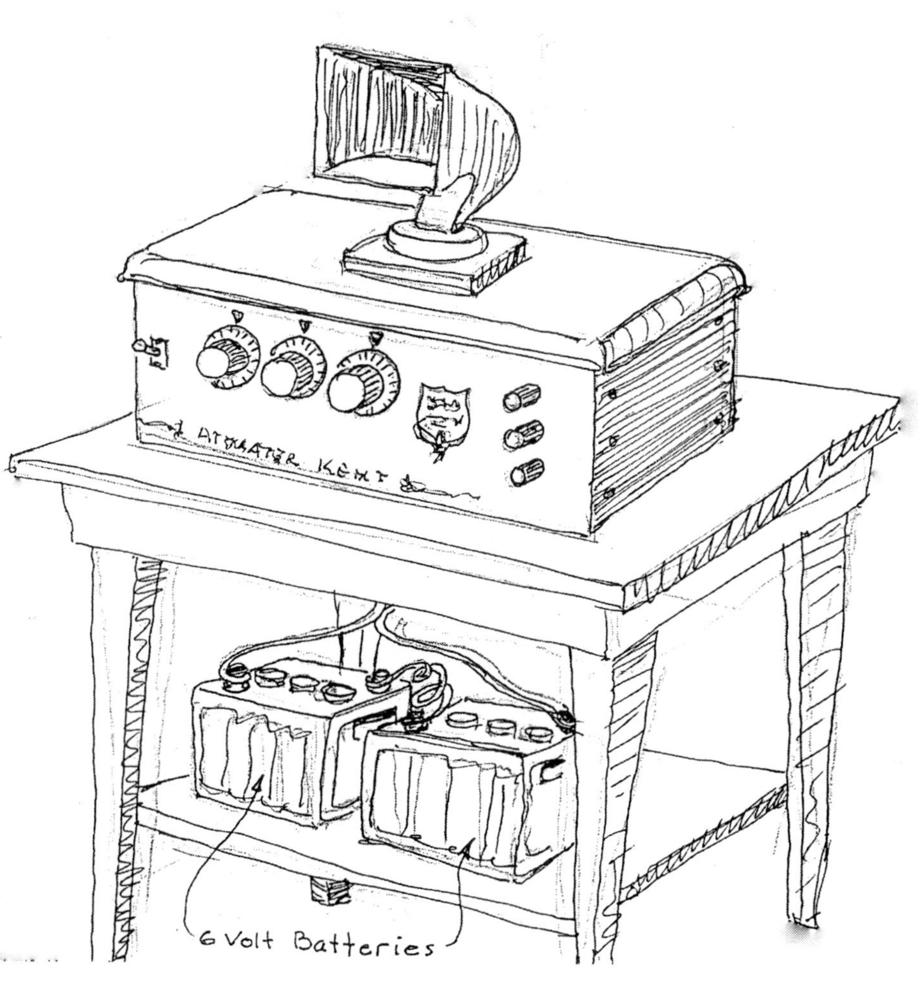

Radio

Chapter Eight

Wheatland

Since my parents moved to Wheatland before I was a year old, that little berg is my hometown and there are no memories of Oakland, my place of birth. Looking back, that move was a fortuitous one for me because of the advantages of growing up in a small town where the outdoors was just off my front porch. With a population of five hundred, it was easy to know almost everyone and to feel comfortable with my surroundings. We had a movie/dance hall where the old silent movies were accompanied by Margaret Selinger on a piano and later, when the town was flush, on a small organ. One of the plums was a free pass when you took a turn at pumping the organ. The view of the screen was from an odd angle but it was free. In those days the film was highly flammable and often one would see a spot on the screen that melted and spread; you can see it now in the introduction to the TV series Bonanza. The audience would begin a restless shuffle, most times quieted by a call from the projection booth, "Okay, fire's out," or sometimes, "Please leave by the side doors." The hall never burned down, and in later years the film changed from nitrate to acetate; if truth be told, that probably spoiled some of the fun of going to the movies.

We had a main street and a big beautiful railroad station. (See illustrations.) That was the one Grandfather took me to see when I had wondered what the distant whistle was, remember? There were two groceries (one with the entrancing name of Nightingale's), a hardware store, pool hall, post office, ice cream parlor, barber shop, blacksmith shop, doctor's office, lumberyard, church, telephone switchboard, community center, high school, grammar school and two garages, one of which now had W. B. BALL—GENERAL GARAGE AND SERVICE STATION emblazoned on a panel over the gas pumps.

All of the foregoing qualified us to be called a town, and in the main we were proud of it. Our streets had not yet been paved, and only Main Street had a sidewalk. On the hot summer days those unpaved streets were dusty, but the water wagon took care of that problem. Jack Phelps sat high in front of the tank, driving the team and controlling the valve that directed water to the four spray spigots behind. It normally took two rounds to do the job, one in midmorning and one in midafternoon. I could hear the wagon coming a block away, and that gave me time to get out and stand close enough to feel the temporary cooling of the air (and get my shoes and pants wet). I can still smell that aroma of wetted dust and see in my mind's eye the pebbles glistening where they were washed clean by the spray.

Our house was two blocks from the railroad and the trains, although you could hear them, were not very intrusive; you could tune them out or tune them in. Mostly I tuned them in because I loved those big black mechanical marvels. My most nostalgic memories are of those nights when I would hear the engine coming down the Bear River grade, picking up speed as it neared town, the engineer holding the whistle rope all the way to warn of the danger at crossings. That whistle always got to me, muted at first by distance, then increasing in both volume and pitch as it approached, and then, as it passed, diminishing in pitch and volume. It was like a long, drawn-out sigh, as if the engine was saying, "Well, that's one more town, how many more will there be tonight?"

There were other sounds like the fire bell and, later, as we got more sophisticated, the siren. These were not welcome sounds, yet for us kids they brought a tingling excitement. We did and yet didn't want it to happen. Damm's Warehouse fire offered excitement enough to last for a long time, and at the same time no lives were endangered and no one was burned out of a home. The warehouse contained baled hay, sacks of grain, and a variety of other stuff. It was a block long, right along the railroad, and the roof and siding were corrugated and galvanized steel. This covering and the fact that it was nighttime were the reasons no one saw the fire until it was too late. Having gotten a good start before finally melting through the roof, the fire was uncontrollable when noticed. The volunteer firemen couldn't get near enough to do any good and, finally, the railroad fire train from Roseville was called in to help. Even with that, the fire burned fiercely for two days and smoldered for ten days after. There was noise, drama, and concern that the whole town might go up as the flames shot high in the air and smoke billowed over the town. We got our adrenaline charge out of that one for a long time.

Every year we had our Rodeo (with the accent over the e). It was held in Roddan's pasture and attracted a great crowd. Both out-of-town and local cowboys competed, and the day always wound down with the barbecue and bean feed. The barbecue pit, dug a day or two before, was about four by six by three feet deep with some rocks mixed in with oak wood. A fire, lit the night before, burned until only coals remained, after which a layer of sand topped with branches of bay leaves was placed, followed by large, carefully wrapped chunks of beef. These were accompanied by corn in the husks, and finally covered with gunnysacks and earth. About eight hours later all was ready to dig up and serve. Meanwhile a hog-dipping pot had been hung over a prepared fire pit and filled with beans and Spanish sauce. Here again, a long cooking period was the rule, and by the end of the afternoon when the bronco busters finished their competition the aroma filled the air as the dust settled. The local women set up oilcloth-covered tables, sliced the homemade bread, and filled the punch bowls, some of which were spiked (and guarded from the kids), and we all stood by as the corn and beef were dug out of the pit. The simple but delicious repast was a fitting climax to an enjoyable day, and people ate and socialized as twilight slowly closed out the day.

We had all varieties of people in our town. There were five hundred of us, and for all my time there it seemed that births pretty much matched deaths. There were poor, middle, and upper strata, and I think about it now with the realization that we were a perfect cross-section of rural America. Some people were always there when cooking, decorating, and organizing was to be done; some always wanted to direct while others worked; some went with the flow; some weren't satisfied with anything. In the main, however, everything worked and the community was a busy and happy place. We didn't have a policeman, and the fire department was whoever got to the fire house, rang the bell, and pulled out the hose cart. There were two people on salary; one ran the water department and the other took care of the street work. The mayor and city council served without salary. We didn't have slums; some of the best homes were at the edge of town and beyond were fields of hops, peaches, alfalfa, wheat, and pasture. For us kids, getting out of town was a matter of a few minutes; in an hour you could be setting up camp for the night by the river, surrounded by willows and oaks. We always took a .22 rifle and sometimes a shotgun, but mostly this was to fire at stumps, cans, and imaginary mountain lions. Speaking of guns, most of us began using them at an early age after extensive training by our dads.

I **recall** some characters. Lottie Jasper was one. She was our vocal news **system**, or, in plain words, a gossip. It all came with much energetic pushing, shoving, punching, and decibel extremes. A question was a series of finger touches until the subject capitulated with an answer. An exclamation was a slap on the shoulder. The recipient of a highly confidential piece of information got a clasp on the arm along with furtive glances around to be sure no one else was listening. Lottie was likeable and willing to pitch in wherever needed.

"Twisty" Harrison, so named because of his peculiar gait, was the town ne'er-do-well. He seemed to be followed by a private little black cloud, was never able to make a decent living, and always needed county help. He was good at one thing, though; there were lots of little "Twisties." To this day I can't recall much about them; they seemed present in the town but sort of invisible, and where they went and what they did in life no one knows.

The Damms!!! This was the Wheatland upper crust. There were two brothers and they ran two big warehouses, one of which burned as I mentioned above, and they owned the biggest and grandest houses in town. The brothers floated in their private ether, not involving themselves in the town's social events, and I recall thinking of them as being carved from a big block of wood as they drove by in their huge Lincoln autos. They didn't seem to like young people, and maybe it was partly because the outhouses at each warehouse became victims of Halloween turnover. There were two sisters in the family, Carrie and Corrie, and believe it or not both had the middle initial B. They were about my parents' age, and it didn't take long for us kids to come up with the obvious sobriquet Carrie or Corrie Be Damned.

Maybe the B stood for Blackford, because they were related to the Blackfords who lived in a big three-story house about two miles out of town. This was a lovely old couple about my grandfather's age, and they had a son known to us as D'wiggy. Where that odd sobriquet originated I never knew. In later years I realized that D'wiggy was a savant. On the rare occasions when he was in town we associated with him even though he was much older than us. One day we learned of D'wiggy's savant side when we were down at the railroad snitching peaches from the cars. As the train began to move D'wiggy said, "I can add 'em." We finally realized that he meant the serial numbers on the cars and that he could do it without pencil and paper. In order to check him, several of us armed ourselves with pencils and paper wrote down the numbers of the slowly moving cars. We put all our numbers together and arrived at a total to check him out next time he showed off his talent. The train was a group of about six slatted boxcars all loaded with peaches, and it took us about an hour to arrive at a total of those serials. When we finished we asked D'wiggy what his total was. To our absolute astonishment it agreed with ours. Today, eighty-one years later, I find it hard to believe such a feat possible, but it did happen. Sadly, D'wiggy, after being absent for a long time, died. It was said that he had hurled himself from a third-story window during one of his "times." We all knew that barred window and that sometimes D'wiggy might be seen there in his "cell," but we weren't sure just why because we liked him. Sometime later, when walking over the slough bridge and going by the big house, we saw that the bars, like D'wiggy, were gone.

And then there was "Cockey" Cunningham. He was the principal of the joint high school and grammar school as I have said, and got his name from the way he walked. He had a sort of rolling gait, and the right leg snapped out at each step. It reminded us of how one opened and closed a hammerless shotgun: a snap and a click and it was cocked. Hence the name Cockey. We finally learned he had a wooden leg and the joint did make a click at each step. He was maybe five foot eight, with thinning hair, and to all of us he was the strict, stern law of the classrooms. We never thought of him as a human being, and it was only later that we came to realize his contribution to our early years. He remained principal of the grammar school after the new high school had been built, and it was when I was in high school that I got know him. He turned out to be a warm and friendly man with a lovely wife and an inviting home. There were no children, but the two of them had an abiding interest in the students and followed the course of us all as long as we were in school. Sadly, I never knew his real first name or I would print it here in respect.

Claude Biggs published the *Wheatland Herald,* and it was the kind of paper every community ought to have. Claude wasn't afraid to tell the truth about anything or anybody. He served as the town's conscience. It was fun to watch the job of typesetting and to see the paper being run through the press. Most of the job had to be done by hand, and it took quite a while to get out the weekly edition.

I could go on, but I can see now as I write this that I am only recalling my love for that small town and remembering what it has meant to me. How difficult it is to transcribe that love onto paper!

WHEATLAND

1874   1974

"First School constructed in Wheatland, 1879."

First School

"Wheatland's first high school located on 2nd floor; Grammer school on first floor and playground in basement. Constructed 1903."

"new Wheatland Union High School"

compliments of Dreyfus and Blackford, Sacramento.

High School

Chapter Nine

Summers 1925 to 1928

hese were the years before high school, and while the rest of each year was filled with activity, it is the summers that stick in my memory. June, July, and August could be outlined in a red-penciled box within which new adventures might be expected. It was a time free of the routine of school, a time to try something different, to feel I was growing up and about to set foot on the threshold of a great new world. I had worked in the shop with Dad in spare hours and during vacations, and although I loved the mechanical part of it a change now beckoned. I'm not sure who made the choice, but I suspect that Mother and Dad, in subtle ways, planted the seed of interest. They also must have arranged the jobs, since I don't recall beating the bushes to find employment. In those years, 1925 through 1928, there was first the cannery, then the peach picking, followed by the harvester and finally the survey party.

The cannery was located on the Horst Ranch about two miles east of town, and was managed by Tom Ferguson. He and Lily (one of my most favorite lovely ladies) and their son, Stan, lived in a fine old home on the ranch, and our families were good friends. I suspect it was because of this relationship that Stan and I got our jobs. Lily and Mother probably decided it would be a good thing to get us out from underfoot, so off we went to the cannery. I thought it strange that the ranch didn't grow any of the fruit that was processed, and all the input (cling peaches) arrived in lug boxes carried on trucks from orchards east of town. Ours was not to reason why, however, but to get to work cleaning up the area where peaches got dumped onto the conveyor leading to the peeling vats. Some fruit got mashed and some survived when the handlers missed the chute, and that was where Stan and I were stationed with wide-bladed manure shovels. The mess went into a refuse bin, but we had to spot the salvageable peaches, pick them up by hand, and put them on the conveyor.

"Hey! This isn't so bad, and they pay you money for it," we thought. We hadn't reckoned on several factors, though, and by the end of the day the view changed. Soon the area was sloppy with juice, our shoes got sticky, and our pants got soaked, starting at the shoe tops and progressing higher as the day wore on. Now and then it was necessary to stop and hose the mess off into a drain trough. While we were doing that, the inexorable falling peaches accumulated. If you have seen the TV show where Lucille Ball is working in the candy factory, you'll know how we felt. At the end of the canning season, which, mercifully, lasted only about six weeks, we were ready for almost any new adventure not having to do with canneries or peaches. Even eating a peach seemed repulsive, and this after previous years when we used to reach in through the slats of a railway car and snitch a peach or two.

Would you believe it? The following year I got a job picking you know what! Yes, peaches! Wheatland held the distinction of being one of the largest peach-growing areas in the world, and the orchards were located along a considerable stretch of river bottom where the old Bear River coursed before it was levied into its present confines. The predominant crop was cling, but small areas were devoted to the Elberta freestone, mainly for local consumption. Clings, used almost exclusively for canning, were shipped out by rail or trucked to the Horst cannery, and they were picked while still firm. They had a good flavor but approached an apple in texture. That characteristic helped them survive the rigors of shipping and commercial canning. In general the Elbertas were tree-ripened and wouldn't survive much handling. Few people could home can them, but Mother had the touch, and I remember having those delicious canned peaches for dessert during the winter months.

Back to the picking. We had a supply of lug boxes at each tree, and as we filled each one we stashed it on top of a previous one until they were six high. A truck came by and we had to load the boxes on board. You wouldn't think that peach fuzz could get to your hands, but it did, so at night a good application of oil helped sooth the dryness away. Fingertips also took a beating from lifting the boxes, but they soon got calloused and sore muscles got toughened. None of this required any brain power, so you could think of other things as you reached, picked, boxed, and loaded for eight hours a day.

In 1927, at the age of twelve, I got a job with a harvest crew. To set the stage, I must tell you a few things. At that time there were no combines with hoppers to feed a truck, so the threshed grain was sacked and slid down a chute to the ground, where it was picked up and thrown onto a truck. The harvester itself had no engine, but as the tractor ahead pulled it along there were chain drives from the harvester wheels to supply the power for threshing and other functions. Fields of today are leveled and carefully manicured, but in those years we took the terrain as it came, with gullies, potholes, and hummocks. Now, off to the job.

Header tender was what I was, and all I had to do was keep the sickles (the oscillating triangular cutters) down close enough to the ground to get all the grain, even the short stuff. Fairly simple, thought I, but remember the gullies etc.? It soon became evident that I had to learn how to anticipate the variations in ground level by observing the top of the wheat, because it was not always possible to clearly see the ground. No daydreaming here, as I learned after digging the header into the ground and getting shouted at a couple of times. After a period of straining my eyes and being in terror that I would break something, I learned to "read" the field ahead and got to be a confident header tender. I stood there behind that big twofoot wheel, moving it clockwise to lower the header and counter-clock to raise it, until I could cut a field to look like a marine with a butch haircut.

I treasured those days with the harvest crews, and the early morning breakfasts, the midday dinners, and the late evening suppers. There were a couple of things I didn't like, though; one was the chaff and the other was the tractor exhaust. Even though we wore bandanas tied around our necks, the chaff worked its way down the neck and into our shirts. Even after a long bath at night the itching still bothered, especially on a hot summer night. The exhaust sometimes got to us on breezy days when the wind blew down the length of the field. As the harvester moved upwind and the fumes blew into our faces, I would feel slightly sick. As we made the round of the field, I recovered in time to get sick again on the upwind course. The older hands seemed not to be bothered; presumably they had been toughened to those noxious fumes over the years. Today, one man can do the job from an air-conditioned cab listening to pleasant music over his FM radio, and when it is time for lunch he calls his wife on the two-way radio and says, "Honey, I'll be at the house in ten minutes."

Survey party! Boy, was I excited. This was a job away from home for the first time, and it would last for the whole three months of vacation! We would stay on a snag boat, in a hotel, on a houseboat, or even at a private home. My Uncle Henry was in charge of the Sacramento District of the Corps of Engineers, and the surveys were in and around various rivers to assess the effect of yearly runoff of silt into the Sacramento River, which is a navigable stream. In those days, a great deal of traffic plied up and down the river carrying rice, wheat, cattle, and other products, and it was important to maintain a clear channel free from silt buildup and debris.

In that first year, when I was thirteen, we sounded the river, took cross-sections of the levees, and shot topography of the area outside the levees from Chico to Sacramento. The work entailed a great deal of brush cutting. A survey line had to be run down the levee, and the sections taken at right angles every two hundred feet. To do this a clear line of sight was required for the transit man. Every foot of the way was solid trees and brush, and we had to clear a path with brush hooks and machetes. The work was hot, dusty, and difficult. Sometimes we had to hang from a tree twenty feet off the ground, holding on by one hand while chopping branches with a machete in the other. Rattlesnakes were numerous, and we were frequently chilled by that ominous sound, so easily recognized. Occasionally we had to kill one, but mostly they slithered off into the undergrowth. On one memorable occasion I heard the rattle and upon looking around found a medium-sized fellow wrapped around my ankle. By that time, we had gotten to accept the snakes as part of the landscape, so, in spite of a moment of fear, I calmly reached down with my machete and flipped him away. That is one of the reasons we all wore knee-length boots and two pairs of socks. Big spiders hung in the brush, and if one fell on us it would bite. It wasn't serious, but hurt like the dickens for awhile. Other things lurked in the tangled undergrowth, but we got used to it all, and before long we felt at ease amongst the creatures.

I had an advantage/disadvantage condition in that I didn't catch poison oak. The "ad" part was that I could slash through a forest of the stuff and only get some brown stains on my body where a falling branch might hit. The "dis" part was that every time someone else ran into a patch, the call would go out for me to get it cleared. In those days I must have cut enough brush and poison oak to cover most of Northern California. Years later, clearing brush on the hillside at our home in Oakland, I caught poison oak!

All summer we went without shirts during the workday, mainly to get a tan and impress the girls when we got back to school. For me it has proved costly, since I have had at least seventy lesions removed, a number of which have been cancerous. Because the problems show up so many years later, there is only the solution of removal of the lesions, with the attendant white spots and scars. I say this as a warning to avoid too much sun and to urge the use of sunscreens so you may retain your schoolgirl complexions.

Chapter Ten

Survey Party

My years on the summer survey job lasted through high school and even into college, so rather than give you a piecemeal narrative I'll summarize the whole experience at this time by hitting on a few highlights that are, to me, most memorable. You remember that I had obtained the job because my Uncle Henry was director of the Corps of Engineers, Sacramento District. Nepotism, you may shout, but I must tell you that toward the end of the job, Bud Fraser, the chief of party, told me, "Your uncle said to me at the start, 'I'm going to have three nephews working with you during the summers, and I want you to work their tails off—don't do them any favors.'" Bud then went on to say that all three of us had never needed any pushing, and in fact had more than carried our share of the workload. I related this to John Waldo (older cousin) and Bob Rich (same age), and we agreed that those summers had been learning and growing experiences for us, and that we were grateful to a tough, profane, caring, and wonderful uncle whose presence up there in the Heavens has almost certainly stirred the place more than God ever bargained for.

To begin, I must introduce you to Bud Fraser. He ran the party all the years I worked there, and to this day stands out as an example of a hardworking, capable, and dedicated government employee. I can still see him, nondescript hat pulled down over his eyes, transit over his shoulder, cigarette in mouth (in those days, Lucky Strike packaged fifty cigarettes in a metal box and Bud consumed two of those boxes a day), on his way down the levee to the next setup at a gait somewhere between a trot and a run. Bud was sort of round and leaned forward as he moved, so that you felt he'd roll like a ball if he had to stop suddenly. For any of us taking notes, the accuracy and rapidity with which Bud turned traverse angles and read stadia topog was amazing, and it kept our pencils flying to keep up.

Each day, precisely at noon, everything would stop for lunch. After we had eaten, we all sought shade and comfort for a nap, which we would try and prolong as much as possible. Bud joined us in these rests and we always hoped he would doze beyond the hour. Even if one of us awoke, the game was to remain quiet as a mouse to avoid disturbing Bud. Never, never did it work! Precisely as the last second ticked off, he would arise with a snort and a "Let's go," and we would lose again. He was patient in explaining things to us, but he never tolerated stupid mistakes.

One year, we had a nephew of Sheridan Downey, a California senator. This guy was gawky, and, we decided, not very bright. He proved it to us one day, and that was the time when Bud came unglued. To set the stage, I will have to tell you how we ran a traverse. (See illustration.) A traverse is simply a series of straight lines with a hub (wooden stake driven into the ground) at each point where the lines have to bend to follow a desired course. Each stake has an indented nail (hub tack) driven into the top to indicate the precise position. From any hub, we had to be able to see the one ahead (foresight) and the one behind (backsight). An instrument called a transit was set up over a hub, and the angle between the foresight and back-sight was measured. Distances between hubs were measured by two men with a metal tape two-hundred-feet long. The man leading was called the head chainman and the one behind, the rear chain. A stakeman carried hubs and station stakes, the latter being smaller than a hub and set every two hundred feet. Each station was marked on the stake. For example, 2 + 00 meant that stake was two hundred feet from the start of our traverse. Assume we were a mile down the traverse; the last stake would be 52 + 80. As we proceeded, the instrument man would set his transit precisely over each hub by centering a plumb bob suspended from the transit over the hub tack. To measure the angle between the line behind and the one ahead, a person called the back rodman held a slender pointed steel rod five feet long and half an inch in diameter carefully on the tack of the first hub behind, and the head chainman did the same on the hub ahead. The rods had to be vertical, so the trick was to hold them lightly between the fingers until they would almost stand by themselves. When the transit man was ready to take his shots, he'd shout, "rod up!" and both foresight and backsight men then were supposed to hold the rods in position. On this particular day, Downey was on rear sight about five hundred feet to the rear. After repeated tries to make his angles check out, Bud was getting frustrated and finally sent someone back to check on Downey. It seems that the guy just plunked his rod down wherever he stood at the call of "rod up," and there were little holes in the ground all over the place, some as far from the hub as eight feet. When the news got back to Bud, he blew his stack and for the first time in my life I actually saw a grown man snatch off his hat, throw it in the dust, and stomp on it. Needless to say, after that Downey was relegated to carrying the lunch bag or packing stakes. We didn't see him the following year, and I suppose he eventually went on to high places in politics!

The summer of the houseboat was a memorable one. We played tennis, Bob caught poison oak, I found out about boxing, and we all ate maggots. John drank honey beer, and I played the saxophone for songfests.

We three cousins played a fair game of tennis, and so did a couple of permanent members of the survey party. It was decided that we would go into Sacramento two or three nights a week and get some practice. There was a city park area that had lighted courts, and we found they were not heavily used. The problem was that it meant a trip of about eight miles in and eight miles back, and no one had a car. The only answer was to hoof it, and because of the work we did all day, we found that to be no problem. At a medium run, it took us about an hour to reach the courts, where we played as many as four sets. At the conclusion, the losers bought milkshakes for the winners. That meant four of the real shakes they used to make in those days, and to prevent too much sloshing as we ran, a rule was passed limiting the intake to two each. Today, I find it hard to believe we did that, but both Bob and John confirm it.

One day, in a dense area of the poison oak, Bob waded in before he realized it, and a couple of days later he started to itch with the telltale inflamed spots. The old baking soda treatment had no effect, and soon blisters appeared, not just a few but spreading all over his body. Lying down was misery, and sleeping was impossible. At this point I called our uncle, and shortly after Bob was in the hospital where he underwent treatment for at least a month. Bob's case was complicated by the fact of his family's dedication to Christian Science, but he finally recovered. Never before or since have I seen such a terrible case of poison oak, and I'm sure Bob remembers it clearly.

We all took boxing lessons from one of the guys on the snag boat. He was a Kanaka, one of several Hawaiians who did the diving to hook the snags below water. Boxing under the name of Kid Kanaka, he had done well until money, booze, and women had softened him and ended his career. We all liked him and enjoyed listening to stories of some of the fights he'd had. Often, he had one of us pose as his opponent to demonstrate a particular combination of blows that lead to a triumph over a tough adversary. Of course, no real blows were struck, but light contact was often made. On one occasion I was the other fighter and the Kid was showing us how a series of left jabs set up his opponent for a right cross. Four light jabs and suddenly my ears were ringing, and I fell back against the steel frame of the bunk beds we used. A small gash opened on my shoulder and blood ran down my back. The Kid was devastated and ran for the first-aid kit at the end of the bunkhouse. While patching me up, he said, "I very sorry; sometime remember old fights too good." The Kid had a beautiful physique; a slightly smaller edition of Max Baer, he fought in the light-weight division. We often watched him swimming around the houseboat, and sometimes saw him at work diving for snags. His grace in the water was a joy to behold, and obviously came from his years in the clear water of the Islands.

One hot day we had taken soundings on the American River, about two miles up from the point where it flowed into the Sacramento River, and had arrived at a grove of cottonwood trees at lunch time. Taking off boots and socks, most of us jumped in for a quick swim to cool off before eating. We then retired to shady spots under the trees as the lunch fixin's were handed out. There was chatter as we dug into our pot roast sandwiches about how good the swim felt and how foolish the government was to pay us for this sort of thing. Someone said, "Boy, these are good today, Cookie outdid himself. What did he add?" Freddie Toy, an old timer, opened the slices, spat, spluttered, and gargled, "God Almighty, you don't want to know!" As I pulled the bread apart, there wriggling happily on the beef was a colony of lovely little white maggots! No one finished lunch, and when we got back to the houseboat that night we confronted Cookie, who swore the beef was all right when he made the sandwiches. There was no evidence left in the kitchen, so we couldn't prove anything, but we were strongly suspicious that somewhere down the river fish were enjoying pot roast and maggots. We told Cookie he should have his eyes checked because if it ever happened again, we'd tie his hands and feet and throw him overboard. For some time after that, lunches were near-gourmet quality. Maybe this experience proves the adage, "What you don't know won't hurt you."

Just across the river from Sacramento was a suburb called Bryte, and it was anything but. Even in those days, one didn't walk through the place alone at night. Most of the homes were rundown and had been converted to gambling dens and drinking houses. This went on right in the open, and I suspect the cops stayed away because it was too dangerous. Four of us decided to have a look at the Bryte night life in order to further our worldly education, and we selected a beer joint to do it. You won't remember, but in those days there was the Eighteenth Amendment that enforced Prohibition. The only effect it had was to drive any decent booze off the market and spawn homemade stuff known as bathtub gin, white lightening, or home brew, and a host of other poisonous concoctions. Anyway, off we went to our evening class in speakeasy lore.

The place we chose had a big screen porch where there were four twenty-gallon crocks of honey beer. We were given a tin cup and told to help ourselves. The crocks had no covers, and on the surface was a greenish foam in which a few flies were either drunk or asphyxiated. It took courage, but the drill was to scrape away the foam and flies and dip the cup into the rather forbidding-looking liquid below. Being a nondrinker in those days, I took enough to taste, but over the evening John must have had six cups. I can't say the taste was bad; as a matter of fact, it was quite good, and the part of the honey not yet fermented made it very sweet. The next day was one of the hottest of the summer, and sometime in the late morning I saw John sitting in the shade of a big old oak tree. "Not like John," I thought, and went over to see what was up. His head was in his hands and he moaned softly, "If I don't die before the day is over, it will be the worst one of my life." Others in the drinking party suffered according to their intake and learned to exercise caution when drinking illicit brew.

Evenings when we were not out playing tennis or slumming I would now and then bring out the saxophone and we would have a song session. The guys gathered around and, looking over my shoulder, read from the songbook as I played the melody. These were pleasant times and nostalgic too, as we sang some of the old favorites, each of which brought back memories to one or another of the group. Sometimes I played and the others just listened. How pleasant this was as the sound floated out over the river and soft echoes returned from across the water. Even more enjoyable were the times when the Kid joined the group with his guitar. These were infrequent for, as the Kid explained to me, "I like play and sing very much, but sometime too sad." I have always wondered where the Kid wound up. He was a lonely man in an alien world, probably led into his transgressions by some greedy promoter whose only interest was to make a buck. I hope he made it back to his native land and had a chance to watch a few sunsets from those beautiful shores.

One time, near Colusa, we rented a boat from a farmer to do a quick check on some problem or other. The catch was that we would arrive on the other side of the river, and since I had learned to swim in a river I was elected to fetch the boat. There were a couple of farmhouses along the shore, and because I didn't want to get caught in dripping underwear I set out with all my clothes on except boots and socks. I didn't allow enough distance upstream for my start, and in an effort not to drift too far below the boat, I tried to beat the current. Bad mistake, because by the time I reached the other side I was a little pooped and a lot scared. Old Man River was about four hundred feet wide at the crossing, and I had been deceived by the lazy-looking, sinuous swirl of the current. With a depth of fifteen to twenty feet, there was no place to let down my feet on the bottom and rest. Next time, I did better and arrived at the boat without a struggle.

One of the guys in the party was Del Stover. He did the driving as we went from one location to another and performed a variety of tasks for Bud Frazer. Del possessed a pleasant personality and everyone liked him, but he lied like a dog. We were always hearing stories of the many experiences he had had, and as tale after tale piled up we began to take notes. It didn't take long for us to amass a formidable total of years at an amazing variety of jobs and professions. Champion boxer, Olympic runner, owner of a chain of stores, writer under a well-known pen name, and on and on. As we summarized these events, it was discovered that, contrary to our assumption, Del, instead of being about forty-five years old, was in fact somewhere around 168! This just goes to show you that you can't judge age by appearances.

Up in the mountains on the Bear River we had our roughest summer. The river flowed through a canyon where the walls were nearly vertical, and we were thus forced to frequently cross the swiftly flowing water that ricocheted from wall to wall. It was hard work carrying the equipment and trying to stay on our feet. Sometimes we would slip and wind up a hundred feet downstream, wet and bruised. The lunch bag went in a couple of times, leaving us with a few wet sandwiches, and Bud fell in with the transit. The instrument got wet and dented, necessitating a long and welcome pause for repairs. Boots became a casualty of the rocks and water, and lasted only about three weeks. We learned one lesson very early. One could not let the chain (two-hundred-foot tape) dip into the swiftly flowing water. Once caught, the chain had enough pull to drag a person into the river. It seems impossible, but that slender tape, only a quarter of an inch wide, exerted a tremendous force when immersed in the roiling waters. To cross the stream, the chainmen had to maintain a constant tension on the chain to keep it always above water. If that failed, the head chain held on and the rear chain let go. Rear was then required to cross and do the whole thing again.

One of the good things about that year was the little hotel off the beaten path not far from our work. The place was deep in the woods, and a hundred yards away ran a stream brimming with trout. Before breakfast we could grab one of the hotel-furnished poles, run down to the stream, and catch however many trout we thought we could eat, and the cook had them steaming on a plate in minutes along with bacon, eggs, and hotcakes. Dinners were just what we needed after a full day in the canyon; five thousand calories of the best stuff you ever tasted. After a short bull session, bed felt glorious, and sleeping was never better than in the quiet and crisp air of the mountains.

This was also the year that John gambled away every cent he earned. In Cisco, where we stayed for a while, there were Chinese gambling and opium dens. In the front section were the poker, blackjack, faro, and other games of chance. In the back, through an open door, were bunk beds where the Chinese smoked their opium. You could see them as they lit up, threw up in the galvanized buckets, and finally lay back to dream. Nothing was undercover; anyone could walk in and sit in on a game or maybe even smoke some opium, although I never saw anyone other than the Chinese doing that.

John was hooked on the card games and never seemed to win. He would ask me to hide his money after he had cashed the monthly paycheck. I hid the stuff under the mattress, in a vase, rolled up in a sock, and a dozen other places, but he always managed to find it and head for the tables. Being flat broke, he didn't have money to buy meals, but he refused to accept anything from us. He went with us to meals but ate only the bread and butter that came before we ordered. His big meal came at lunch, since that was furnished. John's boots came apart just like ours, but he turned down offers to buy him a new pair, applying a novel solution to the problem. When the soles came off, he cut the upper six inches off the boots and, using the lace holes, tied them on for soles. There were about six weeks of the summer left and he came through looking fit as a fiddle, and with feet as tough as shoe leather. A very hardy guy, determined not to involve others in his foolishness. I always admired him for that.

The defunct horse; boy, that was one I won't forget! Brushing out a line one day, I suddenly stepped off into space. Jolted but still standing, I looked around to take stock of the situation. Finding nothing amiss, I stepped—or tried to step—forward, only to find my right foot caught. By this time, a pungent, sweet odor began to permeate the air, and when I looked to see what was holding my foot, to my horror I found both feet in the middle of a dead horse. Now the smell was awful and there were maggots again, more than you can imagine. Freeing my foot, I rushed to the river and scrubbed myself from top to bottom, particularly the boots. Shuddering from the experience, I felt like Humphrey Bogart when he was plastered with leeches in the movie *The African Queen.*

Skunks smell very bad and one has to avoid them, but I didn't, or couldn't, one day. Down around Dixon we had some levee and ditch survey to do where a small tributary emptied into the Sacramento River. Approaching the end of a muddy area we saw a lamb stuck in the mud. It had struggled to free itself but had given up by the time we came along. Bob and I went to help and spotted an old set of stairs that had apparently floated away from a shack during the winter. We figured by moving the steps adjacent to the lamb we could spare ourselves some muddy boots, so, picking up opposite ends, we proceeded with our Boy Scout good deed of the day. What we didn't know was that a friendly skunk had established a nest in the shelter of the steps. As we stood there holding our rescue devise, a deeply offended and greatly agitated animal jumped out and thoroughly sprayed everything in sight. We got the lamb out, though it seemed ungrateful for our rescue efforts. In the short time to the end of the day, Bob and I worked at a respectful distance from everyone else, and on the way back to town we had to ride on the fenders of the truck to spare the rest of the guys. Our lodging was at a private home, and upon returning it was required that our clothes be taken off in the wood shed and washed in a tub of water to which a large can of tomato juice had been added. Scrubbing with juice and a heavy soap rubdown did most of the job for us, but occasionally that pungent odor would return. This was mostly imagination, but the clothes and boots never came clean and had to be thrown away. To this day, when I smell the slight odor of skunk wafted from some distant place, I am reminded of the fully enveloping and piercing stink.

Dixon seemed to be plagued with perils, not the least of which was gnats. "Gnats," you say, "those tiny little things? How could they be a peril?" Well, I'll tell you.

As hot weather dried out the ground, cracks formed running in all directions up and down the levee. Those "tiny little things" made a home in the cracks, and as the sun came up each day, they would sally forth. Not just one or two, but billions! Unprepared on our first encounter, we were driven from the field of battle by clouds of the creatures and, beating a hasty retreat, regrouped for a strategy meeting. It had been found that any opening in clothing was an access route, and around sleeve cuffs and collars a red ring formed from the bites where the insects got trapped. Ears, nose, and mouth were targets, and we could no longer go without shirts and hats as before. Eating lunch was impossible unless you were willing to ingest protein with wings, and I mean lots of wings, buzzing on your tongue and inside your cheeks. The next day, after a brief shopping spree, we rejoined the battle with mosquito netting over our heads. This was held in place by a hat and tucked under the shirt collar, which was buttoned tight. Shirt cuffs were pulled down around gloves and tied. With all this clever armor, we would surely defeat our enemy, right? Wrong! The stinkers somehow found their way under the netting and, once there, they couldn't find a way out. We heard them over the surrounding din of the outside hordes, and the only solution was to squash them through the netting before they climbed up our noses or hid in our mouths. And they still left red rings around wrists and necks, although not as bad as before. It was necessary to drive three or four miles away to eat lunch, and even Bud hated to head back into the swarm.

Looking back from the lunch spot, we could see what appeared to be several gray clouds hugging the levee. As we watched the clouds moved, merged, and rejoined in a constantly changing pattern. The view got on our nerves, and by quitting time it was a great relief to pack up and leave. I will always remember Owen Stanley, as the strain finally got to him. Throwing down his level rod and notebook, he took off down the levee on a dead run, flailing his arms and shouting incoherently. After we caught him and calmed him down, Owen spent the next two days in town and, mercifully, we completed the job in that time.

The gnat tale reminds me of the Wheatland mosquitoes. They were huge and terribly vicious. The only way to escape them was to duck into a metal tank, and as they drove their bills through the steel, clinch over the bill with a hammer. It was critical to count the number of bills locked in place, because if there were too many of these monsters they would fly off with you and the tank! I swear; I swear! The gnat tale is true, but the Wheatland mosquitoes are really BIG.

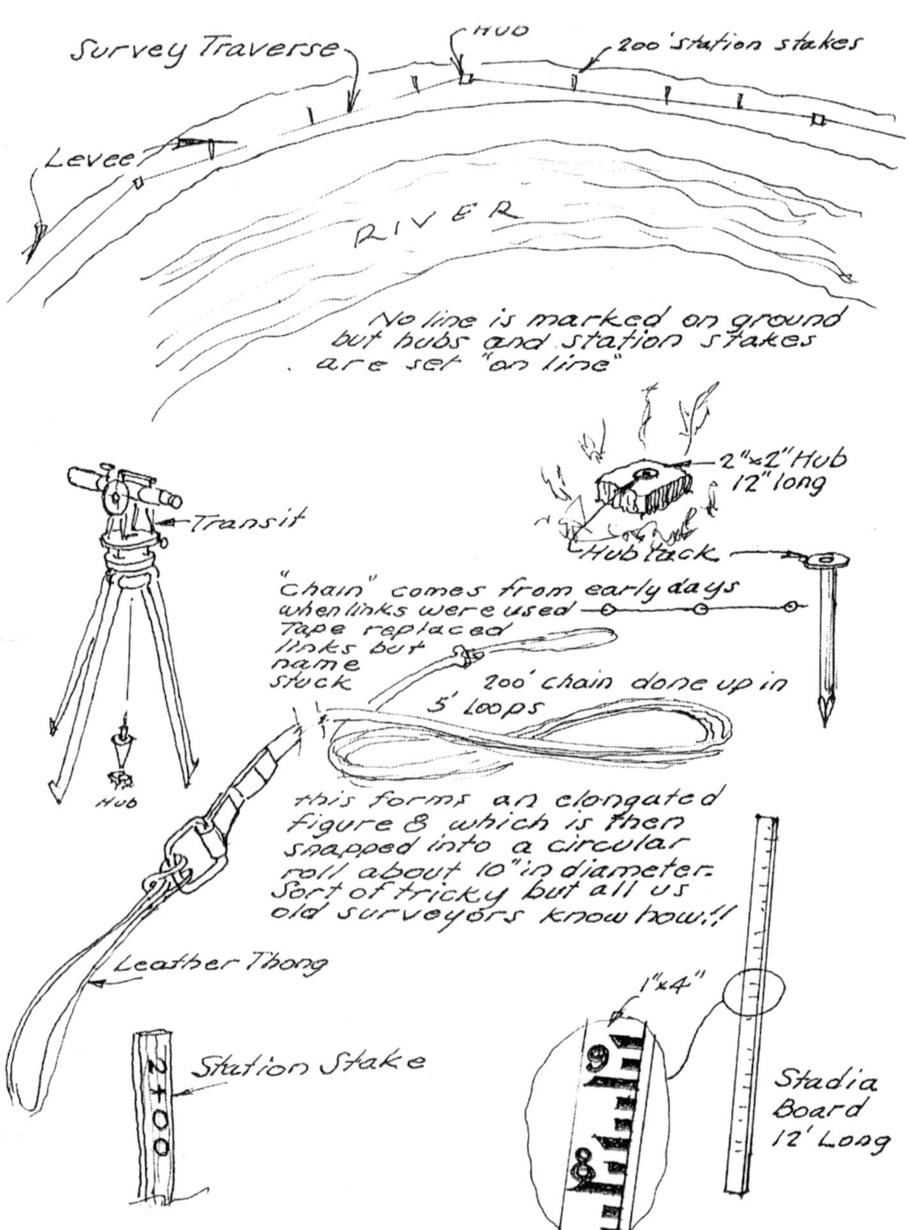

Survey Equipment

Chapter Eleven

High School

When I was in the sixth grade the decision was made to build a new high school. By then we had moved to the house with the barn to be with Grandfather after Grandmother died. I don't recall much excitement over the news of a new school, but that was probably because we were still in the big old barn where I first started school. I had become accustomed to the eight-block walk, and the change to a two-block walk didn't mean much to me. However, by the time I started seventh grade foundations were being set and I could watch the progress from our house. I made regular observations and now wish I had photos to show you. It would be nearly two years before I entered those hallowed halls that became an icon of my hometown like the beautiful railway station. Progress has relegated those two to the dust heap of the past, along with my old house with the barn. The adage "you can't go back" is true; but I can remember!

Wheatland Union High served our town and the surrounding farming community, attending to the education of about 125 of us and doing a fine job of it. The main building was vintage 1925, with some of the soft lines of that period of architecture and none of the flat featureless planes of today's boxes. The Spanish pattern of design with a hint of the Moors made for a wonderful old edifice topped off by the ubiquitous red tile roof. Two other buildings completed the campus: a fine gym and a well-equipped shop.

The main building housed an auditorium with mezzanine and main floor seating about two hundred people, and had a stage complete with a gold-trimmed velvet curtain. Other facilities included classrooms, teachers' lounge, music room, home economics room, sewing room, chemistry lab, and a few other assorted spaces, all in all a rather complete facility for a student body of, give or take, 125. I might also add that with six faculty members, we all got a good education. None of us going on to college had to take "bonehead" English or remedial math, and Miss Silva saw to it that our Spanish met the test.

Our sports menu was basketball, baseball, track, and tennis, and we did pretty well in the league, which included Marysville, a town of twenty thousand people in those days. We were known as the Pirates and somewhere in the memorabilia are a couple of seat cushions with the old logo. Also tucked away in the boxes are some of the letters I earned in the various sports. The only uniforms we had were for basketball, and those were provided by the PTA. We bought our own tennis rackets, track shoes, baseball spikes, and gloves. Our performance in the games lacked sophistication, but there was unlimited enthusiasm. Maintenance of equipment was up to us and our mothers. When things got torn they were mended; if a tennis racket string broke, I was the restringer; when a baseball lost its cover, friction tape was substituted; if a bat broke, we used hot glue and friction tape. Have you heard the expression, "Keep the Spaulding up"? This comes from the days when most of the bats were made by the Spaulding Company. They burned their logo onto each bat so that when the bat was held with logo up, the grain of the wood was parallel to the horizontal. In that position the wood was strongest and wouldn't break as it struck the ball. If the Spaulding faced forward or back, the bat was sure to break.

Track and field was a minor sport in our league, but I did fairly well with the discus, and thereby hangs a tale. There was a meet held in Gridley or Colusa, I forget which, and five of us were to compete. As we got our numbers, we were told that a football throw had been substituted for the discus (my event) because someone had been injured by an errant platter a couple of weeks ago. We didn't have a football team (not enough kids), but most of us had played around with the pigskin so I knew how to throw one, more or less. Disappointed, I thought, "What the heck, might as well try it anyway." I hadn't reckoned with our teacher/coach who, noting that there was a gusty wind blowing, told me, "I'm going down about half-way and I'll watch the trees next to the track. When I see a gust hit them, I'll wave my hat and you throw as hard and high as you can." I stalled around a bit until I saw the hat waving, then I heaved the ball. It seemed to float forever, and when the dust cleared I had won the football throw, thanks to a cagey coach.

In my junior year there was THE GREAT BASEBALL GAME, the one making us champions of our league. Wheatland and Marysville had finished the season with a 6–0 record, and a playoff was necessary to determine top dog. A flip of a coin dictated that the game would be played in Marysville, and we knew the location didn't favor us. On the other hand, they did have a real park with fences, bleachers, and a well-tended playing field. They had uniforms; we had spikes and caps and an assortment of jeans and shirts. The guessing had it that we were about even; they had more good players but we had Frank Spencer, a very good pitcher who later nearly made it to the San Francisco Seals, a Coast League team of that era.

After a hard-fought game into the last half of the ninth, we led by one run, 6 to 5. Marysville had men on second and third, thanks to a bloop hit and an error, but there were two outs. Their second baseman was at bat and he was a good hitter. Everyone was quiet, their supporters hoping for a hit and ours hoping for an out. A hit would put them ahead; an out and we were the champions. Frank would up and delivered; a ball. Four more pitches had the count at 3 and 2. Brocky, our catcher, called time and walked out to the mound for a word with Frank. Finally, the moment of truth; Frank wound up, served a fastball, and the crack of the bat told us the chilling news—a hit! But wait! Out in center field Vernon Baker had started a run for the ball, a sinking line drive. With his glove on the turf, he caught the hard-hit ball in the web between the thumb and forefinger, and we were the champs! It had been suggested that if we won it would be the better part of valor to head for the cars and get the heck out of there, since our rivals were not noted for their sportsmanship. Vernon got to the car ahead of me, and four other guys arrived shortly after. Mother had the engine running and off we went, just ahead of some mean-looking losers. Vernon kept that ball, and it is to this day mounted in a holder sitting proudly on his mantle at his home in Wheatland. There is a faded photo of it at the end of this tale. How do I remember all the details? Not long ago, I stopped by to visit Vernon and he had some notes preserved along with the ball, and we relived the whole glorious event. Who says you can't go back?

After Frank graduated, Chet Stineman, a southpaw, and I, a right-hander, shared the pitching job. When not pitching, I played the hot corner (third base), and Chet held down first. We were juniors in the great year, but in our senior year, although we had a fair season, we didn't win the grand prize and Marysville got its revenge. Chet had a good curveball but no fastball; I had both a good fastball and curveball, but was sometimes wild as a hooty owl.

A school band/orchestra class was part of the curriculum and boasted a membership of twenty. I had originally taken piano lessons, but finally switched to saxophone because I was too lazy to practice the piano. Something about the sax led me to practice with enthusiasm, and I got fairly good on the instrument. Most of the band were beginners, and I was sort of nominated as the general helper. I would sit with the violins and play their part or do the same with the trombones, trumpets, or others. This taught me to transpose to any key and to sight-read, so when playing in college dance bands later I could sit in with nearly any group and hold my own. Later, I found that there were many fine musicians in bands who could play rings around me and there remained no illusions of a musical career.

Many social activities kept us busy. There were music nights, dances, plays, picnics, pancake feeds, and sometimes an assembly to hear a visiting dignitary speak. We took advantage of every holiday to put on some kind of show, and always the auditorium was lavishly decorated with native flora.

I vividly recall a play we put on. It was set in Holland and we built a sort of Dutch windmill base, a home for the main character, as the centerpiece of the stage setting. The structure consisted of cardboard with a few pieces of wood to hold things together. There was one blade of the windmill visible adjacent to a door and window, and we even had some flowerpots on the window ledge. When painted, the whole effect was very convincing. I recall only the one line leading to my downfall. A group of visitors were to come on stage and I was to open the mill door and greet them with a speech containing, in part, "Mit un heardt fooll uf hoppiness, I velcome you." Trying to maintain the accent was too much for me, and what I said was, "Mit un fart hooll of happiness." I looked at my guests, who were doing their darndest to act like nothing had happened. One of them couldn't hold it any longer and exploded in laughter. This did it for the audience, and they too roared as I stood there with the red rising slowly up my face. As things quieted, I doggedly went back to the beginning and got it right. No standing around after the play to accept plaudits that night. I slunk out the back way and beat a path for home. When Mother and Dad got home later, Dad said, "I thought your accent was pretty good."

One Thanksgiving is burned into my memory as the time of the narrow escape. I had access to a Ford shop truck with a large bed on which a hoist had been mounted, and we had used this to gather bales of hay, pumpkins, and all kinds of plants to place around the auditorium. On our last trip, loaded with tree branches and kids, we started to make the turn into the school yard, but the truck didn't turn! The steering wheel was loose in my hands as I frantically applied all of the feeble brake power available on those old Fords. Ahead loomed a telephone pole, with its guy wire pointed toward us. At the last moment, the right front wheel ran up the ditch along-side the road, and the truck veered just enough to clear pole and wire. Heaving a great sigh of relief, I thought, "Boy, we missed," only to see the wire neatly sweep Carol Akins off the running board where she had been standing. My next thought was, "My God, we've killed Carol." Everyone (four people) jumped out to pick up the corpse, but before they could get to her she rose unsteadily to her feet, brushing off dust and grass. All the while, with my heart in my throat, I was bringing that beast of a truck to a halt, not being able to see Carol arise. Wondering how I was going to break such awful news to the family, I became aware of the happy laughter of my relieved passengers. I wasn't a murderer after all.

The Model T Ford had an arrangement using a planetary gear reduction in the steering wheel hub, connected to an exterior tube running down to a flange bolted to the plywood firewall between the engine and the driver's compartment. (See illustration). The tube had torn loose from the firewall and then rotated without having any effect on the front wheels. Dad's shop was a block away, so he came over and fixed things in short order, but that ended our decorating for that event. I must confess that the plywood had been badly treated when we used to go hunting because we often would disconnect the exhaust pipe from the engine manifold to hear the loud roar of the unmuffled engine. The result heated the firewall and hastened its demise. I think Dad knew this, but he never said a word.

Chemistry lab offered opportunities for inventive fun. We found that mixing sulphur and potassium made a mild explosive. Take a spoonful of the stuff, wrap it in a flat paper package, and whack it with a hammer or other suitable impactor, and it would go off with a loud bang. Finally, after things got too noisy, Mr. Fjeldstedt, our chemistry teacher, impounded the supply of ingredients and peace once again reigned. We had one more trick up our sleeves, though: the old sodium/water bomb. Take a medium-sized test tube, fill it half full of water, put it upright in a standard rack, wire a small piece of sodium to the bottom of a cork, tightly stopper the test tube, carefully carry the upright assembly outside and toss it in the bushes. In a short time, the sodium, in contact with water, will produce a gas and BOOM goes the bomb. This little game was the perfect crime in that it gave the criminal time to leave the site before the explosion. Soon the sodium supply was locked away, leaving us without ammunition.

In our senior year it was decided that, except for binding and photo printing, the yearly FIAT LUX should be done by hand, thereby lowering the cost. I got the job of doing the artwork and page borders, and everyone shared in preparing written materials. (See illustrations.) The work was done on a mimeograph, an ancient hand-crank machine with a mean and fractious personality. Things to be reproduced had to be typed or stenciled on a mat having a porous fiber base overlaid with wax. A typewritten stencil gave a good, even result, but drawing turned out to be difficult. Maintaining a steady pressure on a stylus held in the hand took practice. I found that I could make some of my own styluses from large nails by grinding the ends to the shape needed for a particular purpose, and this helped. Two hundred copies, seventy-two pages, and many inkings later, we had the Sacramento Bee do the cover and binding and our job was finished! I still have a copy and marvel at the progress made from mimeograph to today's computers. We could have done the job so much better and faster if we'd had the computer on which I am typing this tale. See the illustration of the stenciled sketch of that lovely old high school.

What will things be like fifty years from now when you girls are in your 60s and 70s? Perhaps you will be able merely to think what you want and it will appear in full color from a printer that holds a year's supply of paper that can be changed in texture and color at the touch of a button. As an attachment for only $5,360.00, plus $500.00 shipping and handling, you will be able to purchase an automatic binding machine.

A soccer field served as a track where we practiced discus, shot put, hurdles, and running. Each spring the grass came up green and luxurious, and by summer the practice areas were dust paths. There was one other activity, during the time of fresh, new, dew-laden grass, in which four of us with vehicles at our disposal participated. We called it car soccer. You started at one end of the field with the car under the goalposts and took off headed for the other goal, gathering as much speed as the slippery field allowed. At a strategic point, you turned the car sharply, causing a spin. The object was to make as many revolutions as possible and end with the car's rear under the far goalposts. About two full turns was the limit, and great care had to be exercised to avoid knocking over the posts. At that time, my vehicle was a 1926 Buick open touring car with huge wooden spoke wheels. Each time we carefully washed all the mud from the wheels and fenders before returning home. The washing and drying of those wood spokes, plus the side load of spinning, loosened them and that required a shim job to tighten things again. After a couple of times redoing the wheels,

Dad was heard to mutter, "I don't know why these damned wheels need so much attention." Again, I think he knew, and as I recall those days I say to myself, "How could I be so lucky to have such a great dad?"

Finally, we graduated—all thirteen of us—and went off in our chosen directions heading for the future. See the illustration of part of the 1933 class. I thank that school and its teachers for a wonderful time of my life, and for a good preparation toward my future.

Oh, I almost forgot. See that rectangular tower over the central entry of the school? On a clear, cold morning after Halloween in the year 1932, there appeared, fully assembled, a beautiful four-wheeled buggy perched neatly on the peak. This caused no end of fun and some grumbling, but we had a great principal, Mr. Williams, who suggested it would be appropriate if the offending vehicle were to be removed by the following morning by those who put it there. Turns out it was harder to get down than up, but we did it without breaking a single tile.

SENIORS

EVELYN GLENN
Spanish Club, 1, 2
Dramatics 2, 4
Class Officer 3, 4
Treasurer S.B. 4
Office 4
Editor Annual 4
Editor Paper 2
C.F.S. 4
Pres. C.F.S. 4
Fiat Lux Staff 2, 3, 4

WILLIAM B. BALL, JR.
Basketball 1, 2, 3, 4
Speedball 1, 2, 3, 4
Tennis 2, 3, 4
Track 1, 2, 3, 4
Baseball 1, 2, 3, 4
Pres. S.B. 3, 4
Pres. Class 1, 3
Pres. Debate Club 4
Art Chairman 1, 4
Dramatics 1, 2, 3, 4
C.S.F. 4
Spanish Club 1, 2

STANLEY FERGUSON
Baseball 1, 2, 3, 4
Basketball 1, 2, 3, 4
Speedball 3, 4
Dramatics 4

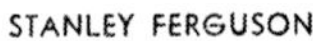

EVALYN LEWIS
Dramatics 1, 2, 3, 4
Class Officers 2, 3
Annual Staff 1, 2, 3, 4
Paper Staff 3 and 4
Spanish Club 1 and 2

FARROND VERSCHOOR
Sec. S.B. 4
Sec. and Treas. Senior Class 4
Dramatics 3, 4
Annual Staff 4
Spanish Club 1, 2
Paper Staff 4
Sec. G.A.A. 4
Vice Pres. S.B. 4

WILLIAM A. ALEXANDER
Basketball 1, 2, 3, 4
Baseball 2, 3, 4
Speedball 2, 3, 4
Tennis 3
Dramatics 1, 3, 4
Pres. S.B. 4
Pres. C.F.S. 4
Asst. Bus. Mgr. A. 3
Bus. Mgr. A. 4
Debate 4

CECIL RODRIGUEZ
Speedball 2, 3, 4
Basketball 1, 2, 3, 4

Yearbook Cover

Yearbook Jokes & Snaps

Chapter Twelve

The Fordolet Tow Truck

This venerable vehicle deserves a place in history for its unfailing four years of service to a bunch of wild high schoolers, and for its unflagging duties as a tow truck in my Dad's business of auto repair. If one can feel a warm spot in the heart for an inanimate object, then I do for that truck, because it never complained, never failed to start, and survived an occasional grievous injury with dignity. It was well known around town, not always, I might add, with affection, except by all the kids it transported on hunting, fishing, camping, and school decorating junkets. It wasn't very fast and it wasn't very pretty. (See illustration.) There was no top for sun and rain protection. No self-starter, no seat belts, no air bags, and no stereo FM with CD. It got us where we wanted to go and back—with some limitations—without failure.

To begin with, I must tell you that its genetics were doubtful. It was a Ford, sure enough, but due to an operation performed by my Dad there had been a transfusion of Chevrolet. It came about this way. Finding the pulling power limited, Dad cast about for a solution. A bigger engine might do the job, but the engine compartment space was too small. How about adding gearing? That would do the trick; but what gearing? On a trip to a Marysville parts ship, Dad found they were using a wrecked Chevy to scavenge parts and the transmission was available. So there was the solution. The Chevy gear shift transmission added three forward speeds and one reverse speed to the Ford planetary transmission, and there we had all the pulling power we needed.

I recall seeing the truck being cut in two pieces, its frame being lengthened, and the new transmission being installed. Now we might have called the resulting vehicle a Fordolet, but on the outside it was still Ford, so it never got renamed. Painted a nice bright yellow with big 32 x 6 tires in the rear and 30 x 3? in the front, and a hoist affixed to the bed, it was a formidable-looking machine. All sorts of gear combinations were possible, but strangest of the bunch was when both transmissions were in reverse. Contrary to what one might think, this combination resulted in forward motion, and with the engine at nearly full throttle one could walk alongside and keep pace!

I don't know how many miles we drove the truck, but it never seemed to use any oil, and one of the guys was prompted to speculate, "Maybe it makes its own oil." If the truth were to be known, I suspect Dad saw to all the maintenance, including oil. Nevertheless, I always went through the ritual of "preflight" check, which consisted of air, water, gas, Chevy transmission grease, and differential grease. The last check before cranking was to see that the spark lever under the steering wheel was in its fully retarded position—because if it wasn't, the guy on the crank might get "kicked." This could break a wrist as the crank flipped backward when the spark plug fired before the piston reached its top position. We always fancied ourselves standing in front of a World War I Spad, hands on prop, shouting to the pilot in the cockpit, "Contact!" before pulling the propeller to start the engine. Open the throttle a little (it was also beneath the steering wheel), pull up the crank, and we were ready for the dawn patrol.

One of our favorite sports often took place at night with a driver and three guys holding shotguns. We would drive out of town four or five miles to a convenient wheat field and begin a circling maneuver around the field boundaries, using only the rather faint headlights to see by. At a strategic moment, the spotlights on the hoist would be turned on and a search begun for the prey of the night. The prey were always rabbits, and the hunt was then on in all its fury. Shotguns blazing, truck roaring, and driver trying to follow the fleeing animals, we tried to account for as many victims as possible before heading home for the night. Lest you think of us as monsters, it is necessary to tell you that rabbits were then a major problem to the farmers, and they encouraged our hunting forays. At times of rabbit overpopulation, drives often took place where many hundreds of the creatures met their doom. Because of tularemia, we were warned never to touch a critter, and after our night hunts they were left to the scavengers. After the drives they were burned.

The rabbits got even one night. I was driving as we followed a fair-sized group. They were just out of range ahead when suddenly they veered sharply to the right. It was too late when I saw the ditch, the cause of their turn, and down into it we plunged. Leaving me only a second to shout, "Hang on," the truck plowed up the other side and came to a grinding halt with its front axle and wheels pushed back under the engine. The front transverse springs stuck out at all angles, and the sight sobered us as we assessed the damage. After a council on the way out of this mess, we got to work. There was a big old oak tree at the nearby fence corner, and by backing the truck, and with the guys pushing the front end to steer, we were able to hook onto the tree, crank the hoist, and lift the damaged front end clear so we could get to the problem.

A lot of hammering with a fence post and tree limb, and things got straightened enough to tie in place with wire salvaged from the fence so we could drive slowly and prayerfully home. Bill Alexander fortunately had a Ford wishbone in his garage and we stopped by to replace the badly twisted one from our accident. A little more work and a good wash job, and the truck bore no evidence of the horrible night. On future hunts, a spotlight on the hoist was always pointed ahead as an aid to the dim headlights.

I wonder what ever happened to the old truck. Did it languish in some junk yard, slowly rusting away as it waited for a bunch of crazy kids to take it out for just one more night rabbit hunt? Strange that I lost track of it when I left home, and now, sixty-odd years later, I feel sad not knowing. Every now and then as you drive the rural byways, you see an old tractor or auto sitting out by a bard or in a back yard. Are these treasured mementos or just junk, too much a problem to dispose of?

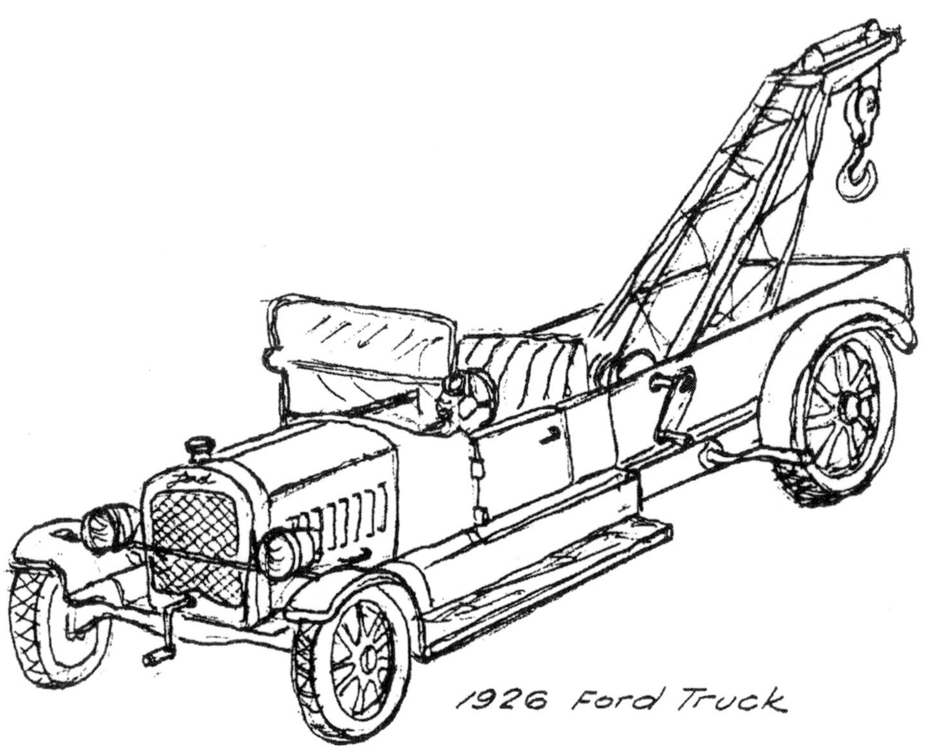

1926 Ford Truck

Chapter Thirteen

Bear River

I begin this chapter with a feeling of nostalgia, maybe sadness, perhaps even a feeling of remorse that I can't return to the river that meant so much to me as I was growing up. I can close my eyes and see so many details. The place where the stream narrowed as it passed beneath the rail and highway bridges, the tree-lined levies and the concrete dam where we fished for salmon. The sweeping curve where there was a sandbar on one side and a deep pool on the other. We learned to swim there. We found a deserted cabin and made it our headquarters. Then there was bear weed, a plant two to three feet high with leaves dull on one side and shiny on the other. I never knew the real name, but we would form the leaves into a shape like a plug of tobacco and chew it. Taking a drink of water after chewing, the taste was deliciously sweet. We sometimes dried the stuff and smoked it, much to the disgust of our mothers. Today I still get a tug of emotion when I think of the Bear River. It was the place where we began growing up.

That old river, originating high in the Sierras, coursing down through our foothills and providing sustenance to agriculture, also offered an end-less source of adventure for us "pioneers," as we fancied ourselves. In pairs, or threes, or fours, we would set out on a Friday afternoon with a bedroll, a frying pan, some assorted stuff for cooking, eating utensils, and our defen-sive weapons. These latter items included a hunting knife (it was considered essential that the knife be handmade) and a rifle or shotgun. In those days, the best material for a knife blade was an old file, since it was hard and tough and could be sharpened to a razor's edge. Handles came in a variety of designs; leather discs stacked on the file end and polished, deer antlers, wood, and, rarely, metal. Mine was wood with carved finger grips. I still have a scar where the knife slipped off a can of beans I was opening and plunged into my leg.

One winter outing had to be salmon fishing at the Bear River dam. About twelve miles east of town, the concrete structure—250 feet wide and maybe sixty feet high—had been built in the early '20s to store winter water for summer irrigation. It had three rectangular outlets on the downstream face, controlled by geared handwheels accessible from the crest walkway. One of the outlets remained open all year and it was here that we had our greatest fishing. At that time spear fishing was legal, and, while we could more easily spear a fish in the riffles below the dam, we were fascinated with the salmon swimming up through that glassy arc of water from the outlet.

After ruminating on the possibility of attacking the fish while it was in the column of water and in plain sight, we took ropes with us on the next trip. Our plan was to tie the rope around the fisherman's waist, take a couple of turns around the handwheel shaft, and have the guys on the walkway lower the spear carrier down to the level of the outlet. From that strategic position it would be simple to plunge the spear into the hapless fish and bring him to shore down below. The spear in this case had what we called toggle points. (See illustration.) The points were hollow and slid over the three tines of the spear end. The toggles, attached to a quarter-inch rope by means of wire loops, would detach from the spear when embedded in the fish, and the spear could be tossed aside so we could deal with the fish using the toggle rope.

All this sounds simple, but the execution was more than we bargained for. In the first place, locating the fish in a rectangular column of water was a trompe-l'oeil. He wasn't where we thought he was; as a matter of fact, if we were in just the right position, there appeared two of the same fish because of the refraction effect of the water-air interface. As a result, aiming the spear took some guessing and many misses. When spearing a twenty-pound salmon for the first time, I got a real surprise and was pulled into the outlet stream by the weight of the fish and my own eagerness. The guys holding the anchor rope around the gate stem finally let go, and down I went into the churning water fifteen feet below, still hanging tightly to the toggle rope with my fish attached. Cold, dripping wet, but triumphant, I held my salmon up for all to see. That experience and practice made us fairly good at the game of outlet fishing, and the catches were enough to supply our families and many of the neighbors with all the salmon they could use. Sadly, those days of plentiful fish in the annual run are gone, and I doubt if a single salmon now makes its way up the Bear River.

In the late spring we had fun with another kind of fishing. This entailed the use of the traditional willow branch, five or six feet of any old fish line, a number six hook, and a small piece of red cloth. Our venue was any of the small creeks flowing into the river, and the season was short because by summer's advent everything dried up. Our quarry was the multitude of perch that miraculously appeared each year. Believe it or not, we had only to dangle that little piece of cloth three or four inches above the surface, and presto! a fish obligingly leapt from the water onto the hook. The size of the fish caught could be regulated by the height that the cloth was held above the water. We threw most of the catch back, keeping only a few of the larger ones to fry for dinner. Later on, as the ponds dried, raccoons, foxes, and crows cleaned up the survivors. We assumed eggs had been laid and somehow sank into the mud to await next spring's nourishing waters. Each year as I feel the coming of spring fever, I think of those eager little jumping fish.

Sometimes it was good to go down to the river and just walk; maybe three or four of us, not talking much, picking up a few flat rocks, making them skip along the surface of the water and watching the ripples dapple the stream. We'd stop and sit under some overhanging willows, pick some long strands of new grass and chew the sweet stems. Now and then there would be some bear weed and we might pick some to take home with us. These brief walks along the river seldom lasted more than an hour or two, and then we'd jump into the old Ford tow truck and head back to town. Many years later your grandmother and I, before we were married, took one of those river walks, sitting under the willows, chewing the grass, wading in the pools and getting soaking wet on a warm spring day. See the illustration of your soaked grandmother.

Of course, we all had chores around home, but the system was to work like the dickens a day or two ahead of time so the weekend was free for a hike or whatever else we might plan. A hike usually started shortly after school on Friday and gave us a good three or four hours to get to a good camping spot. At four miles per hour on the generally flat country, that offered a radius of twelve miles to set up camp. Exploring often cut the distance down, but any time we found a good spot, particularly near the river, was the time to camp. A campfire, some food, an hour of tall stories, and the bedrolls began to look pretty enticing. With the dying embers of the fire and a little before-sleep chatter, we dozed off to the lovely, haunting calls of a pair of owls and the now-and-then chatter of a lonely coyote. Bears and cougars either avoided us or perhaps had never inhabited that area. Of rattlesnakes we were wary and never had a problem. We tended to avoid each other, and, on the rare occasion of a close encounter, our artillery took over.

One of the favorite spots was a meadow bounded by a fence on three sides. About one-third of the field was marsh, where frogs and minnows abounded. This food supply attracted herons, both white and blue, and one of our favorite sports was to shoot at the big birds. Mind you, we weren't trying to kill the creatures, only to frighten them. We'd hit the fallen tree on which they perched or splatter mud near them, and the effect was spectacular in two ways. First, the beautiful takeoff with those wide wings struggling for altitude, and second, the evacuation of the bowels to reduce takeoff weight. The stream approached fifteen feet in extreme cases, and for that reason we called them "shit-a-rods," even though that was a foot and a half short of the official measure. To this day I can't see a heron without thinking of that name.

Not more than a quarter of a mile from the meadow was our deserted cabin. (See illustration.) Chet Stineman and I were the first in our gang to stumble upon it. About twelve miles east of town and not far from the Bear River, it lay in a small clearing with faint evidence of former gardening in a patch about a hundred feet square out front. On both sides and to the rear oaks, scrub pine, and brush sheltered it in a protective cover so that it was nearly invisible from a few feet away. I suppose others had seen and maybe used it before, but to us it had all the romance of a lost continent, and it became the treasured hideout for the several of us explorers. Laid on a foundation of flat river rock, the walls framed a single, dirt-floored room in which there was an ancient spring bed, a two-lid woodstove, a handmade table with two small benches, and, on one wall, a set of shelves. A door flanked by two windows (no panes) with drop-down shutters faced the clearing, and beyond that, through the trees, the river. Out front, a fire pit had been carefully laid out with selected and fitted stones and out where the garden started was a hole that probably had been a cistern. It had also been lined with stones and originally supplied water for the garden and other uses. Time had taken its toll, however, and the hole was filled with dirt, leaves, and branches.

The cabin itself was built from milled lumber, so it was post-log-cabin days. Outside, the walls had the patina of age from wind and sun and rain. Rusty nails plus the curling of some of the planks indicated that long years had passed since the first noise of saw and hammer shattered the peace of that little forest. No one in town knew about the cabin, and we often wondered who the builder was. A prospector? A homesteader who moved on to better digs? Someone who wanted to get away from people? Had he sat out front smoking an evening pipe after dinner as he basked in the warmth of the embers from the firepit? Was he big, small, with a beard, old, young? We'll never know, except that he was a small part of the river of humanity moving by into obscurity. However, he left us a cabin and for that we thanked him, wherever he was.

I remember where I learned to swim. It was in a pool formed at a bend in the river. Upstream the water spread out in a wide, shallow set of sparkling riffles; where it began the turn a sandbar had formed and deflected the flow to an opposite bank, on which a heavy stand of willows had grown. Here the water narrowed and the faster flow dug a sizeable pond with a depth of five feet or so. In the summer, the river slowed to a leisurely pace, and the shelving sandbar made an ideal slope to get into progressively deeper water and finally into the pond. At each depth I could dog paddle and experiment at staying afloat until, before I knew it, I was in the deep part of the pond and SWIMMING! After that, I was doing the side stroke, back stroke, and the crawl, and boy was it ever great with no clothes in that cooling, gentle water! A few years later a swimming pool was built in town, but it was never the same. Too much chlorine, too many people, and bathing suits were required. Sometimes, when the pool was too full, we hiked out to the river and jumped in just for the memory of it.

Long before our time, the ancient river had left another gift to everyone along its path. Before levees were thrown up to control the waters, the winter runoff ranged widely over the flat land on either side of the main channel, bringing silt from the mountains. This formed what we called river bottom, or bottomland, and it was rich in nutrients with enough mountain granite sand to make ideal soil. Watermelons, cantaloupes (we called these muskmelons), all kinds of fruit trees, and vegetables grew like Jack's beanstalk. Extensive farming developed after levees controlled Old Man River, and it was this industry that shared a tiny part of its bounty with us river walkers. Watermelons and muskmelons were always better when shared before the morning sun had warmed them, but cherries, apricots, and peaches were great any time the farmer wasn't around. For you unfortunate city dwellers, it is hard to know the rich, sweet flavor of vine- and tree-ripened things. Just imagine sinking your teeth into a fully ripened, firm, yet yielding freestone peach or eating from the cluster of dark red Bing cherries just plucked from the overburdened tree. Think of the deep red of the watermelon, with its moist, sugar-sweet heart awaiting your first juicy bite.

Those are poignant memories, and as I sit at this keyboard my mouth fills and my taste buds can almost conjure up those long-forgotten delicacies. Old Man River was fun, solace, adventure, sustenance, and learning. It was all that we kids could have hoped for. I will be forever grateful for the opportunity to have lived near Him and I must also thank my mother and father for allowing me the freedom to partake of that largess.

THE CABIN

Chapter Fourteen

College

$\mathcal{F}$inally, high school and all the hunting, fishing, and hiking were at an end! Although there had been many summers away from home on survey parties, this was different. The ties to home were to be more tenuous. No longer would I be coming home from a few months of work or to be in the sheltering cocoon and the familiar environment; I would be a visitor from time to time, and this was a sobering thought. There was the West Point incident, wherein I had gotten a nomination (through my uncle in the state senate) to take the annual Academy examination. I passed the exam with rather high grades but after an extensive physical series was downgraded to second alternate. The reason? malocclusion; in other words, teeth not meeting properly. In those days they were very picky. Who knows what my life might have been had the teeth passed muster.

After the West Point issue we had talked about whether it would be better to go to Cal at Berkeley or Sacramento Junior College, but those discussions had been sort of abstract and, until the time of decision, didn't seem real. Suddenly we were on our way, suitcase, clothes bag, saxophone, and shaving kit in the trunk of the old Oakland, me in the back seat with Dad driving and Mother in the passenger's seat. The destination: Sacramento. Why Sacramento? Wheatland High had prepared us well for college and my grades were good enough to be accepted anywhere, no entrance exams needed. Maybe we thought it would be better for a country boy to start at small city school rather than the megalopolis of the San Francisco Bay Area. In light of later events it might have been better to have chosen to begin at Cal, but who could have read the future?

Arrangements had been made for me to stay in Sacramento with a family living about a mile from the school, and I was to have a roommate.

Upon arrival we were shown the room, which was a lovely airy one with a view over a nicely kept garden. Looking around I was horror-stricken to see on the dresser several toilet articles, amongst which was a bottle of cologne. My gosh, I thought, what kind of thing have I drawn for a roommate? In those days I didn't even use shaving lotion, let alone cologne, even if it was men's. Feeling uneasy, I went out to talk with my host family, who told me my room buddy had gone shopping with his mother and would be back in an hour. At this point Mother and Dad departed, leaving me with a hollow feeling in the pit of my stomach and an uncertain view of the future.

Cologne aside, Forrest Lackland turned out to be a great guy. We had something in common—music. He played trumpet and violin, an unlikely combination, but for two years we shared many wonderful times in the music business. Our friendship lasted fifty-nine years, despite our different interests and infrequent get-togethers. Forrest's mother was a lovely woman and I recall with great fondness the occasional weekends we spent at his home in Vallejo. His dad had been a naval officer, and sometime in the early '30s had succumbed to some tropical disease while on duty in South America. Gramps lived with Mrs. Lackland, and Forrest told me how he patrolled the well-kept garden out front. Seems that the local dogs were making a mess of things until Gramps bought that BB gun. With a few sessions from the front porch, while Gramps polished his aim, the dogs were persuaded to make a wide detour around the Lackland property and it soon got to the point where no human presence was required to keep the yard clear.

Forrest took entomology and I took engineering, but we had a common interest in dance bands. One day in the first month of school I saw a notice on a bulletin board asking anyone who was interested in trying out for a dance band to show up at an address in town on Saturday afternoon. Both of us went, and both of us became members of the Tom Curry Eight. Tom was a trumpeter and arranger. Some of his stuff was very difficult to play, but with practice, held in the basement of that long-forgotten address, we got to be a pretty good bunch of musicians. Curry was an absolute stickler about execution, and there were even sessions when we practiced synchronizing our vibratos! Some years after Sacramento, Forrest heard that Tom was having success preparing arrangements for Benny Goodman and other Big Band groups. Of his future beyond that we never knew. In the two years of our band experience it became obvious that it was tough to stay on top of the music game, but our hope was that Tom would carve out a good spot for himself. (See illustration.)

We played up to three times a week, mostly on Friday and Saturday nights with a rare Sunday gig. It is hard to describe the feeling of playing in a well-rehearsed group. There is the satisfaction of hitting the notes together, right on the button, and hearing the harmony of the other instruments pouring deeply into your soul. Drums we had, but they didn't overpower everything else. The melody line was dominant, with emphasis on musicianship; and those melodies of the thirties are still with us. And hey girls! The guy held his gal close and danced rather than jerked and gyrated.

We did attend school in addition to our dance jobs, and the professors were some of the best of my college years. Mr. Thorpe, a West Point grad and World War I artillery officer, taught descriptive geometry and machine design. He was tough, but only because he wanted his students to do well. The grading was determined by four exams during the semester, but if you thought you could do better, you could take a fifth exam if you were willing to accept that as the final grade. My memory of Mr. Thorpe is still clear; you could hear him coming down the hall in a stomping gait, accented by his wooden leg. He lost the real one in the war. Unsmiling, in his laconic way he'd say, "Good morning, class, have you studied well for this morning's exam?" He was always available for help on any problem, but was not tolerant of those who failed to put forth an effort. One of the all-time best, I'm sure he got a special seat up there in engineers' heaven.

Mr. Teale taught surveying, civil engineering, and calculus, and was very good at each of the subjects. He was also a West Pointer, but graduated after the war and had not seen military action. I recall one event during a field class in which we were being instructed in the use of various surveying equipment. Mr. Teale showed us how to do up a two-hundred-foot tape and did it properly; but as he undid the tape it began to twist, as it will when undone in the wrong direction. He knew he was in trouble, but was uncertain about the cure. Finally, unable to stand it any longer, I said, "Mr. Teale, if you turn the tape around it won't twist." He regarded me with a cold, imperious eye and said, "Mr. Ball, when I need information from a member of this class I'll ask for it." I was embarrassed by the rebuke but later was amused to watch him off to one side, when he thought no one was looking, shifting the tape from one position to the other and noting how it unrolled without twisting as he got it right. I wondered how many years he had struggled with twisted tapes. At our final class Mr. Teale came to me and said, "Thank you, Mr. Ball, for the tape tip." Of course, I never let him know I'd been working on summer surveys for five years. By the way, girls, if you want to know how to double-throw a tape, go back to chapter 10.

Apart from engineering there were two memorable electives, public speaking and history. Both were taught by an Englishman who at some time in the past had done a spate of Shakespeare while at Cambridge. His history was everything from the time man first began to realize he was man to the day we sat in class. Dates were less important in this class, but you were expected to know the general order of events. To this man, history was the shaping of the world in which we lived. It included all the creativeness, brutality, intelligence, and love the human animal has lavished on this planet. His classes were always full and you were lucky to get a spot. Public speaking was an opportunity few engineers got in most curriculums, and we learned diction, phrasing, projection, and other attributes of good presentation from an old English thespian. I regret I can no longer recall his name, because I'd like to record it here for the world to see.

I tried out for track and baseball, but soon found out I was no match for the physical ed. competition and settled for a gym class in which I selected wrestling in spite of my skinny build. Surprisingly, I did pretty well because of the strong legs and back muscles developed in rowing during summer surveys. One problem, however, was the action called bridging. This is where a wrestler uses neck and head to lift his shoulders off the canvas when an opponent tries to pin him. The instructor always had us do the exercise (with someone sitting on our stomachs) at the beginning and end of the class, which was the last one before lunch. For the first half of the semester I would go to lunch with a neck so tired I'd have to use one hand to hold my head while eating with the other. We were graded by wrestling in a sort of round robin competition with other members of the class, and I managed to squeeze out a B.

As time went on our band got more requests for jobs, and we made a few bucks at it. There was one regular weekly assignment we got in Manteca. This one included a half-hour radio broadcast from the dancehall, and we thought we'd hit the big time even though the air waves probably didn't get beyond Stockton or Modesto. The schedule started at nine, and at ten we'd go on the air for an hour, take a fifteen-minute break, and then play again 'til three a.m. For this we got the magnificent sum of four dollars each, and to make it seem more we asked that it be paid in half-dollars because the stack was higher. That time in the morning, after packing our instruments, wasn't the best time to drive home, so we often stayed at a local hotel. For eight guys and a girl singer we got two rooms. The gal got her own room, and the rest of us got the other. We could get some sleep with five guys across the bed and the other three in chairs or on the floor with a pillow. Only one person registered for the room and, after he went upstairs, the others would saunter up one at a time. We thought we'd pulled a fast one on the innkeeper, but come morning as we left he told us he knew what was going on and, but since he always listened to the broadcast and because we didn't mess up the room, he just looked the other way.

Many jobs, many different experiences; some good, some bad, but all interesting. Forrest had an ancient Chevy with a rumble seat where we packed our instruments. It failed us one night outside Stockton in a rainstorm. We were in tuxes but had to get out and push the car under the shelter of a nearby service station. With a Prince Albert tobacco can and a bit of wire salvaged from a fence we managed to jerry rig the fuel pump and get home.

Since I sometimes played with a different group, I thought it would be great to have my own transportation. So I bought a 1921 Harley Davidson motorcycle for $26 and rigged a bracket on the rear for my instruments. After a kinked throttle wire caused me to tear up someone's lawn and nearly knock down a palm tree, and a tube popped out of the rear tire and threw me into the gutter, I decided motorcycling was not for me and sold the darned thing for $30. After that I used public transport or borrowed Forrest's car.

Toward the end of the second year in Sacramento I sat in as first sax with Dick Jurgens while his regular sax man was out ill. Jurgens' was the top band in the area, and I felt privileged to be asked to sit in with his band. (He later went on to become one of the better Big Bands of the late thirties and forties.) We broadcast from the Senator Hotel across from the Capitol three nights a week for three weeks, and it was about that time that Jurgens scheduled a road tour. I thought it would be great to go on such a tour, but the regular sax man returned and after playing with professionals I realized I wasn't good enough to compete, so I settled for an engineering career. These days when I hear a top instrumentalist I think to myself what a good choice I made. I am reminded, too, that when Duke Ellington, Tommy Dorsey, or other top bands came to town we would go, not to dance, but to sit by the bandstand and listen to some of the most talented musicians play some of the greatest music ever. What a joy that was. One night we went to see a young Lionel Hampton playing the vibraharp at a little joint in downtown Sacramento. I'd guess he was about our age and even then a prodigy. He still plays like an angel.

My introduction to prejudice came in Sacramento. Farm laborers had been imported from the Philippines to provide the farmers with a source of cheap labor. Crude living quarters were constructed on the farms but, in a total disregard for common decent human relations, no recreation facilities had been provided. There had been Filipinos but no Filipinas in the work permits. Naturally, the workers, with what little money they earned and with what little spare time they were afforded, sought the nearest towns for shopping and solace. Patronizing the river area and the red light district of Sacramento on the week ends, they often showed up in large numbers, to the consternation of the local denizens. The result was conflict; stonings, clubbings, and stabbings became a frequent occurrence. Police looked the other way as much blood was spilled. To make matters worse, the Filipinos began to wear zoot suits, those high-waisted pants with long ornate watch chains hanging to mid-calf, accompanied by a jacket bottoming at the knees. This subjected them to derisive taunts and further abuse (they were called Filly Goo Goos, Gooks, and Skibbies), and to protect themselves the workers began to walk the streets in groups of six to ten. It seemed that warfare might break out at any time. Finally, at the urging of more sensible citizens, the City Council issued strict guidelines to the police and slowly decency began to prevail. Today, fifty-nine years later, we've done some better, but there is still a long difficult road ahead. If only we could meet one-on-one, rather than in warring groups, it would help.

I cannot leave this chapter without a few words about Forrest G. Lackland, who was my friend, roommate, and fellow dance-band member. We shared many experiences during our two years at Sacramento College. We were different but developed a mutual respect. He visited my family in Wheatland several times and I his in Vallejo. We both transferred to Cal together, but there our separation began. His classes and boarding house were on the opposite side of the campus from mine in the engineering college and the fraternity. With divergent interests we didn't see each other, and now, as I write this, I wonder why. Upon graduation he took a job with a pesticide company in the Central Valley and I went to work on the Coulee Dam in Washington. Forrest and Lorraine were married some time in 1940 and shortly thereafter Forrest joined the Navy. His shop, The Indianapolis, was in San Francisco and we offered Lorraine a place to stay while she looked for an apartment in the city. It was a pleasant time for us to meet and become friends with Lorraine. After the war they returned to Fresno where we visited them a couple of times before they bought a motel in Carmel (The Green Lantern). We stayed there twice before Forrest decided he couldn't stand the motel business and they moved to a suburb of Sacramento. It wasn't long before we found they had moved to Mississippi, where Lorraine had grown up.

After about a year they were back in Sacramento and, shortly after, came to visit us at the mountain house. Serin was with us for the weekend and was looking forward to seeing someone I had talked about so much.

The visit was a disaster! A side of Forrest I never knew, or one that had just emerged, surprised us. He was violently antiblack. The conversation became so disturbing that Serin had to leave the room and Grandmother was visibly upset. I tried to cool things down, but the visit ended with Forrest still railing about "those people."

The next Christmas card said they were back in Mississippi again, but it was not for long. A brief note on a later postcard said they were back in Sacramento. Very strange, I thought, and phoned to see if just Forrest and I could get together for a little talk. After getting several postponements I gave up. Finally I wrote a long letter reminding Forrest of the great old times and saying I hoped we could stay in touch. It was some time before I had an answer, not from Forrest but from a person in a home for Alzheimer's patients where Lorraine had been committed. It went on to say that not long after Lorraine had been settled Forrest had died from a heart attack. I will never know what went on in those last few years, but at least I feel better for having told you the story.

The 1934-1935 Band at Sacramento College
Keith Unash at Piano; Back Row: Forrest Lackland, Ray Conway, Tom
Curry, Chet Gore; Front Row: Ted Sepponen, Bill Ball, Tony Richter

Chapter Fifteen

Cal, Boeing, Oakland Airport

The University of California at Berkeley had an enrollment of ten thousand students in 1935, the year of my matriculation. Daunting is the word that comes to mind as I look back at it now, a huge megaloinstitute sitting there with not a familiar face or welcoming sign. I stood in the middle of that great campus, a Lilliputian among Brobdignagians, wondering which door to open. There was a big one labeled "Engineering," and it was the entry to a new world of learning. Where Sacramento had dealt in textbooks and theory, here were buildings full of monster testing machines capable of bending a truss of heavy steel or crushing a twelve-inch column of concrete. There were laboratories with large diesel engines where one could plot the heat cycle of a single cylinder's motion. The electric lab had motors, transformers, switch panels, and meters where one learned about resistance, capacitance, inductance, and power consumption. There were professors who could fill a twenty-foot blackboard with equations, symbols, numbers, and the next assignment, and do it in a single hour. All of this lay ahead, waiting to be a part of my next two years. Mother and Dad had driven me down from Wheatland and, after sharing my wonder at the campus, found the place of lodging where I had a room reserved. By then it was time for them to leave for home, because it was a good four- or five-hour trip.

It had been arranged that I would stay at a place called Bowles Hall, situated east of the campus and north of the football stadium. After finding the place and unloading the saxophone and a couple of suitcases of stuff, Mother and Dad left me standing on the front steps of my new home. I confess to a feeling of emptiness as they drove off in the Oakland sedan. I watched until the taillight and spare tire disappeared around the final comer, then turned and faced my future.

Bowles Hall accommodated about four hundred students with small individual rooms, a large sitting room, and a spacious dining area. Sort of English/Norman in architecture, the hall had a broad veranda and steps leading to an inviting entry. In all respects it was a beautiful facility, except that I felt isolated in my little cell. Maybe being further from home I succumbed to that old malady, homesickness. I was there just two months when, to my great relief, I received a bid to join a fraternity. The invitation came by the way of John R. Jahn, a man I had met during my survey party days in Sacramento. He had been involved in developing a method of survey using a camera instead of survey instruments, and I did some work for him in the office of the Corps of Engineers one summer. I didn't know it at the time, but John was an alumnus of Theta Xi, and when I got to Cal he gave my name to the fraternity as a possible prospect.

Theta Xi occupied a big old three-story house on the corner of La Lorna and Le Roy, north of the campus. An all-year stream ran by on the north side, and I recall we would use that deep, cool ravine to escape some of the hot days of late summer. The pen-and-ink sketch at the end of this tale will give you an idea of the old house. (See illustration.) My room was on the top floor behind the window on the right. With a touch of nostalgia I remember that the house is no longer there. When I joined the fraternity the membership was down, and the few members were struggling to build up the group. Finances had become a problem and things didn't look good for the future. That year, nineteen of us pledged and all were to live in the house, so the tide had begun to turn. The spring semester saw another ten members joining, and we were on our way to a full house and financial security. The unsung hero of this saga was a small, intense, devoted guy named Steve Plunkett, our house manager for that first period. Every member of that first-pledge class was impressed with Steve's sincerity, and his enthusiasm for the future of the house infected us all. He is listed in my Theta Xi registry as "address unknown," but I, and I'm sure many others, will fondly recall his presence and guidance.

We were a diverse bunch of guys from a variety of backgrounds, and I feel that the experience of working and living together for those two years was invaluable. The TX handshake, the motto, the meetings downstairs in the old, locked chapter room, the gold and pearl pin, and all those kid things meant much to us, and I'm not embarrassed to admit it today. During my second year I served as president and found that task stimulating and rewarding. There is a new house now, and new young men to maintain the fraternity, but some of us old guys are still involved.

As I look through the directory, other names evoke memories. There is Clyde Deal, a saturnine sort of guy who loved sailboats. The last I heard of Clyde he had navigated a small sailboat from England across the Atlantic to New York. Al Croft, a pleasant and likeable man, was lost in the Pacific Ocean and lies somewhere in the deep with his submarine. Len Dieden, a scholarly type, became a judge in the Oakland courts. Lou Smith, a modest country boy, was a fine end on Cal's '38 and '39 football teams. Both he and Len are now dead. Charlie Parker played a mean sax and we had some great duets. Rotund Ted Hubert was as light on his feet as a feather, and your grandmother loved to dance with him. Jim Castle, a superb athlete and heavyweight boxing champ, was gentle as a lamb. Dave Robertson roomed across the hall and had an old World War I high-power binocular we used to observe the sunbathers on the sun deck of the sorority two blocks below. So many friends, so many good times, so many memories. We've gone our separate ways and lost contact one way or another. Seems like we should have kept in touch but it is difficult, particularly since we have flown off to the four winds and our interests have been so different. I thank them all for their friendship.

During my second year I got a job working in San Francisco at the Resettlement Administration. That office had the assignment of preparing designs for the migratory labor camps to house refugees from the Oklahoma Dust Bowl. John Jahn again appeared as my benefactor, since he had been assigned to the San Francisco office, and called to see if I would be interested in a part-time job. This was four hours a day, five days a week, and it offered me an opportunity for more experience in engineering before being thrown out on the cold cruel world after graduation. My supervisor was Art Crawshaw, who turned out to be another one who would help me along in my career.

Working in San Francisco was an experience I will never forget. The city itself had an ambiance that was a palpable thing. You could feel the pulse of it the moment you stepped off the ferry and into the Ferry Building. My routine included an early-morning start, a jog down to Shattuck Avenue, and catching the Key Route Red Train to the Oakland ferry terminal where I boarded the waiting ferry. (See illustration.) Immediately upon boarding I'd dash downstairs to the food bar, where a glass of juice, a cup of coffee, and a Danish pastry gave me a chance to sit back and relax for a moment. While eating I could hear the never-to-be-forgotten sounds of the big old steam engine as it began to move the ferry out into the Bay. After breakfast and up on deck, it was lovely to look over the water, feeling the fresh breeze in my face as the boat made its way to the city. Seagulls always followed, hoping for a handout, and mostly they were rewarded as they swooped and dove to expertly catch the morsels thrown to them. A couple of dirty tricks were played on the gulls, one of which I saw only once. The one-time trick was tossing one of those small, red, Chinese firecrackers into the air after lighting it. It went off in the beak of the unlucky gull that caught it, but after wobbling a bit he flew off squawking in protest. Several of us surrounded the miscreant who did the deed and threatened to throw him overboard if we ever caught him doing it again. The other trick wasn't so bad. Take a string about two feet long, tie a piece of bread at each end, and toss it out to the throng of gulls. Now and then two birds would grab opposite ends and a tug of war ensued with all sorts of acrobatics. This one wasn't so bad because the bread crumbled and the string dropped off in the air. We approached the San Francisco slip with passengers crowding the bow ready to rush off to their city destinations. The pilings of the ferry slip creaked and groaned, the engines churned the water in reverse, the cables swished as the ramp was lowered into place, and the captain skillfully guided his boat to its moorings. I think everyone enjoyed that maneuver at the end of the trip. I know I did.

Of course, as you know, there are days of fog over the Bay, but the ferries never stopped. You could stand on deck with the mist wetting your face and listen to the captain navigate his way across the waters by the reflection of his horn from the soundboards located at strategic points along the route. A ferry going the opposite direction could be heard, but only a vague outline or nothing was seen as he passed by. A chuffing of engines getting louder and then diminishing might be the only sign of other life out there in the fog. Those old captains were great, and I don't think anyone was concerned when the fog settled in; I know I never was and I don't recall ever hearing of an accident. Sadly, the days of those old boats are gone, mainly because of the bridge and BART, but an attempt to revive the ferry system is being made with smaller boats. The patronage is small, but they seem to be able to manage. I don't know what the fare is now, but in my day 25 cents got you from Berkeley to San Francisco by one of the most scenic routes in all the world! I reserve a place in my heart for the old ferries, some gone, some slowly rotting away, and one or two ignominiously serving as floating restaurants, their powerful engines silent forever.

The first year of classes was easy, mainly because I had a great background from Sacramento. There was time to enjoy other things, including a girlfriend. We first met at a party at my cousin Bob's house in Oakland,

and, without a date, I made eyes at a pretty young thing named Helen. By the time the party was over I had wedged myself in between her and her date and, although I didn't know it then, the die was being cast for the rest of my life. Our first official date happened in 1935 at the Big Game played at Stanford. It rained cats and dogs; the parking lot was three inches deep in water and the football field was a quagmire. By game end the skies were clearing, and as we made our way to the chalets we had rented for the night at Brookdale Lodge (separate rooms for guys and gals, of course), the sun was beginning to dry up the flood. After a time to clean off the mud, hang up the wet clothes, and get dressed for the evening, we were ready for the formal dinner dance. The dining room and dance floor were in a terraced natural setting. A stream ran down a formation of rocks and ferns, and azaleas and rhododendrons grew in profusion around an ancient redwood that extended through the roof of the building. What a superb evening that was, and what a way to start my campaign to win your grandmother. I hope that you both will someday have a date as wonderful as that one.

Then there was the night I almost blew the whole thing! Helen had invited me to a dance her scholastic sorority was holding. Somehow or other I got the date wrong, and on the correct night a couple of us from the fraternity went out to a movie. When I got home that night there was a note on my desk. It read *Helen called and asked to speak to you. I told her you were at the movie and asked if there was a message. She said just tell him I never want to see him again.* A postscript said *Boy you're in deep trouble.* I called the next morning and asked to speak with Helen; her mother answered and said Helen wouldn't speak to me. Fortunately Helen's mother listened to my explanation of having marked the wrong date on my calendar. If not for your great grandmother, Leola Hederman, convincing your grandmother of my terrible mistake, you two girls might not be here today. Can you imagine? Much care on a new dress (and a beautiful one it was), much time in front of the mirror, and then a long silence during which many unkind thoughts were harbored about that thoughtless slob at the fraternity. Such are the vagaries of chance.

Although I had brought my sax, I didn't try to get into a band at Cal. I can't tell you why, but at least one new hobby had piqued my interest. I owned an Argus, a crude forerunner of many 35mm cameras to follow. Not long after I had earned a few bucks working in San Francisco, I bought a used Leica and started taking pictures of the plays and players at the Saturday football games. After selling eight by ten prints at the games I built up enough money to graduate to a Zeiss Contax with an f-2.8 normal lens and a 150mm sonar telephoto. That beautiful old camera lasted me until around 1954, when I sold it and got a Rolliecord 2 1/4 square format. To this day I stick with that format in black and white.

Some of the professors at Cal deserve mention. My favorite was "Little Joe" Le Conte. His family was legend at the university, and there is a building on campus named after them. "Little" was appropriate because he was diminutive. He was devoid of the usual small-man characteristics and was a patient, caring teacher in the finest sense of the word. I took hydraulics from him and I remember it as the best class I ever had. Then there was Mr. Folsom; egotistical, nasty at times, but one heck of a teacher on the subject of aerodynamics. Mr. Wiskocil taught us about reinforced concrete and opened each semester with, "I don't know why all you students want to punish yourselves with this subject, but I'm going to teach it to you whether you like it or not." There were others, mostly fine instructors, highly qualified in their respective fields.

The Cal campus deserves a word. There are many classical buildings and structures, including the Campanile, the life sciences building, the library, Wheeler Hall, and Sather Gate. The Gate was the entrance to the campus when I was there, but it is no longer, the campus having expanded down Telegraph Avenue. The Greek Theater up on the hill is a setting for graduations, plays, operas, and concerts. Sometime when you are near, take the time to walk the campus and listen to the bells in the Campanile and you'll get a little of the feeling I had sixty-eight years ago. Do it for me; it will only take a few hours of your life.

Moving into my second year, things began to come apart. I flunked advanced differential equations, an elective I never should have taken because it was loaded with math and physics majors. I guess it was the trigger, because by the end of the year my grades were getting lousy. Much to the disappointment of my parents, I elected to leave Cal without graduating and attend Boeing School of Aeronautics instead. I had always wanted to be in the airplane business, and this seemed to be the time to do it. I must say I had a fine time in classes having to do with design of parts and complete airplanes. I got top grades. Along with the schooling I took flying lessons in exchange for doing aerial photography. This was a great time and included such experiences as watching new designs being tried out at Oakland Airport and working at a part-time job disassembling big aircraft engines in preparation for required overhaul.

During this time your grandmother-to-be and I spent much time together. There were photographic trips to San Francisco and the beach. There was the time when I got caught by an errant wave as I concentrated on some particularly photogenic rocks and got sloshed chest-high in seawater, along with my camera. It was a long trip home, standing on street cars and the ferry before I could shower and wash off the salt. The camera, after disassembly and a wash in fresh water, was no worse for wear and survived for another twelve years before being traded for a better one. The exciting atmosphere at the airport, with new planes and the advent of Boeing's and Douglas' first generation of passenger planes, drew us to that area on many weekends. All this time saw Helen's family suffering badly from the Great Depression, but it was a time also for us to cement our relationship and it soon led to the announcement of our engagement.

In 1938, the National Air Races were held at Oakland Airport and I was a pylon official. This included the duty of watching the race planes as they made their turns around the marker to be sure they didn't cut the corners. What a thrill it was to watch those speedy little planes dash around the course, engines screaming, wings vertical, and pilots watching the competition while trying to gain whatever advantage possible. In those days the planes were mostly homemade and so small the pilots almost had to put them on like a shirt. Some had retractable landing gear, but the pilot was required to pull up the gear by hand. You could tell when this was happening because the plane wobbled as the wheels were jerked up into place.

Part of the course was over the water, and I will always remember one little plane rounding the pylon and for some reason flying straight on in a shallow dive until it plowed into the water with a huge splash. Rescue efforts were impeded because the water was shallow and some time passed before the pilot was recovered. It didn't matter, since we all knew the pilot had been killed. The plane, eventually recovered, was a mangled, twisted mess of fabric and aluminum that no one could have survived. One other accident happened within 150 feet of my location at the pylon. This one was due to bad pilot judgment. The Waco was a popular biplane in that period, and there was a dealer at the airport who was scheduled to put on a show of the plane's acrobatic ability. The pilot took off, flew a couple of low passes over the area near the spectator stands, and then climbed for altitude to do some rolls, a wing-over, and an Immelman, all fairly simple stunts. Then came the fatal loop. He came in low, pulled up into the climb at the start of the loop, came over at the top, and started down. I knew he was pretty low and watched, fascinated, as the plane gathered speed on the downward curve. The poor guy never had a chance. Experiencing what is known as high-speed stall, the pilot was unable to bring the plane out of the dive. I could see him clearly as he struggled with the controls, trying fruitlessly to pull up. I will never forget that crash; one minute a sleek plane, engine roaring, and the next a sound like a ripe cantaloupe hitting the tarmac, followed by silence. I saw the man being crushed and mangled in the mess in that split second. The crumpled remains didn't even resemble a plane, and I remember thinking how quickly a life had been snuffed out by a foolish error in judgment. The crash truck came out, removed the tangled junk, took it out behind a hangar, extracted what was left of the pilot, and the show went on.

A more pleasant experience just before the races was an example of supreme flying skill. Roscoe Turner was a racer, a public relations man for Gilmore Gasoline, and a stunt flier who often flew with a young lion in his plane (see illustration). Gilmore, the lion, served as a mascot for the gasoline company until he got too big to handle in Roscoe's plane. A cross-country race was scheduled to start from Oakland, and Roscoe (without Gilmore) was in the air tuning up his plane the day before takeoff time when the control tower received a radio call informing them there was a gasoline leak that had flooded the rear fuselage. Since the plane had a metal tailskid, there was danger that, as it touched the ground, a spark from static electricity or from striking the pavement might ignite the gas vapors. Roscoe informed the tower that he would come in for a landing but would keep the tail off the ground, and he requested that someone come out to the plane with a grounding wire to eliminate the static charge. The word got around the airport, and we all watched as the plane came in for that amazing landing. Roscoe had to keep the engine running fast enough to hold the tail up, while at the same time applying brakes enough to stop the forward motion without nosing over. We watched this delicate maneuver as the plane came in and slowly rolled to a stop, tail up. An airport attendant ran out, grounded the plane from a wingtip and then the tail was slowly lowered to the tarmac. Gasoline ran from the fuselage without igniting and as Roscoe climbed from the cockpit we all gave him a resounding cheer to which, always the showman, he responded with a sweeping bow. See the illustration of a model of the plane. He won the race that year, and I will always remember him as one of the great pilots of that exciting era.

Near the end of the year at Boeing the faculty contacted manufacturers seeking placement for the graduates. I had three offers: Boeing in Seattle for $90 per month, Lockheed in Burbank for $85 per month, and Pan

American Airways on Wake Island for $125 per month. While agonizing over these magnificent opportunities I got a telegram from Art Crawshaw, my boss at the San Francisco job, now in a place called Mason City, Washington, offering me a job on a dam named Grand Coulee for $35 per week. This salary translated to $151.66 per month, and there went my ambition to become a great aircraft designer. (Incidentally that salary turns out to be 78 cents per hour!) I couldn't get to Western Union quickly enough to wire back, "Yes, be right there!" See the illustrations of faded copies of that exchange. That left my fiancé with an absent boyfriend way off in some God-forsaken place she'd never heard of.

THE BIG RED TRAINS

Roscoe Turner, Aviator, with Gilmore

Model of experimental plane flown by Roscoe Turner

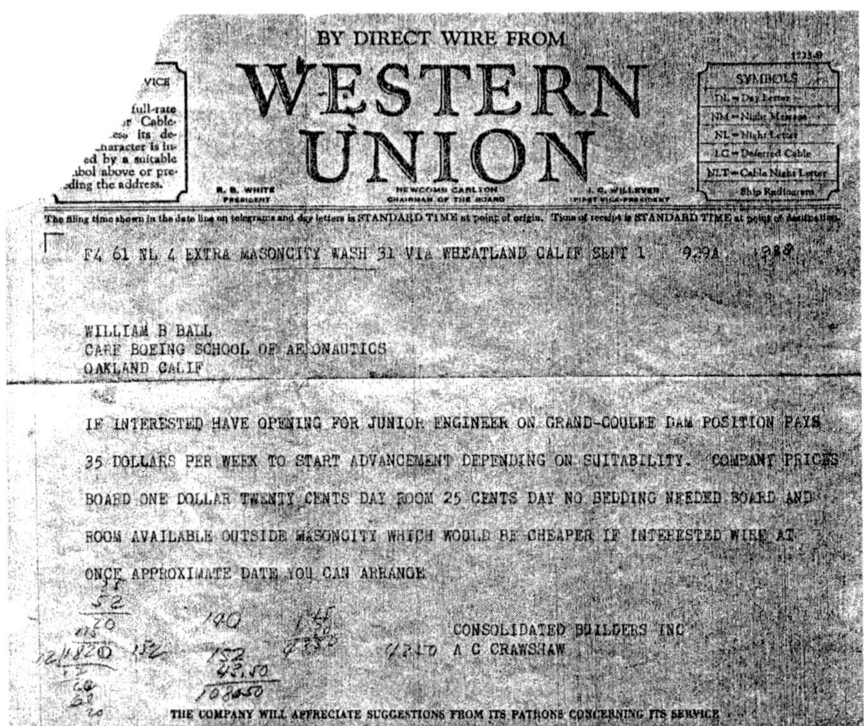

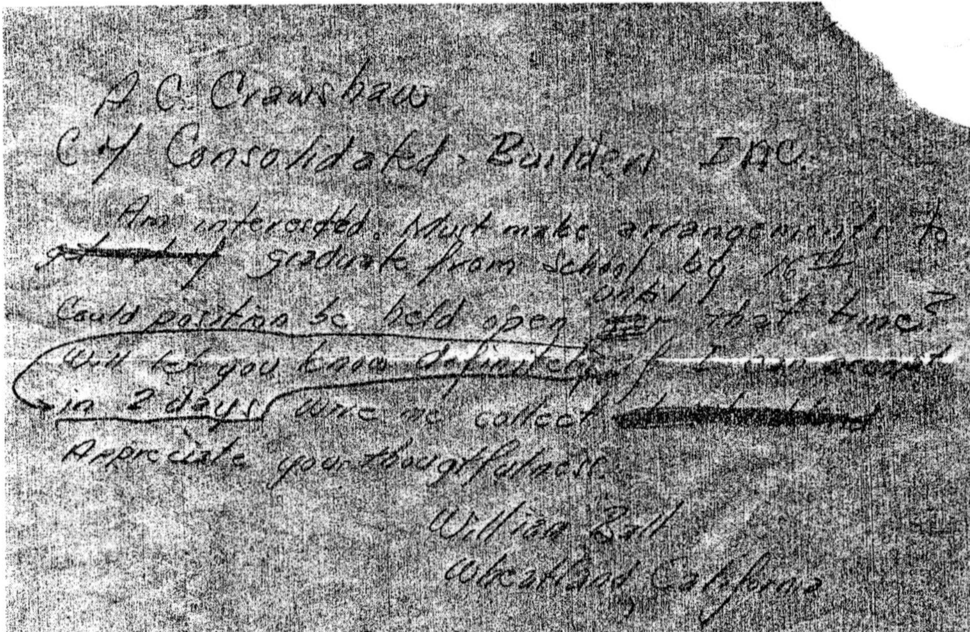

Accepting the job at Grand Coulee, Washington

Chapter Sixteen

The Great Grand Coulee

While going to Cal I had worked part-time in San Francisco for the Resettlement Administration, doing layouts for the migratory labor camps to be built in the Bakersfield area. These camps were to house the people fleeing the mid-thirties Dust Bowl in Oklahoma. Following that, I participated in the site surveys to locate and stake out the facilities. All through this work my boss was Art Crawshaw, who now was my chief benefactor.

My Dad wanted to drive me up to my new job in Mason City and suggested that my fiancée, your grandmother, go along. As I recall it was a one-stop trip, because Dad was one of those people who could drive forever, pausing only for food and pit stops. After the briefest of stays, Dad and fiancée headed for home and I was alone to face the world and my future. After the cloistered atmosphere of academia with its safe, predictable order, here I was, suddenly face-to-face with this huge, swirling, noisy, clanking mass of activity—and I had somehow to find a spot where I could step onto the merry-go-round and grab a seat without falling off. I don't mind telling you that I was scared, but finding Art was the first order of business and so off I went.

At breakfast I was lucky enough to sit next to a guy named Vince Palmer. Vince had been working at the dam for a while and directed me to the field office where I found Art. What a relief to see that familiar face! After bit of reunion and looking at photos of the camps in California, we got down to a description of my job, which seemed rather simple for someone who had just become an engineer. Briefly, my task was to keep track of all form work and concrete poured each day in ten areas of the dam. Additionally, I would be involved in other office activity as time permitted.

There was one other little item: since the project was on a seven-day schedule, so was my job. With the rest of the office on a five-day schedule, I could take off on the two weekend days when my regular chores were finished. Generally this meant a half-day Saturday and Sunday, but as it turned out I often got away as early as ten a.m. and so had time for some recreation. The information I needed came in from the field engineers on four-by-five-inch forms, but it was part of my job to make periodic forays into the field to check on the accuracy of the data and, in particular, to more carefully assess the trash rack details (the trash racks were upstream structures to keep logs and other debris from the turbines). This inspection was a weekly must, but there were additional trips over the dam as well, and these averaged about five or six a month, each one taking about three hours.

After the job description Art arranged to get me a room in the bachelors' quarters, and the next day I moved in. The town restaurant was a short walk in one direction, and the office about a hundred yards in the other. This was convenient but not very inspiring, so after hearing of a room for rent I moved to the home of Mona & Tom Ostliff, where I stayed for the rest of my time at Coulee. Some time later Mrs. Summers, just next door, offered boarding for five of us and provided wonderful home cooking from then on.

Some time in those early days a significant event took place, the evidence of which exists to this day. I wanted to save as much as possible from my salary, so each payday I put money into a savings account, leaving just enough to pay my expenses until the next pay period. I was running a little short when someone came around with a football pool with one remaining square for a cost of one buck. Never much of a gambler, I turned down the offer, saying, "Holy smoke, I've got only $3.50 and that has to last me 'til payday." One of the guys said, "Oh, come on, everybody else is in. I'll stake you to payday if you need it." So I bought the last square, which turned out to be an improbable 5 and 2. The game featured Michigan vs. Michigan State, and after a wild and wooly game the scores ended with a 5 and 2. I worked that Saturday until two p.m., and when I got back to the Ostliffs' there was my $100 neatly packed in an envelope. I don't recall winning another pool since, but what a big one that was! It bought cigars for the guys, candy for the gals, and took me in grand style to payday. One more thing it did: it bought an engagement ring setting and an unmounted diamond. I will forever remember choosing these in a little jewelry shop in Coulee City, pouring over about thirty diamonds on a black velvet pad, selecting one and then picking out the ring. I felt like such a big wheel with all that money, buying those symbols of matrimony. It was a good buy and one that got better each year.

My trips over the job site were, at the beginning, daunting to say the least, because early in my stay the only access to the main dam blocks was by ladder. As I looked down for that first time from the high trestle I wasn't sure I really wanted to risk it: two hundred feet down a flimsy wooden ladder wired to the trestle supports, for gosh sakes! I finally screwed up my courage and began the descent, hanging on for dear life. Reaching the bottom, I leaned back against the ladder and slowly collected my shattered nerves as the adrenalin stopped flowing. Not long after that, the steel ladders with handrails and landings were completed and life became a lot easier. That initiation, while frightening, helped me get used to high places, and before long I became a veteran high walker.

One other incident on the east abutment trash racks gave me a fright. This occurred on a weekly trash rack form check, when I climbed about twenty feet on a wood ladder to get to the top of a block. As I came to the top, the ladder seemed unstable, and upon inspection it turned out it was held by some loose wire that appeared on the verge of pulling away from the form. Looking down at the upstream water flowing by a hundred feet below, I was angry that such careless work might cause a serious injury, or even death, and after returning to the office I reported the matter to my boss. All hell broke loose because, in addition to unsafe work, it turned out that the east abutment foreman was snitching lumber and prebuilt forms from the west abutment on little midnight raids. He would then wire them in place to get credit for forms placed so his costs would look good. That guy, Pop Baker, nearly got fired, but survived after being made to replace the forms he had snitched plus an extra week's supply. He also got a warning that any further evidence of unsafe work would result in termination. I was, nevertheless, very careful around that east abutment area. Interestingly, I ran into Pop at the Richmond shipyards about five years later, and as we reminisced about the Coulee job he said, "By God you sure stirred up a hornet's nest over that ladder and I caught all kinds of hell about it, but deserved it." I lost track of Pop in the ensuing years, but will remember him as an excellent construction man with a little larceny in his soul.

My job turned out to be more involved than it had seemed at the beginning. While the field information coming in on four-by-five-inch sheets was delivered to me from the site office, it required sorting by area and type, and that was time consuming. After a few days of this, I revised the sheets so that the various classifications were displayed at the top of each sheet in bold lettering, and the sorting became automatic as the engineer made his way over the job. This, then, left a minimum of juggling and gave me time for other more interesting things, such as drawing up special details for the repair shop and helping with drawings on buildings. Most form areas were simple repetitive items, but there were things like the penstock inlets and gallery intersections that offered a challenge to calculate. I often got help from Paul Newell, a very bright guy who was sharper at calculus than I. Unfortunately the penstock inlets defeated us both because of the multiple curvature. A rectangular opening of about thirty-three by twenty-four feet transitioned to an eighteen-foot diameter penstock tube, and after struggling with the calculation for a while we gave up. I solved the problem with newspapers. Heading out to the carpenter shop with a bundle of papers, I went to work taping them to the then-completed form. Many of the sheets had to be cut to fit, so I simply counted the number of sheets used and deducted the area of the cut pieces left over. Hundreds of gallery intersections occurred throughout the dam and, although we had calculated those, I did a check with the newspaper method and came out right on the nose.

As winter bore down upon us work slowed over the dam and finally came to a halt, except at the office and some of the shops. During the buttoning-down period we still had trips to make over the dam, and they became increasingly hazardous because of the ice forming on the blocks and making footing precarious. That was the time when we hung tight to the handrails as we crossed the bridges over the open blocks. I remember looking down at the water flowing by in a syrupy, gleaming stream at thirty miles an hour and thinking how little chance one would have at grabbing one of the knotted safety ropes suspended from the bridge. Our fears were well founded because, at the downstream face where the spillway bucket rolled the water, you would often see thirty foot logs being thrown completely out of the foaming turbulence only to drop back again where they were finally chewed to splinters. We all knew the story of the boat that was intended as a rescue craft in the event someone got swept downstream. According to the story (and we all believed it to be true), a crew of two took the boat, a twenty-five-footer, close to the turbulence to see how near they could safely approach. Something went wrong, no one ever knew what, and boat and crew were gobbled up in that voracious maw. Splinters of the boat appeared downstream, but of the crew there was no trace. We were careful when winter cold and silence hunkered down over the dam, and we were glad when the outside work shut down so we could stay inside safe and warm.

Winter was the time for hiking and hunting, and that also meant the weekends were mine. Ernie Jones and I each bought a .22 pistol and 12-gauge shotgun (the pistol cost $16.95, the shotgun $12.95 with a Finnish hunting knife thrown in. Try that today!) Our hikes took us in all directions out of the Coulee and up into the desert, and we gloried in the crystalline air and cobalt sky. Those little adventures ranged from five to fifteen miles round-trip. We used our guns mainly to alert the game of our transgressions into their territory. It really was more fun to watch the birds fly than to shoot them. We often hiked for miles, not talking, just soaking up the silence and majesty of that land. Now and again our reverie would be broken by a grouse thundering out of a clump of brush like a 747 on takeoff. They would unfailingly do this only seconds after we had passed and, by the time we had gathered our wits, the bird was out of range.

This was also the time to help Charlie Melander with his boat-building project and to construct our radio-controlled model plane. We never got the radio installed, because on our final test flight an errant wind current caught that beautiful red-and-white plane with its six-foot wingspan and lifted it out over the river, where it sailed on beyond our view. It must have come down into the water, where it may have made its way to the ocean for all we knew. Both Charlie and I remembered, years later, that sinking feeling as we watched our labor of love disappear forever. We did get Charlie's boat (a sixteen-footer with outboard motor) finished after installing what seemed like a million brass screws. The launching of the *Ruth* was a gala affair at Lake Nespelem, with a touch of good wine on the bow as a christening. For my labors I was promoted to first mate on the crew.

The winter lull saw three of us off to Tacoma for two weeks to help on the quantity takeoffs for the Tacoma Narrows Bridge. Little did we dream that the bridge would come tumbling down twenty-five years later as a result of harmonic oscillation in a severe wind storm. Designers learned from that, and subsequent bridges have profited from the experience. A supplement to that story came to light as the Bridge Authority filed its insurance claim. It seems that the agent who prepared the policy cheated a bit and wrote two policies, one for the Authority and a different one for his company, forging signatures on both policies. The agent pocketed the difference in premiums, thinking that no bridge ever falls down. When the unthinkable happened, the Authority found itself minimally insured.

Twenty-five years later, when I was working on a project in Tacoma, the insurance agent was being paroled from McNiell Island Prison just offshore from my job.

There was a most unusual chief engineer at Coulee. I suppose he might have been fifty at the time, but to us youngsters he seemed ancient. We held him somewhat in awe because of his mastery of the engineering profession. Fred Crocker could design a structure in half a day that would take anyone else several days, and we used to marvel at the fact that he seldom needed to refer to a handbook of structural shapes. Fred had most of that voluminous data committed to memory, a feat we found astounding. In other ways Fred was different, a loner, lost in his own world, hard to get to know. I watched him as he finished dinner in the restaurant where several of us ate, and the routine never varied. All plates would be carefully stacked in descending size and, having saved the little cream server and butter pat, he would lick the butter and sip the cream before stacking them in the pile. He had supplied the restaurant with a selection of foods compatible with his diet for diabetes and left it to them to select his meals. He never paid as he left, and we found that the waitresses put everything including tips on an account that was promptly paid at the end of the month. Automobiles were a mystery to Fred, or maybe he just couldn't be bothered with the details. He seemed to drive in whatever gear he happened to shift to that day, and we all gave him and his old Chevy a wide berth.

When the Japanese bombed Pearl Harbor and sank some of the battleships caught there, one ship seemed salvageable, but there were grave doubts that it could be rolled over and refloated. The call went out to Fred Crocker, and together with another top engineer from Kaiser, Jim Foster, he devised the method and equipment to right the vessel. That ship, I believe it was the *Oklahoma*, went on to play an important part in the war. A few years later I worked for Fred designing mechanical equipment, a most rewarding experience; I will tell you a little story that sticks in my memory. It has to do with my regular task of calling the Spokane Weather Bureau each Sunday for the next week's forecast and taking it in to Clay Bedford's office (Clay was Kaiser's project manager).

Call Spokane, get the data, enter it on the prepared form, walk down the hall to Clay Bedford's office, laboriously and slowly push open the twenty-three-foot-high door, struggle through eighteen-inch-thick carpet, shinny up the twelve inch leg of a ten-foot high desk and push the forecast over the top to the silent, waiting ogre. That done, drop back to the clinging

*carpet, out the door and back to my desk, sweating in terror that I had not
done my job properly.*

That was the dream I had years later, and it was no doubt because
Clay seldom spoke as I delivered my report and I really was sort of terror-
ized. Many years later Clay and I had a good laugh over my dream.

In 1938 Franklin Delano Roosevelt was president and he scheduled a
visit to the dam as part of a political cross-country tour. There was a rush
of preparation for the visit and several of us were assigned as tour guides.
A convoy of five eight-passenger, open-top autos was arranged to take the
president and his retinue around the project. Each auto had a guide, and I
was in number two along with several dignitaries, most notable of whom
was postmaster James J. Farley. The president, of course, was in the lead car
and I remember him still; smiling, head tilted up, cigarette holder at that
jaunty angle. As we made our way, I tried to provide the visitors with a bit
of background on the various facilities. The postmaster was an interested
spectator and asked questions as we went along. At the conclusion he
thanked me for my efforts and said that the tour had given him new insight
into many of the major objectives of the project.

That year I sent the postmaster a Christmas card, my first photographic effort, a picture of the dam, but without a picture of myself. About
a month later I received a letter from Mr. Farley thanking me for the card
and remarking how much he had enjoyed the visit to the dam. He went on
to recall one of my comments about the potential for agriculture as a result
of the pumping system at the dam. This confirmed the man's reputation for
never forgetting a name, and I have remembered it ever since as the true
measure of a great politician.

In 1994, fifty-six years after my first real job working on the Grand
Coulee Dam, Helen and I revisited the old site. We had been back one time
before with Serin and Lori, in 1954, on a camping trip. The original dam
had been completed and water was flowing over the spillway in a beautiful
white turbulence, plunging into the river below and finally curling back up
by the massive spillway bucket. This time there was no water going over the
spillway, much to our disappointment, but a new element had been added;
a third powerhouse with turbines and generators dwarfing the original ones
by a factor of nearly six to one!

We occupied a motel on the east side of the river in what was originally Mason City (named after one of the first contractors), and our room offered a view of the dam. As I stood there looking out over that magnificent structure I confess to a feeling of nostalgia, and in my mind's eye I stripped away all that mass of concrete and replaced it with the trestle, supports, cranes, blocks, and clutter of construction. I could hear the whistle of warning preceding a blast in the pump plant area and then the crump of the blast as I took shelter in one of the penstock tubes to avoid the flying rock that sometimes showered down. Just as plain as if it were yesterday, I saw the concrete trains pulling away from the mix plant on the east abutment and heard the diesel engine as it hauled up to twelve four cubic-yard buckets to the waiting cranes, where the concrete would be lowered two hundred feet to a prepared block, fifty feet by fifty feet and five feet deep. Silent now, it was then a bustle of activity, alive with the puny efforts of man to tame that mighty river. I felt a sadness for the passing of those experiences. There was a deep depression upon the land then, but there in the Coulee was work for many people, and it was to be a great boon to an arid and thinly populated area. It was a time when life was different and somehow simpler; no television, no drive-by shootings, and few of us had autos. We got around by walking, taking the stage, or hitchhiking. A different time, granddaughters, but we thought it was great. Standing there at the window I felt proud that I had played a part in such a magnificent project.

Before closing I will give you some clues on the terms used in the text and introduce you to the drawings and the photo, which certifies that I worked on the project. The photo came from J. V. Mims, an old Coulee buddy, who secured it from the visitor's center at the dam. Following the photo is a tabulation of wages specified for all craft classifications. How would you like to work for those rates today? The main dam concrete was placed for $3.50 per cubic yard. Today it would cost around $50.

All the engineering drawings (see illustration for a very small sample) are contained in the Specification Book prepared by the Bureau of Reclamation at the Denver office in 1937, and I have carefully preserved that book for all of these years as a wonderful reminder of a most important time in my life.

This Certifies That
Mr. William B. Ball
worked on the
Grand Coulee
Dam
and the
Columbia Basin Project

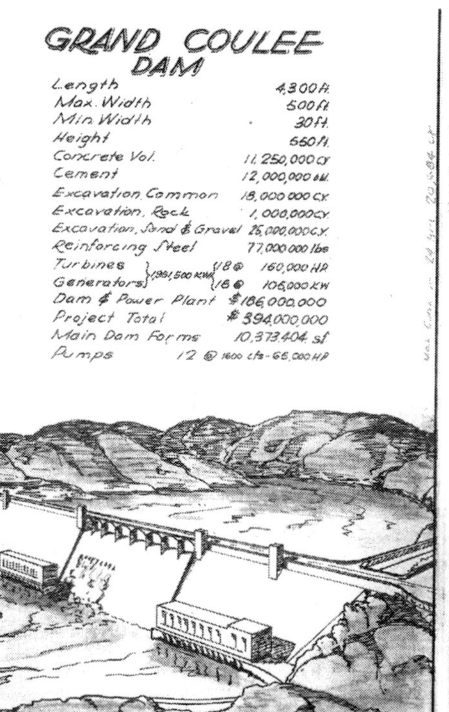

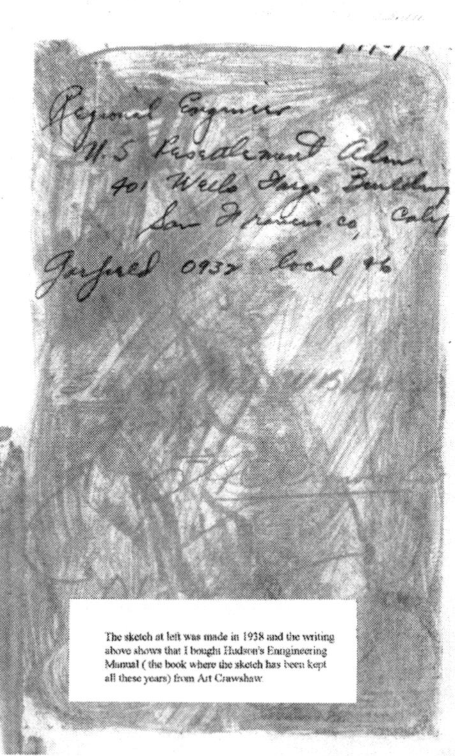

The sketch at left was made in 1938 and the writing above shows that I bought Hudson's Enngineering Manual (the book where the sketch has been kept all these years) from Art Crawshaw

Classification	*Rate per hour*
Crane operator	$1.50
Core driller (carbon or Calyx)	1.20
Core driller helper	.65
Conveyor tender (aggregate)	.70
Conductor, railroad (standard gage Govt. railroad, 30 mi. long)	1.00
Concrete vibrator operator	.75
Concrete pump operator	.75
Concrete mixer operator (under 1 cu. yd.)	.75
Concrete mixer operator (1 cu. yd. and over)	1.20
Concrete dispatcher	1.20
Concrete chipper	.75
Concrete batching-and-mixing plant operator	1.20
Churn driller (keystone, cable, spud, drillwell)	1.20
Churn drillers' helper	.65
Cement screening plant operator	.90
Cement pump operator (Fluxo & Fuller-Kenyon)	.80
Calker, ship	1.20
Calker, pipe	1.20
Concrete finisher	1.20
Concrete finishers' helper	.65
Concrete form anchor setters	.90
Lather, metal	1.20
Lather, wood	1.20
Concrete form (mover) (stripper)	.65
Carpenter	1.20
Carpenters' laborer	.65
Divers	3.20
Divers' tenders	.75
Dumpman	.60
Drill sharpener (machine drill dresser)	1.20
Drill sharpener helper	.65
Dragline operator	1.50
Dinkey operator	.90
Derrick operator	1.50
Electrician	1.20
Electricians' helper	.80
Elevator constructor	1.12½
Elevator constructors' helper	.78¾
Fireman, locomotive	.90
Fireman, shovel, crane, stationary	.75
Glaziers	1.20
Grade operator, elevating	1.20
Grader operator, power blade	.90
Grader operator, pull blade	.75
Grout machine operator	.75
Grout machine operators' helper	.65
Handyman (mechanical)	.90

1938 wage rates on the Grand Coulee Dam project

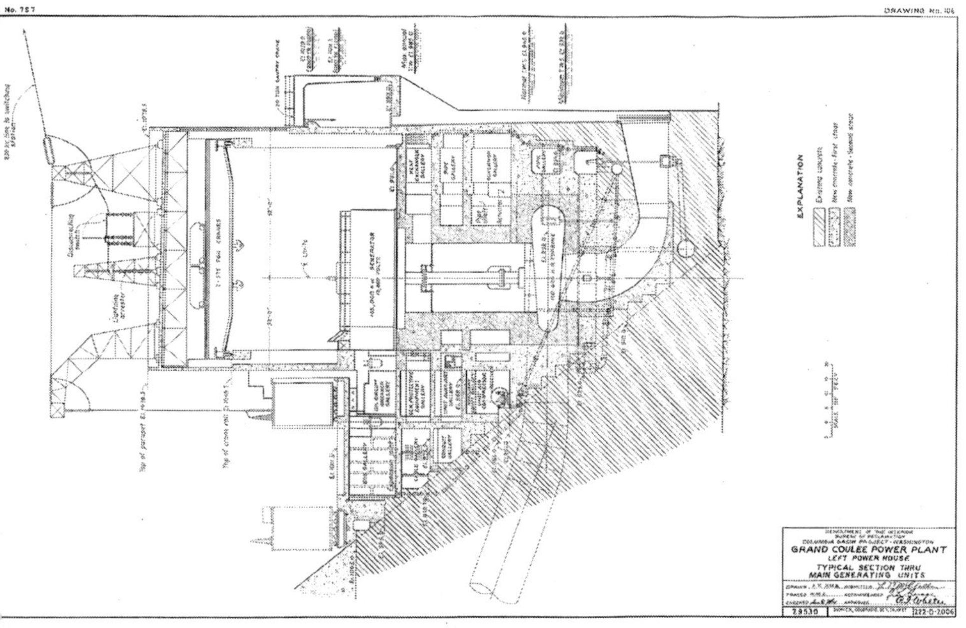

Section drawing

Chapter Seventeen

Marriage and a New Job

During the Coulee time I had been in touch with a cousin, Bob Rich, about the possibility of starting a dredging company. There was a firm in Pittsburg, California, Bundeson & Lauritzen, that had been in the business for thirty years and, with the owner nearing retirement, was seeking someone to take on the operations. Our group would include Bob, John Hector, and me, and we would have access to all of the B&L equipment as needed for the jobs we were doing. We could lease units as we were using them or begin a pay-as-you go purchase over ten years. Full of enthusiasm, we set a date and I left my job at Coulee. I regretted leaving that great bustling job, but a new adventure beckoned and off I went, back to the Bay Area.

There was an important priority before all else. Your grandmother and I had been engaged for more than a year, and apart for most of that time while I was away at Coulee. (See illustration.) It was time to get married, and this took place in the Oakland hills at the home of a Unitarian minister with his wife and a friend as witnesses. Since I didn't have an auto, my parents loaned me their 1939 Mercury sedan, leaving themselves without transport to attend the ceremony. In deference to my folks, Helen's parents also did not attend. After the ceremony there was a quiet little champagne celebration, complete with rice, at the Fruitvale Ave. house in Oakland, and then my new wife and I headed off to Carmel on our honeymoon. Because the roads were not freeways in those days it was necessary, after a late start, to make a stop in San Jose on the way. The drive had been made in a miserable rain, and the following day was even worse. Checking in at Highlands Inn south of Carmel, we thought our honeymoon was destined to be a wet and gloomy one.

Highlands had a main building with about twenty accommodations, a dining room, and a big lounge area. Scattered around the main building, on the steep hillsides, were individual stone chalets, each with a large sitting- and bedroom, a dining alcove, and a big bathroom. On the wall opposite the bath a huge stone fireplace stood, and to the right of that was a wall full of windows looking out over the ocean. Unfortunately there was nothing to be seen through the rain and gloom as we arrived that evening, but the chalet was warm and cozy and we soon dried off and got settled for the night. Listening to the rain on the roof, punctuated now and then by a big splash as a tree unloaded a branch of water, we ruefully contemplated our sodden adventure.

Bright and early we were awakened by a warning knock on the door, followed by the entrance of our waiter with a beautiful breakfast tray. Placing it on the alcove table, he stepped outside to return with an armful of wood and kindling. In moments the fireplace was ablaze with welcome warmth. As we threw aside the bed covers that my shy bride had pulled up to hide from the waiter, we were greeted with an unexpected sight; sun, glorious, beautiful sun. The trees were decorated with a million diamonds left by that drenching rain and the sky was clear as a crystal with not a cloud to be seen. Sitting at the small table enjoying our breakfast of orange juice, coffee, sweet roll, and a baked apple, we watched the roiling ocean as it protested the passing of the storm. Deep blue, punctuated with white caps, it seemed a fitting welcome, and through the windows we could hear its muted thunder. What a way to start a honeymoon and a marriage. There was a whole week ahead and much to explore. As I write this, it seems like yesterday.

Well! Stop mooning and get on with the story, okay? Carmel was brim full of new things for us. We visited the home of the poet Don Blanding, hoping to meet him since Helen had several books of his poems. Unfortunately Don was in the Islands, but we did meet there a weaver of drapes and wall hangings. We bought a small carving from the woodcarver and a tiny glass boat; visited the art galleries; tramped the trails at Point Lobos; ate in the best restaurants; and generally lived in the lap of luxury. To give you a feel for how lavishly we spent, here are some samples: The Chalet at Highlands, $5.75 per night; a steak at Sade's, $6.50 for both of us; a good painting, $100 (we didn't buy), and you could pay for it as you liked without interest; gasoline, 15 cents a gallon. Today those prices are, respectively, $300, $95, $2000, and $1.30. What is worse, Carmel has changed; glitz has pushed aside the old craftsmen, t-shirts have taken over from the dressmakers, and slick art is selling better than the good stuff.

We still go back every year, though, because by poking around off the main streets, worthwhile things are yet to be found. We always buy a couple of French rolls, some cheese, a bottle of good wine, and a half-pint of salad from the Italian deli that's been there forever. Then we go out to Point Lobos, watch the ocean, and enjoy a great lunch. I'll tell you one thing; we can't sit out on that high rock anymore with the surf all around while eating our lunch and feeding the seagulls. It's forbidden—too dangerous! We regret that, but it is the price paid for too many people. The trails are still open to all, however, and there is no restriction on watching the ocean as it dashes against the rocks, flinging spray high into the air, sometimes showering the unwary walker.

In those days entrance to the park was free, as was the "Seventeen-Mile Drive." The old Ghost Tree, immortalized in paintings and photos, has succumbed to the ravages of time, and around by Spanish Bay the road has been cut off by an ugly, mushrooming blight of condominiums. We are glad to have seen and photographed those beautiful long waves as they came rolling into the bay with the wind lifting the spray into a rainbow of colors. One can still see some of it, but the condo owners now have the privileged view.

The week, quickly gone, saw us on our way back to Wheatland to return the borrowed car and pick up a wedding present: a shiny new black Ford coupe. Our first automobile! What a thrill to hold the wheel of that machine. It had a V-8 engine and was capable of speeds approaching a hundred miles per hour. No radio, air conditioner, power door locks, power windows, or power brakes, but who cared. The gear shift and ignition switch were on the steering column, and they were later responsible for a couple of scary moments. I suppose the problems occurred because I had never driven a car with those "modern" developments.

The first event took place one night on our way to visit my folks in Wheatland. A moonless night was pierced by the welcome beams of our headlights as we approached the dogleg crossing of the railroad tracks near the town of Sheridan. I slowed to fifty miles per hour to make the crossing, looked to see that no train was coming, and accelerated out of the final turn. Suddenly, there was stygian blackness—no lights! Guessing where the road curved, I brought the car to a stop, shaking with relief as I realized we had made it without injury to car or occupants. The problem was a wiring harness that had slipped down so the gear shift arm could wear through the insulation. The final turn had thrown the wires against the lever and shorted out the light circuit. By flashlight I looped the harness clear and, replacing the fuse, made it safely home where, the next day, Dad and I made the necessary repairs.

The second little fright occurred about a year later as a result of a stupid error on my part. This one was definitely a case of always having driven cars with switches on the instrument panel. Bob Rich and I were attending to some business over near San Rafael, and I had locked some papers in the glove compartment for safe keeping. As we neared our destination, Bob asked if I had brought the information we needed. I said, "Sure, the stuff is in the glove compartment." He asked for the keys and, without thinking, I extracted them and handed them to him. We were in a gentle curve at that moment, and as I began to straighten out for the road ahead the lock bolt dropped into place in the steering column. Here we were still in the turn with a fixed steering wheel and headed for the ditch. Frantically grabbing the keys back, I managed to insert them and unlock the steering system to get us back in control. We avoided the ditch, but not before throwing gravel and tufts of grass through the fence and into the field beyond. A lesson learned at the expense of some adrenaline, but without other cost!

And now the dredging business. With the three entrepreneurs—Bob Rich, John Hector, and Bill Ball—full of hope and ambition, we set up a few simple rules and regulations. One major agreement was that if any member got called into the draft he would simply walk out of the partnership, leaving the business to the others. Another concerned money; only minimum monthly withdrawals would be taken by the partners so that the business gained the maximum cash inflow.

It began with high hopes, and John Hector was nominated as our salesman and chief promoter. Bob and I were the operations managers, meaning that we drove tractors and operated the suction dredge or clamshell dredge and the dragline. (See illustrations.) All of our jobs during the early period were around the Petaluma and San Rafael areas on the east side of the Bay and, as the business name implies, involved mud and water, some of which we carried home on our clothes at the end of each day. Bob lived in San Rafael, so he had a short drive to the jobs. His wife, Gail, was often our lunch provider. John lived in Berkeley and I lived in Oakland, so we both had a long commute. In those days the bay crossing was by ferry, and it was necessary to time your arrival at the ferry slip carefully to avoid a forty-minute wait for the next boat. The ferries are now history, having been replaced by the Richmond-San Rafael Bridge. The crossing time is now five minutes, as opposed to the old ferry time of twenty-five minutes plus loading time.

We had a variety of jobs in the start-up period, and we quickly found that the bay and its mud had lessons to teach us. The shorelines were treacherous, and what looked like firm footing could suddenly give way and bog down a piece of equipment. Levees that had been there for years could be riddled with rodent tunnels and at the first touch of the dredge might collapse and flood a farmer's field. Mud, dug from underwater and used to build up an area, might need to dry for a year before it could safely support traffic. One of our worst experiences occurred when we were preparing to dredge a yacht harbor near San Rafael. We were to use a suction dredge, and the material sucked up from the harbor was to be used to fill the surrounding areas. To do this it was necessary to build a levee around those areas to be filled so that water and mud could be pumped in and the water slowly drained off through adjustable gates called weirs.

We brought in our dragline to build the levees and were operating it on wooden mats so as to prevent the tracks from sinking into the unstable ground near the shore. The system used three mats; one on which the machine sat, one in front onto which the machine was moved, and one in the rear that was picked up and moved to the front. In other words, we carried a portable roadway to run the dragline on. A mat is made of several twelve-inch-square timbers lashed tightly together with wire rope and spikes to form a ten-foot-by-twelve-foot platform; the machine operator picks one up using the teeth of the bucket hooked into a loop of cable on the mat.

The yacht harbor was to have an entrance on San Rafael channel, and we were starting the levee near the bank of the canal. Of course, we knew this was a touchy area but there was no avoiding it so, with caution, the work was begun. After several hours with no problems it seemed that our caution was slowing the work and we picked up the tempo. That did it! While the rear mat was being picked up, the machine slid slightly on the muddy and slippery mat beneath. As we watched, that pad began to float out from under the machine, much as an air mattress pops from under a swimmer as he tries to climb aboard. We realized we were in trouble as the machine, now clear of the mat, was settling slowly but inexorably into the slop, and we had visions of a $50,000 piece of equipment disappearing into what we had come to call the bay mud—"loon shit."

What to do? Maybe we could get a big tow truck and, with its hoist, pull the dragline to firmer footing. We tried, but to no avail. All that happened was that the truck was pulled toward the mess, and if we persisted there would be two machines in the mud. Still the settling continued. By this time, the tracks were covered and mud was creeping up into the floor of the cab. Despair!—Defeated!—We were exhausted, and to say we had a "sinking feeling" would have been descriptive of our mental state as well as the scene with which we were confronted. Was this to be the ignominious end to the business so hopefully begun a few months ago?

As Bob and I stood ruefully surveying the mess we had gotten ourselves into, a big Duncanson-Harrelson derrick barge was being towed down the canal. Seeing our plight, the crew anchored the barge near our disappearing machine. Reaching over with the big boom they extricated first the cab and then the tracks of the dragline, setting each part on firm ground. Next they reassembled the machine for us and we were able to give a great sigh of relief. We asked what we owed them and the answer was, "Nothing, it only took us a few minutes. Glad to be of help." We wrote the company a note of thanks for saving our bacon!

There were other trials and tribulations during that time of the dredgers, and money was scarce as hen's teeth, but it was an adventure and involved lots of learning. A few months later, John Hector, who had been in ROTC at Cal, left us to join the army. We all could see the tips of those thunderclouds of war rising from the eastern horizon, and John said he was going to join while he had a choice of jobs. I've lost track of John, a good and honest man, but I know he rose to full colonel and served in Germany as a military governor before his retirement. As the din of the saber clashing rose, my draft board became restive and suggested that I get into a defense industry where I could use my engineering training. So, not long after John, I departed, leaving Bob, who continued to run the business throughout the war years.

Sometimes I wonder how different my career might have been as a "dredger." Would it have become boring? Would it have been a dead end like it has for Bob? I can say the experience has been useful in my career as an engineer, because I had hands-on operating time with machines pushing around a lot of bay mud. This gave me an advantage over my fellow engineers, particularly during the shipyard years that were to follow.

Helen Lois Hederman

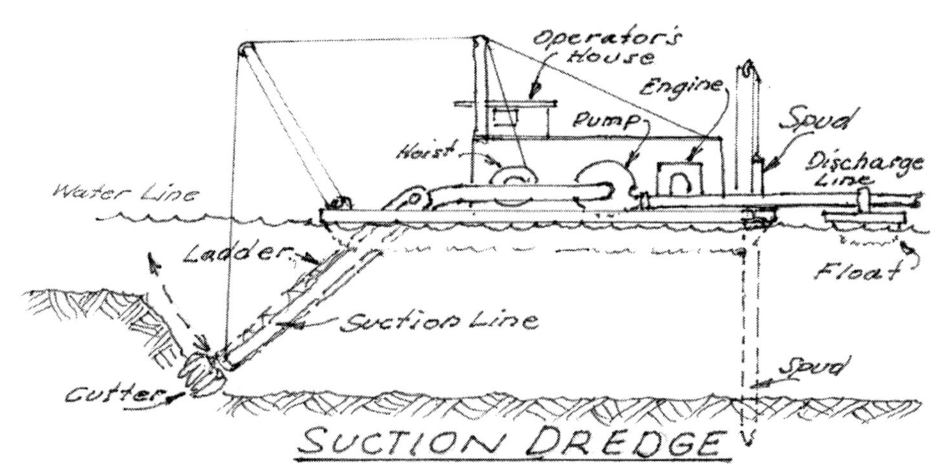

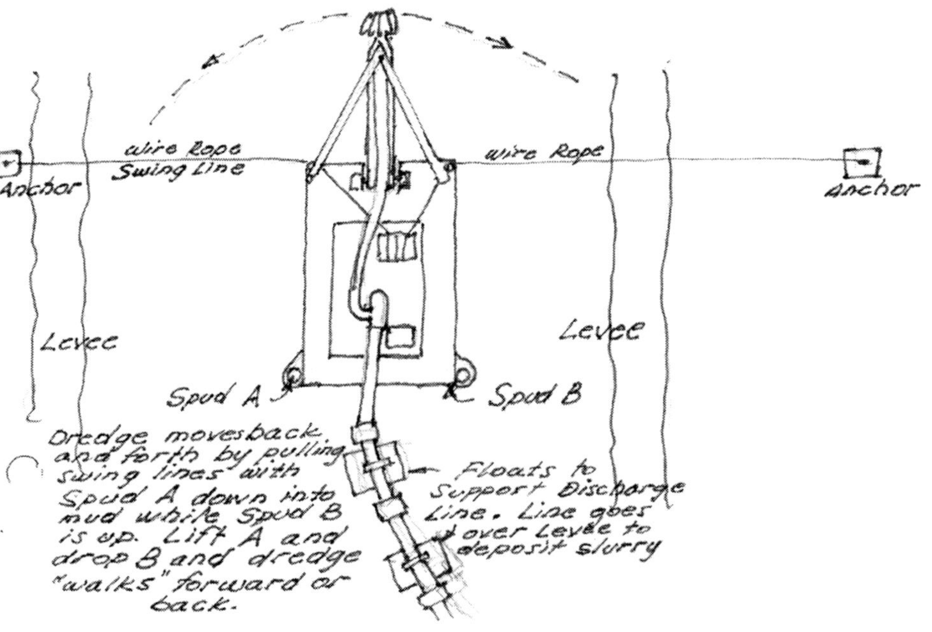

Suction Dredge

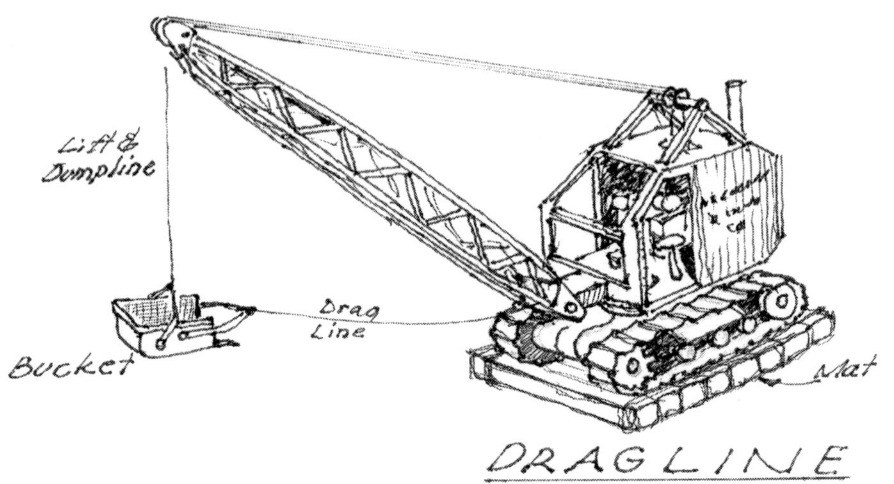

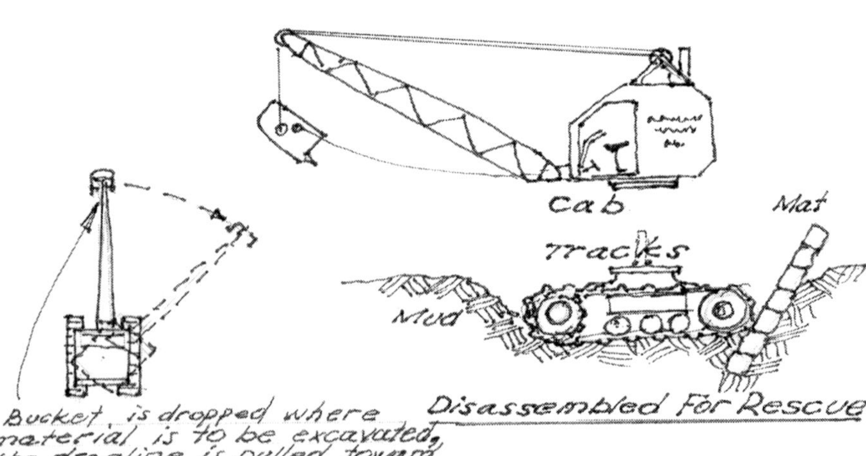

Bucket is dropped where material is to be excavated, the dragline is pulled toward machine causing bucket teeth to dig in thus filling bucket. Cab was then rotated to where material was to be placed. Dragline then released while dump line was held causing bucket to tilt and discharge load.

Dragline

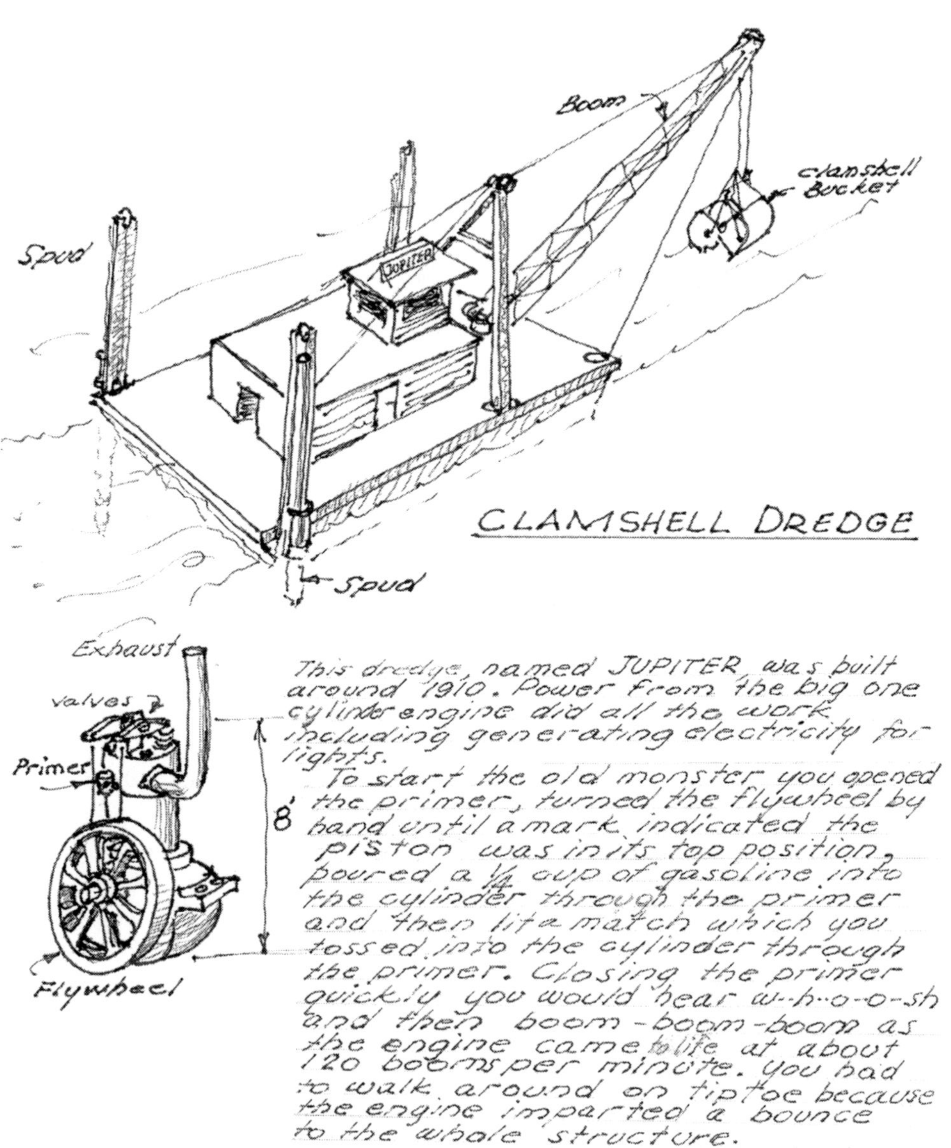

Clamshell Dredge

Chapter Eighteen

Shipyards in World War II

As 1940 drew to a close and the military draft picked up speed, my number floated to the top and I got the "notice." When I appeared for a preinduction physical, my board in the Fruitvale district in Oakland suggested that since I was an engineer it would be appropriate to join a defense industry. Still working at trying to build up a dredging business, the news was disheartening. Not much war work was going on in the Bay Area at that time, but the news had it that Henry Kaiser had concluded a contract with the British to build some cargo ships. There were some antiquated facilities along the Alameda Estuary between Oakland and Alameda, but Henry had chosen to start anew on some mud flats in a place called Richmond.

Not much existed out there except for a small port called Parr Terminal and a channel harboring a couple of yacht businesses. Along the waterfront, miles of tidal marshlands offered plenty of space for development, and the Kaiser team in Oakland picked a spot to lay out a shipyard. With my background with Kaiser at Coulee I had no problem getting a job on the construction of the first of what eventually grew into a complex of four yards. I didn't get the greatest position because of my past association; as a matter of fact I got a stinker graveyard shift as a piling inspector.

Those first four months were during a very cold and very wet winter and were enough to try a man's soul. With mud knee-deep and more, rain that seemed to happen only on my shift, and the constant din of the pile drivers ringing in my ears, I went about my lousy job. It was often cold enough to freeze a witch's heart, making writing in my notebook nearly impossible, and the pages were waterlogged at shift end. Hip boots were part of the uniform, and walking around in the quagmire I would often leave a boot stuck in the mud. Finally I tied a rope from the bootstraps over my shoulders to keep things in place. Because boots have little or no foot support I began to have problems with that arch, beneath and behind the third toe of the foot, called the metatarsal. It got more and more painful until I began using an elastic support. To this day there is a twinge now and then. To thaw out I would, whenever possible, seek shelter in the pile-driver cab where the steam boiler offered its welcome warmth. Lunches were eaten standing around fifty-gallon drums fired with wood scraps, hoping the rain would let up enough to permit a dry sandwich, but boy, did that hot thermos of soup ever taste good!

Piling muddy boots and wet rain gear in the car, I would wearily set out for home in the soggy gloom of early morning with the ca-CHUNK, ca-CHUNK of those damned pile drivers pulsing through my brain. After a wonderful late breakfast, prepared by my ever-faithful wife, life would again take on a rosy glow and the horrors of the night would recede. Fortunately this routine was finally broken when I was called into the office to help with survey calculations and the design of the buildings, docks, railways, and other yard facilities. From then on until 1945, I was privileged to be involved in more of a variety of work than some engineers experience in a lifetime. In the Richmond yards, we built 747 ships of various designs and in the Portland, Vancouver, and Swan Island yards our counterparts contributed another 743 for a total of 1,490. Such a monumental effort had a major effect on the war effort and every one of us is proud of our part.

In the five years at Richmond, a group of nine engineers and five architects did all the design for the four shipyards including, near the end of the war, a variety of studies aimed at creating new enterprises for the growing Kaiser empire. We sat down one day and totaled up the engineering costs for that work, coming up with a figure of 0.5 percent of the total construction cost. In subsequent consulting work after the war, that figure would generally run about 5 percent and the client would be charged 8 percent. In a relatively short time, our little group had become a closely knit, highly efficient organization. We concluded that the Maritime Commission had gotten a bargain and the draft board had received their money's worth by sending us to a war industry.

For me, one important association was with the architects. Like the rest of us they had been herded into war production, and in our office their numbers were higher than usual. All were experienced and highly regarded in their profession. Working with them gave me a different view of our related, but different, disciplines. I learned some of the art of design and feeling for spatial relations from those guys, and have tried to remember those lessons throughout my career. Every one was a cherished friend and I salute them all by recalling one name, Morry Wortman, a talented, ebullient, and gregarious purveyor of charm.

There were times when we worked the night through until breakfast, and times when my pregnant wife perched on a drafting stool to keep me company on the Saturday or Sunday sessions. On some of the all-night gigs, a couple of us would join Harry Bernat at his home in Richmond, where Mary had a wonderful hot breakfast ready for us, and after a couple hours of napping we'd be ready for the fray again. We were young then, but looking back I am still amazed that we did it. Working with that team was one of the many high points in my career, and it stands right alongside Coulee in my life as an engineer. I will remember fondly all those men. Most are gone now—only two of us remain.

Even in the days before we were at war, steel became difficult to get except for material used in ships, so we were obliged to use wood for most of the structures. Accustomed to designing with steel, this required learning new techniques, including the use of devices most of us had no experience with. It didn't take long for us to become proficient in timber design, and at that time lumber was available in sizes not seen today. Can you imagine a piece of timber sixteen by twenty inches with a length of thirty feet without knots? Today such a size is unavailable, and in its place we would use a glued member made up of several smaller pieces, fabricated in a factory, rather than cut from a huge old tree. You might say we were profligate in use of materials, but war is a waster of resources. Today, with most of the big, old-growth trees gone, it is necessary to make better use of the wood we have.

As Yard One, as it was later to be known, rose out of the mud flats, our attention turned to the business of launching the ships that were to be built. To prepare the final launching calculations, management had employed a naval architect. To us "regular" engineers, this work appeared to be a mixture of prestidigitation and legerdemain with maybe a little witchcraft thrown in, and we viewed the process from a safe distance. Safe, that is, until suddenly the naval architect disappeared, none of us knew what happened, and Jim Foster asked me if could finish the job. It was an intriguing but intimidating task, but the intrigue won out and I said, "sure." I set out using civil engineers' excavation calculations to determine the volume of water displaced as the ship slid down the ways. This gave me a buoyancy force to determine when the ship would lift off the ways. Applying some kinetics and dynamics plus a prayer, the job was completed. At the launching I stood watching with my fingers crossed. The champagne was smashed across the bow, workmen knocked away the restraining blocks, and the big hulk began its slide down the ways. It took what seemed like an hour to complete the run, but, wonder of wonders, it all went off as calculated!

While we are discussing launchings, I must tell you the story of the Russian freighter. This happened on the third launching, and I was in a small boat out in the channel to watch the ship from a side view as it slid down the ways. To slow the ship and bring it to a halt, large concrete blocks were placed at intervals in the channel on either side of the ship's path. Chains, anchored to the blocks, were lashed to the ship in such a way as to drag pairs of blocks and use them as brakes. As the ship progressed it would drag more blocks until it was dead in the water. A tug and derrick barge then came out to unhook chains, move the blocks to a new location, and take the ship to the outfitting dock.

On this occasion everything went off as expected until the ship was clear of the ways, and then it began to swerve to the left. Obviously, the drag on the left was working but the drag on the right wasn't. We could only watch helplessly as the vessel continued its slow but inexorable curve, almost majestic in its determination. Now we began to feel concerned; when would it stop with only half the drag, and what about that Russian ship tied up at the Parr Terminal? As our ship came closer we began to see activity on board the docked vessel, and finally we could see men jumping from the deck to the dock and running from the scene.

Almost dreamlike, our ship made contact with the Russian freighter, and the rudder, lashed fore and aft for launching, cut the hull of the other vessel like a giant can opener. Peeling back a hole about forty feet long, it allowed some of the cargo to be jostled around and a few pieces fell into the water. It was then that we realized the reason for the panic of the Russian seamen. That cargo was barrels of HI-TEST AVIATION GASOLINE, and those sailors had visions of a giant fireball. Fortunately, no ruptured barrels and no stray sparks! The yard repaired the Russian ship, and helped make up the lost time for a desperate Russia in the grim struggle to fend off a German offensive aimed at its heartland.

With the eight classes of ships built at the yards, there were three different modes of launching. In both Yards One and Two, the conventional stern-first launch off an inclined way was used. In Yard Three, rather than "launched," the ships (large troop carriers) were constructed in a concrete basin, and when ready for outfitting seawater was pumped in to float them, after which huge gates were opened to allow a tug to tow the ship to a dock for finish work. Yard Four (see illustration) turned out to be the wild one. Built at the end of a restricted channel used mainly for small boats and barges, the space for launching was ridiculously short. When we asked Clay Bedford why he had chosen such a location, his answer was, "There wasn't much choice; besides, I knew you guys would come up with something."

Come up with something we did! For the first part of the ways we used a slope somewhat steeper than was customary. As the ways entered the water we began a downward curve. I still remember the radius, 909.75 feet! Why not 910 or some other even number? Darned if I can remember. Anyway, this arrangement dictated the use of two support points for the ship, one fore and one aft, each of which had to provide a pivoting motion. (See illustration.) The purpose for all this was to plunge the stern of the ship into the water as quickly as possible to provide a braking effect. In addition, each of the pivot devices, called poppets, was built with a wide plywood connector across the ways to offer more braking. We called these arrangements barn doors. All this took the place of the concrete blocks I mentioned before. Here again, I sort of fell heir to the job of designing a workable system and I confess to some feelings of trepidation as I stood by watching the first launching. IT WORKED, IT WORKED, and boy was it ever a spectacular show! As the rear poppet reached the curve, the bow would begin to rise. It would reach a peak about twenty feet above the ways and then plunge back down below the ways as a finale.

That steep stern drop later became the cause of a little dramatic comedy. As the work went on the shipwrights kept adding more parts to the ships in spite of my warning that too much would ultimately dip the stern in too deeply. Because the launch had a little of the Coney Island rollercoaster to it, some of the foremen would ride the ship down. On this occasion the troops were assembled near the stern, prepared to enjoy the show and, since I was convinced there was too much weight on board, I went out to watch. Sure enough, the stern went in and kept going down, down, and down until water suddenly began pouring into the scuppers and up the deck. There was a wild scramble to beat the advancing tide. Some managed to grab something and hoist themselves out of the boiling water, while others got the full treatment and two had to be plucked out of the water by the waiting tug crew. Next launch had no riders, and there was less weight. I never said a word to the guys and they never mentioned the event to me. I still chuckle as I write this.

It was a gloomy Sunday, and I was at work finishing a rush job so we could call in a contractor to give us a bid for grading on Yard Two. I hadn't taken a lunch, figuring on finishing the task no later than two o'clock and then heading for home. I was hard at work at the drawing board and the shouting didn't penetrate at first, but finally it got through: **PEARL HAR-BOR—PEARL HARBOR—THE JAPS HAVE BOMBED PEARL HARBOR.** I remember the chills running down my spine as the news registered. Was it possible? Why? Will they keep going and hit the West Coast? Should I drive home the back way avoiding the vulnerable East Shore Highway? I finally realized it would take another day before enemy carriers could get within striking range and, with visions of bombs devastating the Bay Area, I finished my task and drove home under a threatening, and, I thought, portentous sky. That day was December 7, 1941, and was, as President Roosevelt said in his broadcast that evening, a "date which will live in infamy."

People huddled around their radios that evening awaiting details of the disaster, and on street corners extras were being hawked. From our safe continent we had watched the war in Europe grow in brutal intensity. Now, suddenly, our isolated cell was cracked wide open and we were at war! Soon there were blackouts and I remember the eerie sound of the siren on the Tribune Tower. The first blackout was a new experience, and I recall that after all was cloaked in darkness street lights at Hopkins (now McArthur) and Fruitvale continued to flash their red, yellow, and green as though to signal those bombers that, fortunately, never came. People were much agitated about such stupidity, and one angry citizen tried to climb up and bash out the lights. He couldn't reach them, but later someone pulled the switches and we all breathed a sigh of relief. All this seemed to make our jobs more urgent and more important, and throughout the nation shoulders were put to the wheels of industry. The result is history, leading to the greatest output of planes, ships, and war materials the world has ever seen. In our four shipyards alone we built eight classes of ships, for a total of 747 vessels. We also had the distinction of building a ship in four days, fifteen hours, and twenty-six minutes from keel to launching. After all equipment was installed, the sea trials completed, and Maritime Commission acceptance accomplished, the time from keel laying totaled seven days, fourteen hours, and twenty-three minutes. That record has never been beaten!

Generally, engineers would be the first group into a building and would enjoy the good office space. As the yard added administrative, accounting, and other functions, we would be moved to the next yard. That worked well until Yard Three was filling and we were only beginning to lay out Yard Four. Suddenly our luxury space was gone and we were moved to the mold loft, an area about six hundred feet long, eighty feet wide, and twenty feet high. It was located above the plate shop, where all the hull plates were cut for attaching to the ship. Much riveting, drilling, hammering, and overhead crane action took place in the shop. In the loft there was a wooden floor where all the layouts were done and where templates were made for the fabrication to be done below. Since not all the space was needed for template work, we were given a sizeable area at one end for engineering. Our boss, Einar Larsen, had an office within our area and we were all surrounded by eight-foot-high partition walls. Apart from having to climb a thirty-foot spiral stair to get to work, things didn't look too bad. Not bad, that is, until we settled in.

The six-hundred-foot sweep of space had its own weather; winds whipped down that length and curled over our partitions so that we had to wear our hard hats with a shawl of cloth tucked under to shield our necks and shoulders from the cold gale. The din down below deafened us, and I remember at home someone would speak to me and I wouldn't hear them because I had learned to shut my hearing system down. When the big cranes below picked up a load and moved down the rails, our drawing boards shifted under us and we often drew unwanted squiggles that had to be erased. Pink Pearls (erasers) disappeared fast. We complained to deaf ears, but finally one day our time came. Einar was in and out of his office, and as a result did not feel the full effect of the environment until the day of the phone call. The call came through during a period of delicious noise below and he was struggling to hear, holding one hand to the free ear and going through contortions with the phone. In those days, wastebaskets were made of cardboard because of the shortage of metal, and I concluded the one in Einar's office would make a good insulator. Seizing the opportunity, I stepped into the office, upended the contents on his table, and dropped the basket over Einar's head. I wasn't sure it would stay, but it did, and as he finished the phone call he slowly lifted the basket and said, "I see what you guys are going through." Within ten days we were out of that hellhole.

It was, however, almost like going from the frying pan into the fire, for we wound up in an office without a roof. This was at Yard Four and construction was now underway. Everyone appreciated leaving the mold loft even though it was to move into an office without a roof. We hollered about this when our drawings got dusty, but no one seemed to hear until the road oil incident got some attention. The roads and parking lot had been graded and gravel had been laid, and, one evening as we left, the road oil spray rigs arrived. Everything, it seemed, except our building, was being expedited. Next morning all our drawings had freckles. The fine spray of oil on roads and parking lot had floated into the roofless building and settled on the drawings we'd left the night before. Some sheets were salvageable, but others had to be done over. This time our howls got attention and a roof was constructed in two days during the hours when we were not working.

Before we leave the tale of the shipyards there is one more important launching to tell about. Leola Serin Ball came off the ways on June 28, 1943. In those days many people were growing "Victory Gardens," and we had a vacant lot across the street full of a variety of vegetables. Your grandmother put in a great deal of time cultivating and watering, and we figured that digging and hoeing would be good exercise during the pregnancy. One day I arrived home after a long day at the office to find that my diligent wife had put in a strenuous stint of weeding the corn and potatoes. Both of us were tired, but we decided to take in an early show at the Diamond Theater, two blocks away. After the movie and our short walk home we were ready to hit the hay. Settling into the welcome comfort of the bed we were startled by a clatter and a crash as the mattress and springs jolted to the floor. Between giggles we managed to reassemble boards, springs, mattress, and bedclothes, and snuggled down once more. Early the next morning we were on our way to the hospital where our first daughter was born. Did the jolting get things underway? It took a week to get wife and daughter back from the hospital, and they were transported in an ambulance. Today it's home on the second day and transportation is by the family car.

Along about this time there was the Spruce Goose; the wild and wooly ill-fated partnership between Henry Kaiser and Howard Hughes. Henry watched his ships go to sea, some to be sunk by U-boats, and was concerned as the battle of terrible attrition continued. Always full of ideas, he said, "Let's build a flock of big cargo planes and fly the supplies over the submarine menace." Gene Trefethen was assigned the task of organizing the program, and a proposal took form in the mold loft. The book, twenty-four by thirty inches and bound in leather, weighed about sixty pounds, and I lugged it down the spiral steps, took it to Oakland Airport, paid a terrible sum for postage, and saw it off to Henry who was in Washington, D.C., ready to make his pitch to the War Production Board.

There followed a hectic period during which we made layouts of planes being assembled on shipways, sliding off into the water (see illustrations), and being towed to a station where wings were attached. There were sketches of various configurations: eight engines, seven engines, six engines, four engines, one fuselage and two fuselages. Sketches showed a plane in the water off the coast of Africa while people unloaded the cargo into small boats, and another showed a plane at a dock. To avoid use of aluminum, the flying boat's structure was to be wood. This, of course, is the reason for the name "Spruce Goose." Several people accompanied Henry to Southern California to obtain information so that we who remained in Richmond could do the modifications required to adapt a shipyard to airplane construction.

As time went by, tales began to filter back of late-night meetings and fruitless attempts to tie down details. Howard Hughes seemed to exist in a world of his own, unassailable by outsiders, regally marching on his own course, deaf to any communication. After a valiant try to achieve cooperation, Henry and Gene, frustrated in their efforts, gave up and we packed away all the work we had done on what we'd hoped would be a major strategy to defeat the U-boats. As you may know, Hughes went on to build one huge flying boat, flew it about two miles, brought it down, and mothballed it. (See illustration of a model.) Later used as a tourist attraction in Southern California, the plane was recently disassembled, barged to Seattle, and reassembled for tourist display in the Northwest. An ignominious end to a great idea.

We built roads in and around Richmond, we built a rail line from Oakland to the yards, and we built a ferry slip to accommodate ferries from San Francisco. Somewhere there still may be a drawing of the commuter train unloading platform, with a little dog sitting underneath, with my name as designer and bearing a date of about mid-1942. About half of us started in the yards in our mid-twenties, and by the time the war ended we had accumulated the most intensive experience of our careers. It was said that Clay Bedford had only to write a note on a slip of paper and throw it in the office door and we would parcel out the work and have drawings, estimates, and schedules in a week or two.

Two assignments of the later shipyard days remain etched in my memory. The most difficult one had to do with a helicopter. Henry had heard about a revolutionary machine invented by young Stanley Hiller, and proposed a partnership to develop a production model for military use. I was sent to the Berkeley Armory, a big gym-like building originally used for ROTC training. Here four of us, with Hiller, started the design for the proposed new machine. My job was to design the control system and fuselage. What a nightmare it was. To give you a feel for the task, I must describe briefly the rotors and their function.

To begin with, this helicopter had no tail rotor to keep the fuselage pointed where the pilot wanted to go. There were two rotor blades, one above the other, and turns were accomplished by increasing the pitch of one rotor and decreasing the pitch of the other. The fuselage would then turn in the direction opposite to the rotation of the increased pitch rotor. It was simply a matter of the fuselage absorbing the torque difference, since the increased pitch had a higher torque than the lower pitch. To move forward, the pilot would tilt the whole rotor assembly down in front, giving a forward component to the lifting force. He'd do the reverse to back up, or he could tip to any direction. If both rotors were lifting equally, the machine would simply hover. To climb, he'd increase pitch equally on both and up he would go. Pitch would be decreased for down. When moving forward the blades rotating in the direction of flight had more lift than those retreating, so the pilot would lower the pitch of the advancing blades and increase that of the retreating blades. This is called cyclic pitch control, and is accomplished automatically as the assembly tilts. All this is done by the wobble plate. Next time you see any helicopter, notice the small ring below the rotor and note that it connects to the blades by short control arms.

Now think of another set of blades above, and see if you can figure out how to get all that monkey motion done at the top. One can't go around the bottom set because the blades turn in opposite directions. Can't do it. Here is where the nightmare comes in. The lower rotors are driven by hollow shaft and the top blades by hollow shaft. Pitch control of the upper blades is driven by threaded tubes through the upper hollow shaft, while wobble control is driven by a threaded tube going between the hollow shafts. The pitch and wobble control for the lower blades are just like a normal helo. All this mess of controls had to be led to a pair of foot pedals and a single joystick so a pilot could fly the machine without going bonkers, which is what I nearly did as I developed the system. (See illustration.) I used to go home at night and dream about control arms, tubes, shafts, and wobble plates.

To watch the controls in action I built a crude strobe using a sewing machine motor turning a cardboard disc with evenly spaced holes around the circle. I could vary the speed of the disc and, looking through the holes with a strong illumination of the control parts, I could slow the motion, speed it up, or stop it. In the early stages of design, we equipped small electric drills with a single set of blades and a big vane to slow the turning motion so we could study different stabilizers. A great deal of information was gained from using those two simple devices.

Our helicopter flew and did very well, but the timing was wrong; we were too late as the war was winding down and Sikorsky helos were filling the need. (See illustration.) Two machines were built; Kaiser took one to a plant in the east where it may still be, and Hiller took one with him when he moved to Fairchild Aircraft. What an adventure for me though! I still have a large finished drawing of our machine. Someday ask me to show it to you.

The second assignment mentioned above concerned railway cars. In order to speed construction of ships at Richmond, we built a large assembly building where major sections of ships could be fabricated and then trucked to a vessel on the ways at Yards Two and Three. Six hundred feet long, with two sets of tracks running the length, it had prefab bays along each side. Management thought such a structure would be ideal for manufacturing rail cars. I was called to Clay Bedford's office and asked to take a trip to St. Louis Car and Foundry. Obviously this was to be an industrial spy job, and my cover would be to act as an expert in the use of aluminum for lightweight rail cars. I had no real information on the subject and suggested a couple of days of library research before leaving. Tough—tickets were already purchased and an appointment made with the president of the car manufacturer. My leaders promised to have some information at my hotel when I arrived in St. Louis, and this would give me an evening to become an expert.

I arrived at the office, catalogs in hand, and prepared to try to bluff my way through the ordeal, and after a few minutes discussion the president suggested we have lunch before going out into the plant. After a very pleasant lunch with several management people whom the president thought ought to hear my story, I began to feel as though I had done a superb job of fooling everyone. As we prepared for a trip into the shops my ego was deflated by, "Mr. Ball, we know why you are here, but we do compliment you on your presentation. Now we will show you how we do our job." With that I was introduced to every detail of the process of making railway cars, and quite an education it was! We were thinking of using as many as *eleven hundred* people in our shop; they had forty. We expected to make about four cars a day; they could make eight if necessary.

Other cost-saving methods left me dumbfounded. To cast wheels they placed molds in a nearby steel plant, and when a cast iron order for some other customer was completed the mill poured what was left over into the car company's molds. When an order for spring steel wound up with extra material, the car company's waiting trailers would get the leftovers. Those materials were almost free for the taking, and we had never contemplated such an arrangement. Needless to say, our people were astounded by the story I brought back in my report. No rail cars were ever built in the assembly building or any of the other yard buildings, and they all ended their glorious life destroyed to make way for a new generation of industry in Richmond. My first and last job as an industrial spy was an embarrassing but highly educational experience.

Now the war in the Pacific was over. Hiroshima and Nagasaki had been obliterated in the first nuclear conflagrations in history. With D-Day in Europe soon to follow, it was time to plan for the postwar period.

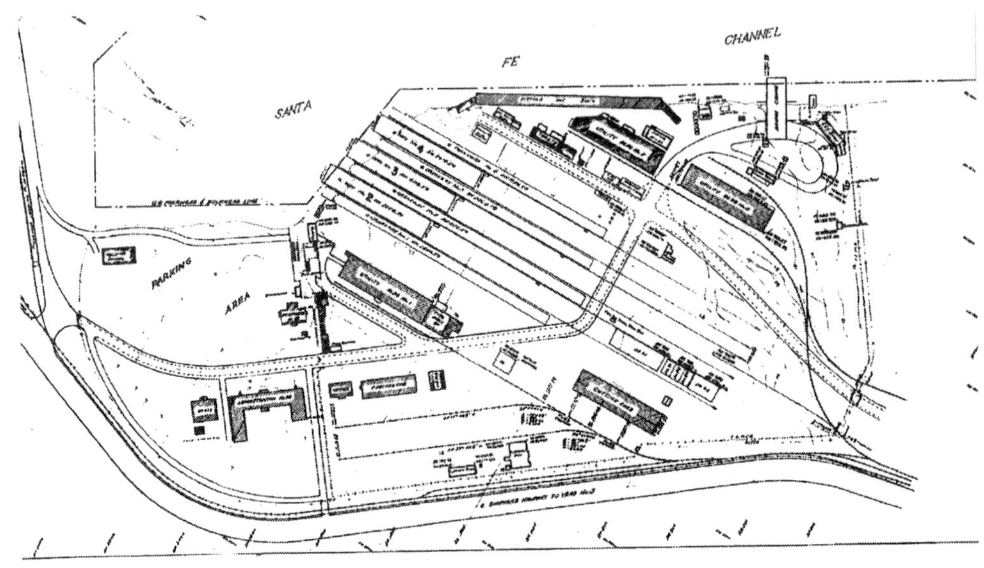

PLAN OF YARD NO. 4   **FIG. 1**

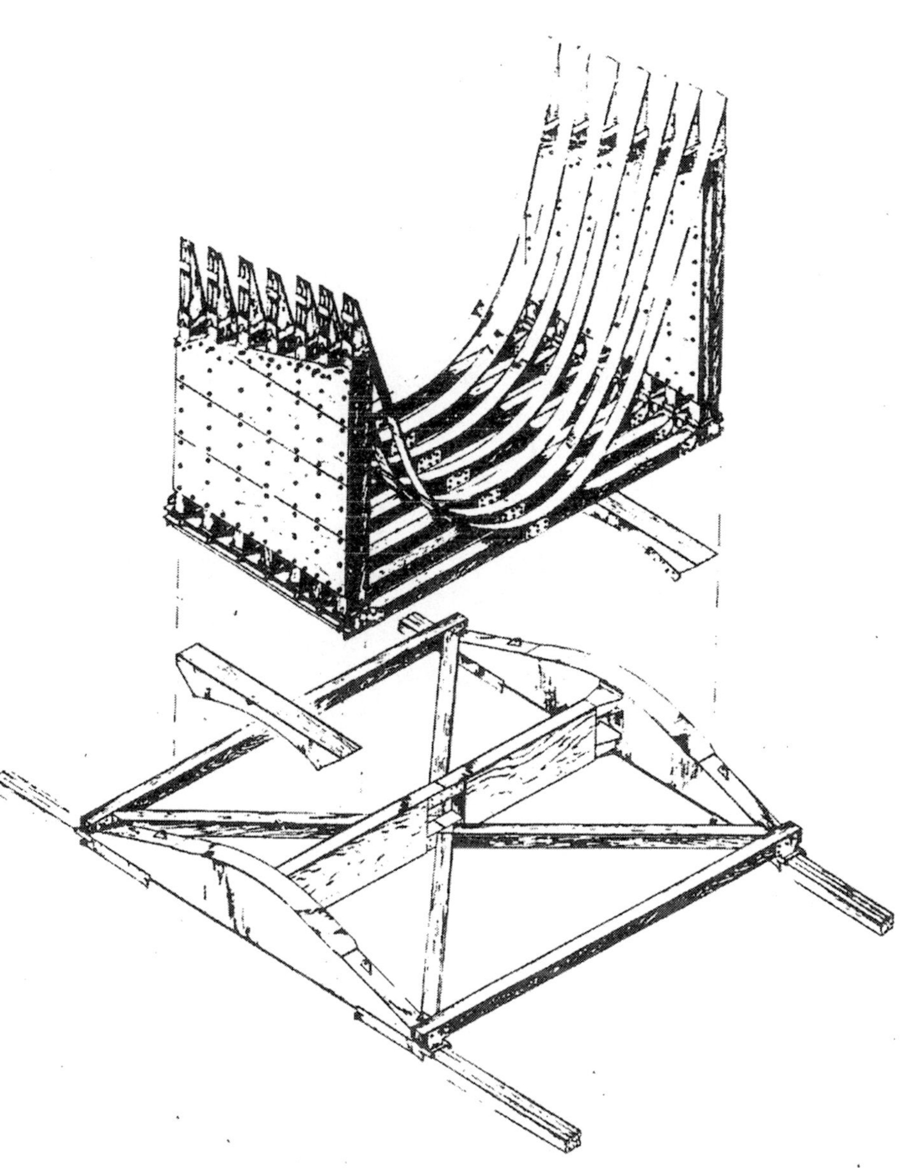

ISOMETRIC OF FORE POPPET FOR FRIGATE

Model of the Spruce Goose

Flying Boat Sketch

Flying Boat & Hanger Sketch

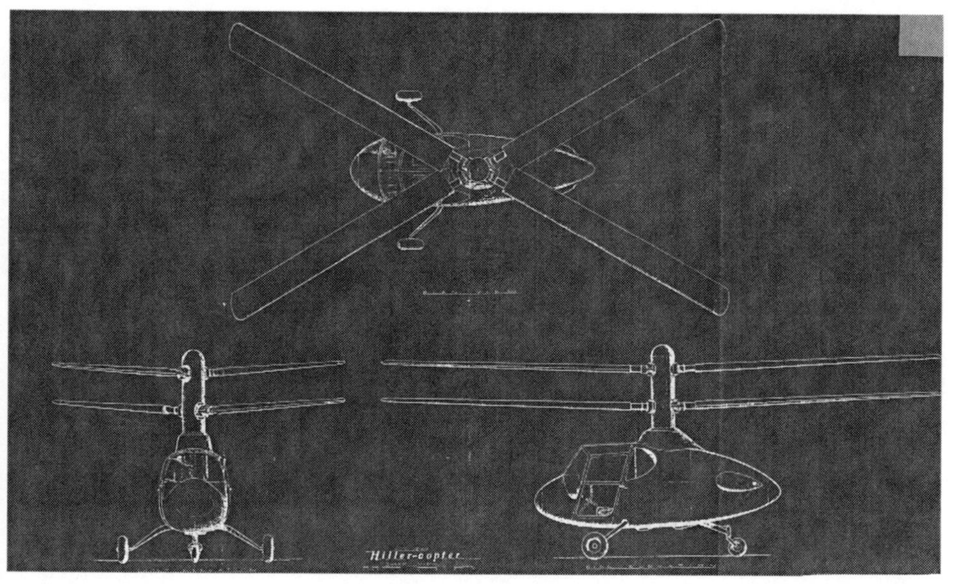

Hillercopter Prototype Sketch

Hillercopter Flight Test

Chapter Nineteen

Post War 1946-1950

Finally, after five long years, the bitter and tragic grinding of the war machines had come to an end and we looked forward to a time when we would no longer feed humanity into that grisly mill. Auschwitz, Buchenwald, Hiroshima, and Nagasaki were behind us and now the time of healing and rebuilding was ahead. Lives disrupted or interrupted by conflict needed redirection in a fragmented world. Suddenly we realized that it was not only soldiers and refugees but we ourselves who had to find new direction. After intense concentration in an effort to be a part of the victory we now savored, the home-front troops had to find new jobs in industries converting to peacetime production.

The Marshall Plan, probably one of the greatest efforts in history to heal the war-torn continent of Europe, followed by MacArthur's leadership in reorganizing Japan, gave hope and promise to millions of people. I remember the conflict in my own mind—why not some help for us, redoing our lives here at home? But then we were not uprooted from our towns and farms, nor did we die on some nameless, muddy battlefield; rather, we had jobs to look for in an economy that could only surge ahead in the years to come, so it was time to get out there, join the crowd, and find a future.

Leaving the shipyards and the people I had worked with for so long was hard, but I hit a sort of compromise. Four of us with similar ideas decided to set up an engineering office and strike out on our own in the consulting field. Bill Bertwell, Morry Wortman, Al Fingado, and I rented space above Benetar's Drugs in San Francisco and, through Morry's earlier efforts, landed a job. Everything looked rosy: a five-hundred-home development north of Richmond adjacent to Highway 80, with a sewage disposal plant, water, and electrical distribution, roads, and design of five typical homes; a three-year program with enough income to give us a good start. Two architects and two engineers about to make a name for themselves! Not long before this I had taken the tough, two-day exam for a civil engineer's license and passed it, Bill had a structural license (the toughest of all), and Al had his architect's ticket, so we were fully qualified to practice.

We hired a survey crew, began layouts of the area utilizing the terrain to provide the best bay views, and were about four months into the venture when the program was suddenly canceled. What a gloomy office it was that day as we paid off our surveyors for their half-finished work and contemplated our future. Al said he would stick with us, but would also seek private work designing residences. The rest of us went out beating the bushes and managed to get some work, but it was not encouraging. We did the most menial tasks, like tracing for other engineers and detailing structural steel, but in the long run the whole effort sputtered out like a guttering candle. We gave up as a team; Bill landed a job with Sverdrup and Parcel, a fine engineering firm in San Francisco, Morry went back to Kaiser, and I decided to have one final fling by myself.

That fling was difficult. I spent most of the days looking for work and then spent the nights doing what I got. The most frustrating part of it all was collecting the bills. That experience revealed a part of human nature I found disturbing. I had clients who would present me with a problem and, after I had engineered a solution, would say, in effect, "That turned out to be pretty simple, you mean to say that those three drawings cost that much?" I did do some interesting things during that time in spite of such miserable clients. There was a fast drying plant for foods, a cardboard box plant, machinery for production of window screens, and a yacht harbor. The income was not as interesting as the jobs; I had a family to support and was getting tired of paper drapes for the windows and unpainted furniture with six coats of paint.

Anyway, it was off to Fibreboard, which turned out to be a terrible mistake. I was never allowed to do any meaningful engineering because everything had to go through Leland S. Rosner, a consulting engineer in San Francisco. It seems that Rosner had married a Fleishacker (owners of Fibreboard) and all work over $500 had to be done by him. Things I could have done in an afternoon took two weeks of work in Rosner's office. After six months of this, plus the long commute from Oakland to Antioch, I threw in the sponge and told your grandmother, "We'll have to starve if I can't find anything else."

Along with all this turbulence, on September 21, 1948, Helen Lori Ball joined the family and we had much to celebrate. Our trials and tribulations of the business were forgotten as we welcomed the new addition, and Serin had a sister to keep her company. We also had another round of early morning feedings to attend to.

With the euphoria of the new family member abating, it was back to reality. What to do about earning a living? I was convinced that either I didn't have the ability to be a businessman or the economic climate wasn't right for the start of an engineering firm. In either case, the conclusion left only one alternative; get the heck out there and find a job. It was a simple solution, except that I never before had faced the need for a full-fledged job search. Always before someone had asked me to take a job and there were friends to welcome me through that first door.

I must admit to an empty feeling of concern as I began leafing through the Yellow Pages searching for engineering firms and employment agencies. Making a list and establishing a priority for contacts, I updated my resume and prepared to begin my search. Completing the resume and making some copies over a weekend, I was set to assault the barricades on Monday. It never happened! On that fateful day I had an early morning call from Bill Bertwell. "Sverdrup and Parcel needs a good mechanical engineer. If you are interested why don't you come over to San Francisco and see if you'd like the job?"

Talk about timing and luck! That was the beginning of two years of the most technically rewarding engineering of my life. Powerhouse heating and ventilating, selection and layout of heavy duty cranes for generator and turbine maintenance, design of an extensive fish ladder and selection of water supply pumps, design of the penstock gate-lifting system, all for Ice Harbor Dam on the Snake River; preliminary design of a supersonic, variable-throat wind tunnel for NASA; design of the very large Bascule Bridge over the ship channel near Sacramento. On this last job, because of the size of the span of the bridge, it became necessary to use two large gear racks driven by two electric motors and a complex of gear reducers. (See illustrations.) To provide an even distribution of gear loads and to prevent runaway in case of a gear failure, I devised a form of limited-slip differential, which you can see on the drawing. I was right proud of this then, and, as I look at the drawing today, I still am after forty-six years. Helen and I visited that bridge many years later, and when I told the operator I had done the machinery design he took us down into the equipment bay beneath the bridge deck for my first look at the actual system I had put on paper in the office.

I must not leave the S and P work without paying tribute to Leif Sverdrup himself. His work as an engineer in the Pacific theater of war under General MacArthur is the stuff of legend. His firm, headquartered in St. Louis, is greatly respected in the engineering profession for its ethics and high level of technical standards. Every member of the San Francisco office felt the warmth of Sverdrup's personality, and we were all accorded his respect for our professional positions. Leif received many honors from his adopted country, the United States, and from his native homeland, Norway, and throughout his life made many contributions to both nations. I will always be proud of my association with Sverdrup and Parcel.

Once more I was offered a job, this time back with Kaiser for the third go-round. The decision was a difficult one. My association with S and P had been a wonderful experience and the future seemed bright. Would rejoining Kaiser in the recently formed Kaiser Engineers be a wise move? I would be heading the mechanical group on a big project to build an aluminum plant in Chalmette, Louisiana, and there were other projects in the near future. So, not without some regrets, I left S and P and headed off into a new job. I recall having some misgivings over that decision, but many years later, looking back long after retirement from Kaiser Engineers, I know it was one of the best moves I ever made. It has led me around the world, into more kinds of projects than I could have imagined, and it allowed me to meet an exciting spectrum of people. How lucky I have been!

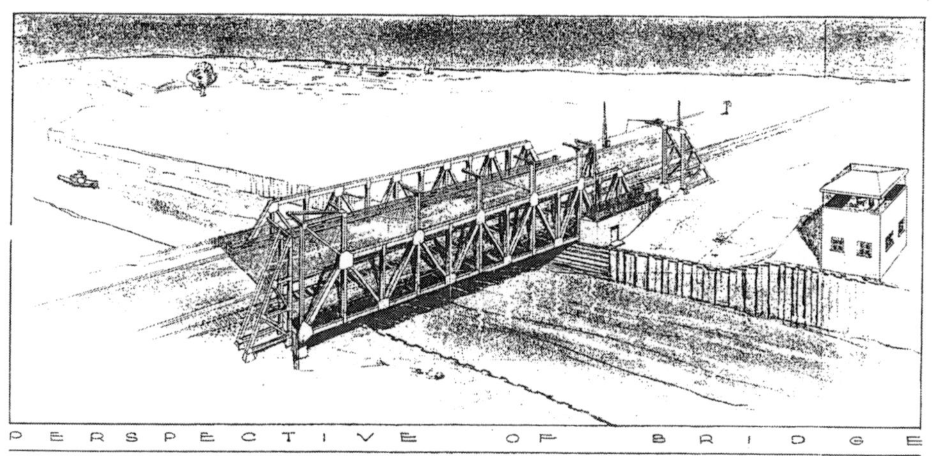

PERSPECTIVE   OF   BRIDGE

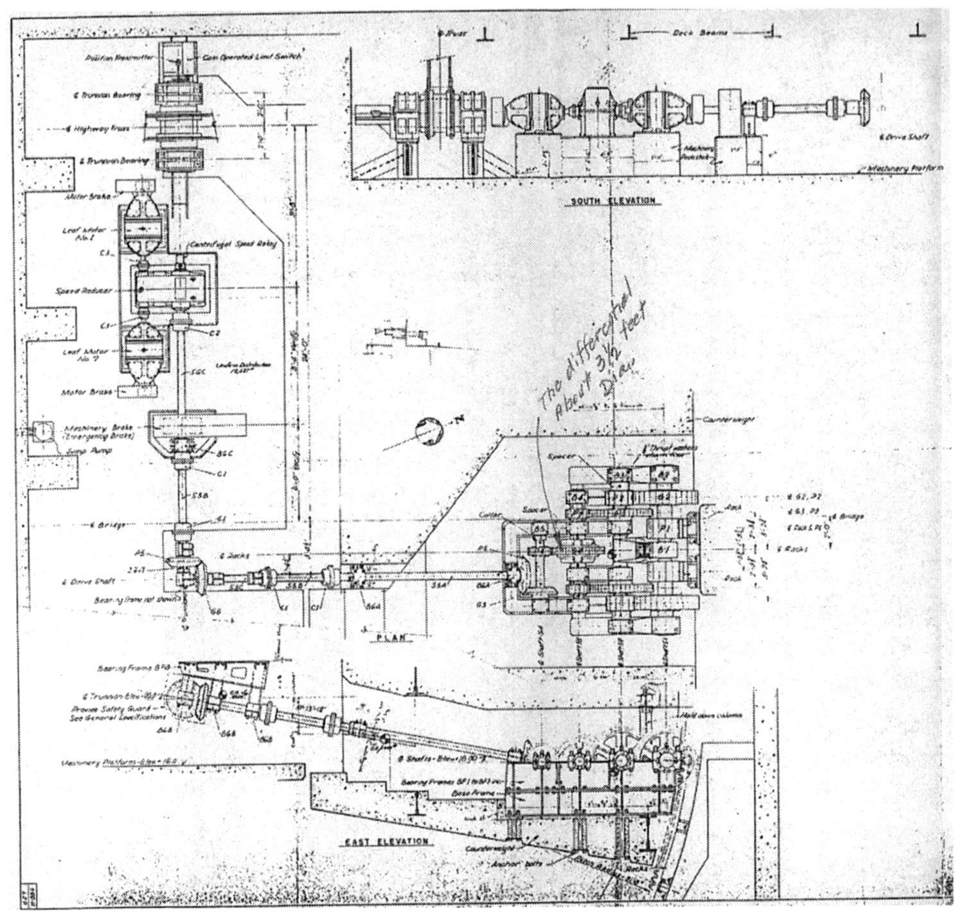

Blueprint—Bascule Bridge

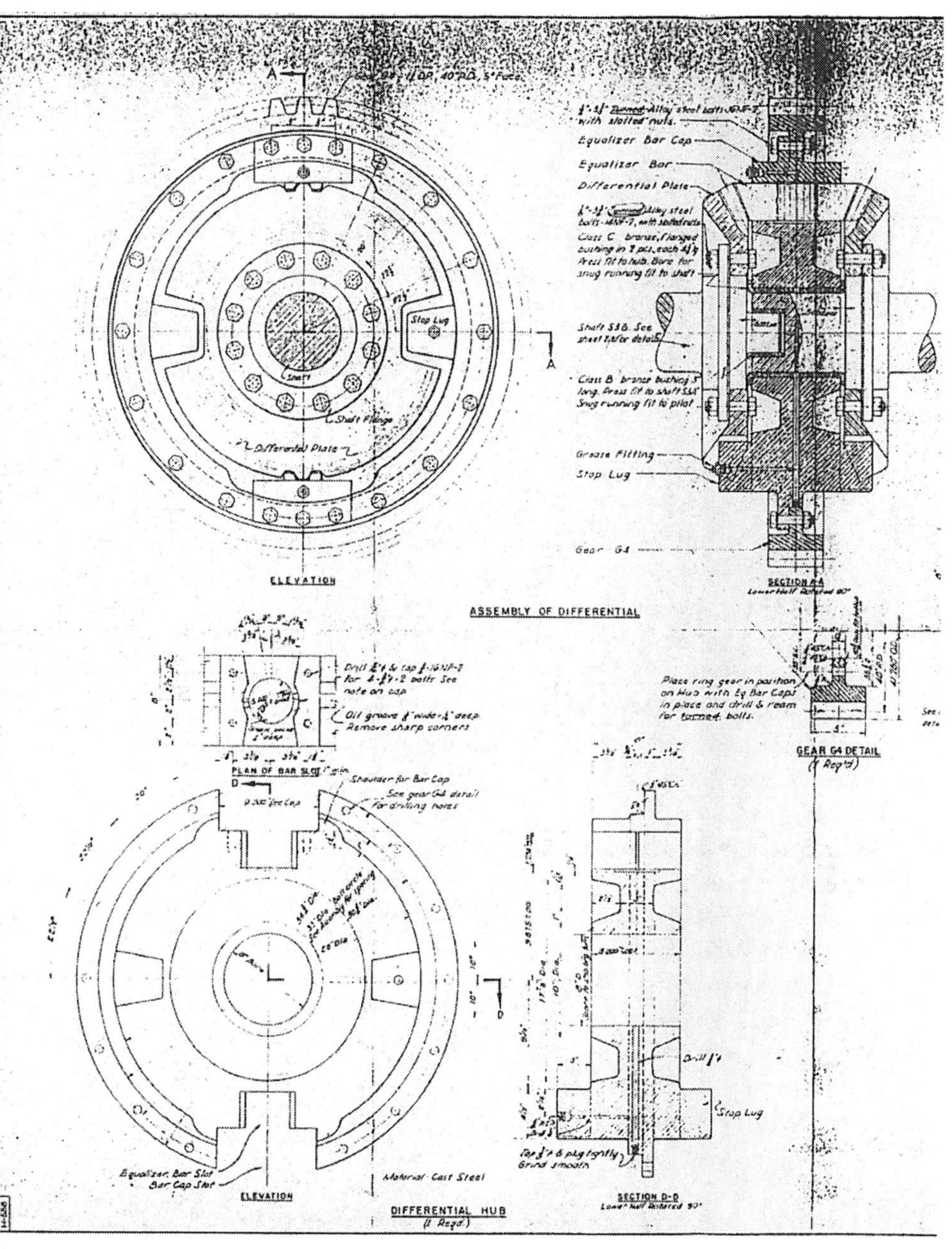

Limited Slip Differential

Chapter Twenty

Back with Kaiser

Again, I was back with the company where I began my career, only this time there was a brand-new name, KAISER ENGINEERS. Already I knew many of those great engineers such as Jim Foster, Clay Bedford, Fred Crocker, Ralph Knight, Pat Donaldson, and others who helped catapult Henry Kaiser's rocket into the stratosphere. These talented people loomed large in my decision to return to Kaiser. There were other reasons too; I had worked with men in the Kaiser Richmond shipyards where we had built four yards in record time. Our work also contributed to the production of more than four hundred ships, one of which was completed in four days, sixteen hours, and twenty-four minutes, an all-time record. Perhaps the real enticement was a big project brewing in a place called Chalmette, Louisiana, not far from New Orleans. Something brand new to me: an aluminum plant, and a big one at that! This project was triggered by the War Production Board's declaration of surplus for two aluminum smelters in the state of Washington. This occurred at the end of World War II, and Henry Kaiser immediately jumped at the chance to get into a new business, particularly since the price was 25 cents on the original dollar. Buying the plants at bargain-basement prices, and recruiting personnel who had operated those plants, he was off to the races! This move became the start of a major business for both Henry and the fledgling Kaiser Engineers, and I was in it at the beginning!

With Henry's recruited aluminum experts at our elbows, we learned what was needed to produce that bright, shiny metal. My job was to head up the mechanical group of the engineering task force that had been formed to design the plant. Project engineers were recruited to supervise the design work on the various plant elements, and we took our general directions from their specifications. What we did in those eleven months so Henry could push the button to tilt the ladle and make that first pour set a record never before or since equaled. Few who remember it are around today.

This plant was designed to generate its own power using the plentiful natural gas available in the area. Because delivery of the conventional steam-driven generators could not be obtained in time to meet the desired schedule, it was decided to install Nordberg gas-engine-driven generators for the first two pot rooms because of their fast delivery schedule. These machines were big, twenty-foot-diameter affairs much like overgrown air-craft engines, except that the crankshaft was vertical and the generator was attached directly beneath. The choice of the Nordbergs led to what was to be known as "The Great Explosion."

I was high atop the carbon plant building, attending to a problem with the dust-collection system. From that vantage point, 125 feet up, I could see the entire plant spread out around me. As I stood taking in the view, there was a monster explosion. I could see smoke coming from one of the big exhaust stacks outside the Nordberg building. As I watched, wondering what had happened, there appeared ten or fifteen twenty-foot smoke rings curling lazily into the blue sky above. Before the rings had dispersed, a mass exodus of workmen charged out onto the wooden walkway placed over a muddy area. One man slipped on the wet walk, and a half-dozen other workers followed him into the mud. There was much splashing and churning as they made their way to higher ground and, as they thought, to safety. Soon fire trucks pulled up, sirens blaring, looking for the expected conflagration. Pick-up trucks zeroed in on the site and before long muddy workmen, fire crews, and supervisors had gathered and I could hear them shouting at each other in an effort to find the cause of the explosion.

When calm finally returned it was found that the first engine would not start because the timing system had not been properly set. When it was reset and the engine cranked up again, the natural gas fuel that had accu-mulated in the exhaust system blew up with the first ignition. The smoke rings were caused by successive firing as the running engine cleared out the muffler. The guys in the building said the noise inside convinced them that the whole place was doomed.

Then there were the cockroaches! I had gone to the plant manager's newly rented house for dinner, and after we had eaten I offered to help move some things around in the kitchen. As we lifted the refrigerator, about a dozen cockroaches came charging out looking for a new place to hide.

Several other moves resulted in similar performances, and when the manager's wife shouted, "I can't stand these things," a local citizen who had also been invited to dinner said, "Once you get everything located they'll stay put and you won't see them; they do their wandering at night." Pat never got used to them. She said, "I can hear the damn things running around at night."

About a year after Chalmette, San Terry and I were assigned as project engineers on jobs for Great Lakes Carbon Co. We were the first project engineers chosen in-house, and from that time on it became the normal practice.

The Great Lakes Carbon Co. job I was assigned was in Niagara Falls, New York, and my work began right in the middle of winter. That winter saw record storms all across the nation. As our flight lifted out over the Sierras on the way to a meeting in Chicago we saw the entire range blanketed in white, and as we approached the summit the pilot called our attention to the City of San Francisco passenger train stalled in snow banks reaching as high as the cars. Snow cats could be seen crawling through the drifts, taking passengers from the train. The Great Plains were snow-covered for miles, and when we got to Chicago for our meeting with the client, the city was blanketed with drifts of up to four feet of snow. Our landing at the airport was exciting, as we came down in a canyon formed as snow plows piled the snow off to both sides of the runway. The Windy City itself had suffered a near-record snow, and many streets were still unplowed. In that time, 1953, soft coal was still being used for heating and in the still-prevalent steam locomotives. As a result, the snow had a cover of coal dust and the gutters ran a dark gray stream. I remember this because my new hat blew off, and before I could recover it had floated twenty feet in the grimy mess.

Finally arriving in Niagara Falls, we were greeted with thirty-nine inches of newly fallen snow. Driving back and forth to the job posed no problem for me, since I had driven in Sierra snow and knew enough to allow plenty of slither space for any traffic stops. With Dave Carlson, who worked for me on the job, I managed to take in some of the tourist sites, including the tunnel under the falls where one could look out at the thundering water sluicing by a few feet in front. We took the footbridge to the island where you could watch the water rushing by on either side. That island has since eroded away and fallen into the river below.

One evening we walked across the bridge spanning the river that divides the US and Canada. We were headed for the General Brock Hotel on the Canadian side, where there was a fine restaurant on the top floor. From that vantage point we could see the colored light show playing over the falls. What a beautiful sight it was! A particular memory remains: wind blowing downriver from the falls carried tiny ice crystals, and as they struck our faces it felt like thousands of needles prickling the skin.

I should add that Sam Terry's job was in Morganton, South Carolina, the furniture capital of the United States, and he took the time for an interesting tour of the plants.

Sam and I finished our work at about the same time, and for a few months until our next projects we did some small studies and proposal work. Sam's new project was in Baja, California, developing facilities for a gypsum mine being operated by Kaiser Cement and Gypsum. My knowledge of his job was sketchy, but I recall that he had modified a fishing rod to fit into a small suitcase so he could take it with him on trips down there where the fishing was great.

Developing facilities for a sand and gravel plant at Steilacoom, near Tacoma, Washington, was my next job. This was once again in the middle of winter, with much snow and ice. Don Barry and I spent long hours in the field and would get back to our hotel in Tacoma around nine in the evening. Cold and wet, we first had a hot buttered rum, even before showering. These drinks were prepared in the old way, in a big ornate mug where the ingredients were heated with a hot poker. These drinks were a lovely compensation for the long, cold days!

One other memory of that job had to do with the plugging pipeline. Many thousands of years ago, melting glaciers had dropped a near-perfect mixture of sand and gravel that was now being used to make concrete. Some of the sand was separated from the gravel to make plaster and other similar building materials. That sand was taken to the serpentine storage structure by pumping it along with water. From the pump station the slurry (sand and water) was pumped through a ten-inch pipe to a flume above the storage. Running along the ground a couple hundred feet to a sloping pipe, the slurry was delivered to a flume running the length of the storage. Sand was automatically graded by size as it flowed along the flume. With the system completed, it was time for a trial run and we turned on the pump motor. After a few minutes the motor breakers blew and we found that the pipeline completely plugged. After several more attempts, we called the manager of Kaiser's sand and gravel plant in Pleasanton, asking for advice. Arriving the next morning, he watched a demonstration and said he could not imagine why it did not work.

Puzzling over the problem at lunch, the expert said that slurry was pumped on several spots at the Pleasanton plant without a problem. As he thought further he told us he did not remember any sloping lines and wondered if that might be the problem. "All were either horizontal or vertical when I first arrived at the plant. Could that damned slope be the gremlin in the system?"

I had a slender tower built to hold the sloping section vertical, and our troubles were over. It worked like a charm. (See illustration.) Some cagey old operator had solved the problem years ago and we had to learn it the hard way.

A final pleasant note. Two men, employees of the former owner, stayed on after Kaiser bought the plant. Both were hardworking and willing to labor long hours with us to put the new plant into operation. They were also dedicated fishermen and would walk down at noon to a small stream nearby to catch a steelhead salmon, which they would take home to process by smoking. Both brought their lunches, most of the time with some smoked salmon. One or the other would offer me a piece of the delicious fish. What recipe they used I can't say, but I have never tasted anything better.

The original owner, Hefernan, had three sons, all working in the business. Some time in the past one of the sons found a trace of gold in the material being excavated and shut down the plant to search for more of the precious metal. When the father saw what was happening, he said, "We have made a fine living off the sand and gravel business, don't let me catch you wasting any more time looking for the small amount of gold out there or I'll send you packing."

I learned of this story from John Hefernan, the last of the family and plant manager when Kaiser bought the business. It was on a weekend voyage around Puget Sound with John and his wife in their sixty-foot cabin cruiser, a beautiful ship with the latest in radar, ship-to-shore radio, and quarters for six. When we sailed into a sheltered cove to spend Saturday night, John asked if I would like to call my wife. I still remember that call;

your grandmother was so excited to be talking with me on a boat several hundred miles from home that she called Serin and Lori to listen in on the call. I had several visits and dinners with the couple in their lovely home on a hill overlooking the Sound. I remained in touch with them until their deaths within three months of each other in 1968.

In those days I would drive to the Oakland Airport, catch a twin-engine plane to San Francisco, and meet a waiting four-engine DC-4 for the flight to Tacoma. That plane had a Plexiglas bubble atop the fuselage used by the navigator for sextant observations on overseas flights. On a recent flight over the Atlantic, the bubble had blown off from the interior cabin pressure, unfortunately taking the navigator with it. As a consequence all flights in those planes were restricted to altitudes under ten thousand feet. That was all right in the summer, but as winter bore down on us with its wind and storm, things got rough, sometimes leading to a stop in Portland for lunch because in-flight service was impossible. Finally Dave and I decided to take the train. It was a relaxed trip, beginning with a great dinner, then a good night's sleep and breakfast before arriving in Tacoma the next morning at 7:30. Ten days later we returned by train, again a pleasant trip. We decided we would do it by rail until winter was past.

With heavy rains at the lower elevations and snow above, it was obviously not a time to fly, so we were off on the train again. Around ten that night I was awakened by a sudden grinding stop. In a few minutes a porter announced there had been a mudslide, but that equipment was on the way to clear a path. We got to the job five hours later.

For the return, heavy snows were reported at all elevations and once more we chose rail, assuming the airways would be storm-tossed. At two a.m., another shuddering stop. This time it was a huge avalanche. We stayed stalled until we ran out of food and saw a murky sun trying to light up a leaden sky. With nothing else to do, I put on my work boots and heavy jacket to step outside. A porter said we had passed a small town a mile back and it would be at least four or five hours before the tracks were cleared. Dave and I walked back, hoping to find a phone so we could let our wives know we were all right but expected to be delayed. We looked around the small town hoping to find a bite to eat, but nothing was open. On the way back we vowed never to take a train again. We were twelve hours late into Oakland.

I made two more trips to the job, returning home Christmas Eve and again at the same time New Year's Eve. One more trip remained, this one for a review with the client, scheduled for January 15, and Grandmother wanted to go along, see the plant, and visit her aunt and uncle in Seattle. We managed to squeeze in our annual pilgrimage to Carmel on January 9.

The day of our trip dawned bright and clear, but with a near-hurricane wind. As we taxied out to the runway at Oakland Airport, I saw the grass alongside the runway laid flat in the wind while a large group of seagulls hunkered down flat on the ground. One attempted to fly, but was blown backward and gave it up. The pilot began his takeoff run, and as the wheels left the runway, a blast of wind lifted the plane almost straight up. Recovering, the pilot went into a slow turn to cross the bay, only to have another blast turn us nearly upside down. Grandmother was gripping the armrests so hard her knuckles were white. I put my hand over hers to offer comfort, but truth be known I was scared stiff. The flight to Tacoma wasn't much better, and when we got to our hotel one of those hot buttered rums helped to sooth the nerves. After a look at the plant Grandmother spent several days with her relatives, returning a day before the flight home. I had to tell her I was stuck for a few more days but she should go on by herself. She wasn't sure about that, but the flight home was a smooth one and a kindly gentleman pointed out things of interest on the way. Grandmother's first flight was one of the worst I ever experienced!

Here in the early 1950s I was truly back with Kaiser and among friends and people I knew. I felt at home, but I could not have imagined what lay ahead for me in the years that were to follow.

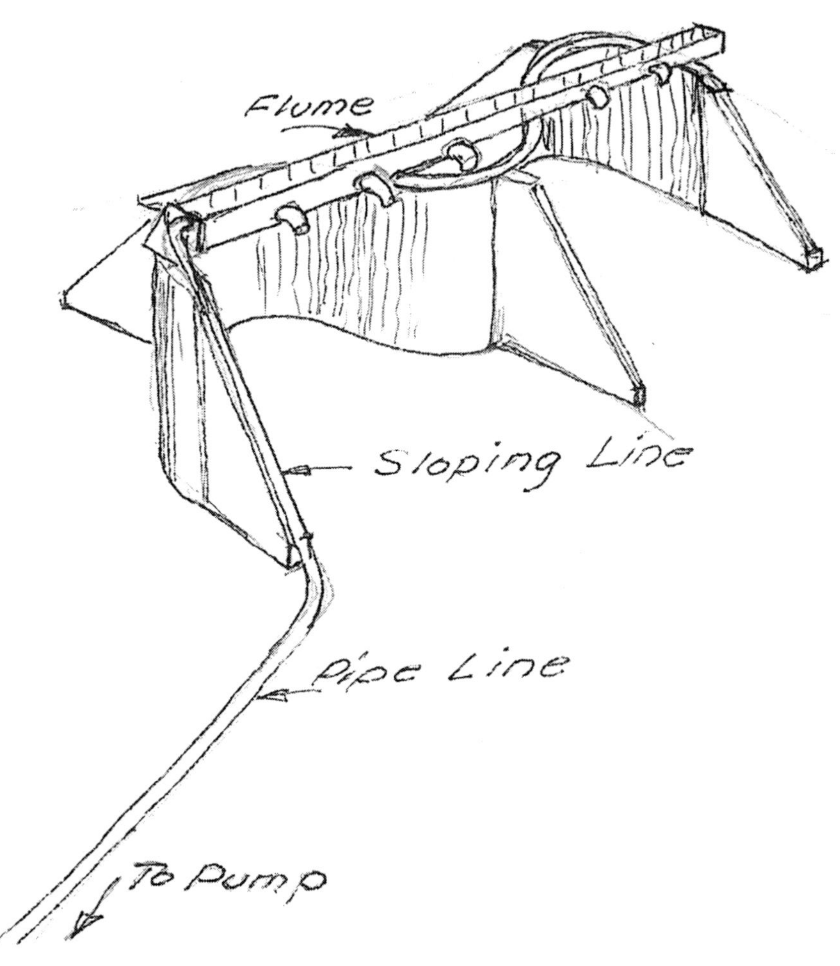

Sloping line

Chapter Twenty-One

Autos in Argentina

*I*n 1954, after the intense activity of the aluminum plant in Chalmette and the Great Lakes carbon plant job in Niagara Falls, I found myself in a variety of studies, proposals for new work, and, finally, a study of the Willys jeep. Kaiser had acquired the Willys plant in Cleveland, Ohio, and asked Kaiser Engineers to prepare a review of the many attachments being developed for the famous little workhorse of World War II. The attachments included a posthole drill, a large-swath weed mower, a gang plow, a small hoist unit, and an insect spray device.

I was assigned the job, and after a cross-country trip during which I interviewed both dealers and users, I submitted my report. I found that, while the jeep could perform multiple tasks, it was not as efficient as a machine made expressly for the job. In my report, a sixteen-by-twenty-inch, thirty-page document, complete with photos and performance data, I recommended that Kaiser/Willys should not promote the sale or use of attachments, and the company accepted that conclusion.

Not long after the jeep report, Kaiser's big venture into the automobile business was feeling the pressure of competition from Ford and Chevrolet. Sales were too few to make the auto business profitable for Kaiser, and Henry was looking for some way out of the dilemma. It came from the mayor of New Orleans, de Lesseps, whom Henry had met while selecting the site of Chalmette for the aluminum plant we had built in 1950. Mr. de Lesseps had met Juan Peron, Argentina's president, during talks on trade relations. Somehow at that meeting the subject of automobiles had come up and Peron had said that there was a real demand for automobiles in Argentina.

How this discussion got back to Henry I do not know, but he saw an opportunity to avoid a possible collapse of the Kaiser-Fraser company. The solution? Pack up the whole Kaiser-Fraser operation and move it to Argentina. The magnitude of the plan didn't faze Henry Kaiser. He pointed a finger at the automobile group and told them to GO. Then he pointed to Kaiser Engineers and told us to see to the task of building a full-scale facility in a place most of us knew only from articles and maps in National Geographic. Because I had been involved in the conversion of the Willow Run World War II bomber plant to assembly line production of automobiles in 1948, I was asked to move to Argentina as chief design engineer, and I accepted.

I could not have imagined the events into which my family and I would be plunged on that assignment: Kaiser's first overseas job, experiencing a different culture, doing all the engineering in the metric system, getting used to new foods, and experiencing a revolution. Half our pay was in dollars, deposited in the US, and half was in Argentine pesos. The peso part was based on an exchange rate of sixteen to one. That rate was never realistic and soon the real rate had climbed to forty-eight to one, while our exchange stayed at sixteen. Needless to say, that black-market rate put a strain on our pocketbooks, and had it not been for the fact that the company paid for our rent we would have had a difficult time making ends meet. We could have bought pesos with dollars, but that was discouraged because it would add to the inflation. So we tightened our belts and put up with it, vowing never to get trapped in that kind of deal again.

So many different, wonderful, exiting, frightening, and new experiences occurred on that assignment that it would almost take a book to cover them all. Perhaps I will tell you of some of them in later chapters, but for the moment I will keep it to the Christmas hurricane and the revolution.

The auto plant was to be located in Cordoba, a city about four hundred miles inland from Buenos Aires, the capital and port city of Argentina. Your grandmother, our two daughters, Serin and Lori (your mothers), and I took off in May of 1955 for Chicago, where I left them to go on to New York while I detoured to West Virginia to collect drawings and details of the separately located press plant. I rejoined the family in New York, and we boarded Areolineas Argentinas for the long flight to Buenos Aires. Arriving at night, we were met and escorted to our temporary quarters at the City Hotel located on the big square around which were the Casa Rosada (the president's home), the Navy Ministry, the old government building called the Cabildo, and an historical church. Embedded in the walls of that old building were cannonballs from an earlier revolution. Little did we dream, as we settled into the hotel, the fate to befall that church and navy building.

Our office was three blocks from the square, an easy walk in the cool fall weather, and I took the opportunity to have lunch with the family in the hotel. Some part of Grandmother's day was occupied in house-hunting so we could get out of the hotel. That was a difficult job because so many of the homes she was shown were old and poorly heated. With winter coming on and with it the promise of record cold, the search seemed impossible. Then it happened!

Several firms had expressed interest in fabricating and erecting structural steel for our plant, and our experience thus far had been that there was a disparity between ambition and capability. I had accepted a lunch invitation to visit a facility on the outskirts of Buenos Aires. Following the lunch there would be an inspection of the steel fabricating plant to determine its capability for meeting our specifications. During lunch we were discussing details of the job using a mixture of Spanish, English, and two-way translation. There was a phone interruption and then our hosts were conversing sotto voce. Both the translator and I caught one word, "bomba." We were told there had been a bombing around the Plaza de Mayo, the square on which our hotel was located, and that we would be taken back to our office immediately. I was particularly concerned because my family was still in the hotel near the Plaza.

That return trip was memorable! The closer we got to our office the more congested the streets became. Thousands of people were on the march toward the city center. We were caught behind a street car filled with shouting passengers carrying sticks, baseball bats, shovels, and even a pick. The car was riding on its axles, with people hanging on the hand grips and others hanging onto them. With the crowd all around us the driver threw up his hands, looked at us and with a shrug and said, "Impossible, Senors."

At this point we left the car and crossed over to a side street that would get us back to the hotel. All thoughts of the office had long since vanished, being replaced by concern for my family in the hotel. We were, at that point, about seven blocks away. Taking a last look at the car I saw the driver sitting calmly as the sea of humanity flowed by, and with a last wave we set off. There were sounds of sporadic gunfire from somewhere ahead, but it was hard to tell just where it was coming from. Charged with adrenaline, I led the way at jogging pace. We'd made about three blocks when the rattle of gunfire echoed down our street, this time accompanied by the whine of ricocheting bullets. This was serious business and we dove for a nearby doorway until things quieted. Once more before we reached the hotel we had to duck for cover. Once there we banged on the heavily shuttered door. A peephole slid open and we were identified and admitted through a small steel door. After a relieved reunion we got some of the details of events. It was reported that planes with Navy markings had attacked the Casa Rosada with bombs and machine guns. Not a great deal of damage resulted but, as we later learned, Peron had called for the Peronistas to assemble at the Plaza with rifles and pistols, and this accounted for the problems we encountered on our way back.

That night we slept under a heavy wooden table on the lower floor of the hotel. Nothing happened, but for the next three days we were virtually captives. On the second night, the hotel manager asked if we would like to see the fire near the Plaza. Climbing to the roof top, we saw the old church across the Plaza erupting in flames. Three other churches suffered the same fate that night, and we were filled with a mixture of anger and concern. We later heard that the Peronistas had torn up pews from the church, piled them at the doorway, and set fire to the pile. Many irreplaceable old books and manuscripts were also lost to the conflagration.

On the fourth day, with food running short and tempers rising, we were told to be ready that night to take a walk to a spot where cars would be waiting to take us to the American Embassy. One suitcase, preferably a small one, per family. Sometime after midnight about twenty frightened people followed an American diplomat on a ghostly march under drizzling skies through the deserted and deadly quiet streets of Buenos Aires. Now and then a dim light reflected from the wet street, and I could see drops splashing from the footsteps of our walkers.

We overwhelmed the Embassy, but the staff managed to gather up enough food to quiet our rumbling stomachs. Milk was for the children, but the grownups washed things down with weak coffee tasting faintly of dish-washing soap. The next day we were parceled out to a variety of places and our family drew the Alvear Palace Hotel, which was to be an adventure all its own.

Even if you saw *Evita*, you would not have known about the monument Peron was going to build for his dead wife. This was to be a marble column five hundred feet tall. On a mezzanine fifty feet up, mummified in a sealed glass sarcophagus, Evita would be on view for generations to come. With Peron deposed, this outrageous project was terminated. Two shiploads of marble were turned back, leaving the Italians wondering what to do with all that material.

There followed a period of unrest. Sporadic police activities and false alarms kept us on edge even as we returned to work. We soon got to know the signs of impending trouble by watching the residents hurrying out to the local food stores, then scuttling home to leave quiet and empty streets. That became our signal to leave the office and head for wherever we were staying at the moment. Sometimes it would be a tank rumbling through downtown shooting up an office building suspected of being a shelter for dissidents, but more often than not it was just a false alarm. It was tough on the nerves, but we were still getting the job done.

The Navy had carried out the bombing of the Plaza De Mayo, aiming at the Casa Rosada (Pink House), used as a residence for Peron and the seat of government. Several different bombs were dropped, including a five-hundred-pounder. Machine gun fire from the planes pockmarked several buildings nearby. One of our people left for lunch a few minutes late and was trying to catch up with others when the big bomb fell near him. He died from a concussion. This unfortunate accident affected us deeply, and showed us that life or death is sometimes just a matter of a few seconds.

A couple of days after the bombing, a group of Peronistas assembled around the navy building and with rifles, pistols, and several machine guns systematically shot out all the windows. The result was a huge pile of glass around the base of the building and tattered Venetian blinds dangling from the open window frames.

My family and I were temporarily housed in the fifth floor of the Alveas Palace, a beautiful nineteenth-century hotel with a rather elite clientele. Our room looked out on a wooded park. One night we were alerted by sirens, and as we looked out from the darkened window, a police van pulled to a stop. Six men jumped out and disappeared into the woods on a dead run. Silence, then a terrified scream followed by four shots. More silence and soon four people emerged from the woods with two more carrying a bundle that they threw in the van. Then, after all were aboard, the vehicle departed, leaving behind only the silence of the night and the feeling that we had witnessed an execution.

One amusing incident is worth recounting. Soon after we moved to the new hotel a food shortage occurred. A waiter who had taken it upon himself to keep us informed of impending problems told us that there would be nothing for breakfast. I had seen another waiter with what I took to be puffed rice and asked our waiter if some was still available. My fractured Spanish left him puzzled, but I tried again. This time he brightened and said he would be back. Twenty minutes later, answering a knock on the door I opened it to behold four small bowls and a heaping bowl of popcorn. Along with the popcorn came a pot of coffee and two slices of bread. Have you ever had popcorn for breakfast?

On the twenty-eighth of June, 1955, with the food supply returning to normal, we had a birthday party for Serin. At one end of the hotel dining room was a big grill where we could watch the chef preparing things to be broiled. I had never seen anything like it before. It was vertical, about fifteen feet long and five feet high. Anything to be grilled was placed in small wire baskets and hung on the vertical frame. I wasn't sure this was a practical arrangement but it was spectacular. Our dinner was excellent, with filets for Grandmother and me and hamburgers for Serin and Lori. At the end Serin was served, with a flourish, a small cake with a single candle. To top the sumptuous celebration we were served Pavlovas, a variation on Baked Alaska.

Shortly thereafter we were moved from the city to a home in the suburbs where we stayed until finding a home for ourselves. Quiet did not return to Argentina until after a serious fracas in Cordoba, the site of the auto plant we were building. This resulted in the departure of Juan Peron aboard a Uruguayan destroyer; he took with him several suitcases of cash and, oddly, six or eight Vespa scooters.

We mailed our Christmas cards that year under close scrutiny by four soldiers armed with automatic rifles. It was a long walk up those many stairs trying to look nonchalant with our bundle of cards to drop in the post office.

You probably didn't know that Evita had a fleet of small Mercedes autos masquerading as ambulances. They were used to transport workers to various vacation spots. Somewhere in the process, Evita was collecting a pile of money, presumably for charity. It actually wound up in a Swiss bank, and after Evita died, Juan Peron attempted to claim it for himself with no luck. It no doubt disappeared into one of those "friendly" Swiss banks.

After the Cordoba fracas, things quieted down and a trip to the jobsite was arranged. Seven adults and four children made up our party, and the four-hundred-mile journey was by railroad. We were among about a hundred passengers in five cars. I won't describe the meals or the smoke from the coal-burning locomotive, but the toilets deserve a place in history. They looked like any normal commode, but when you lifted the cover the fearful din of wheels on rails filled the compartment. Looking down, you saw only a gaping hole and the roadbed flashing by. It was intimidating; I was afraid I might fall through to the track below.

Booked into a lovely hotel at a resort, we found ourselves alone except for a few service people. Dinner was at eight p.m. for the children and ten for the grownups. I still recall that first dinner. We had celebrated our arrival with champagne followed by several cocktails, all of which made dinner a pleasure, even the pickled partridge—or was it quail—and the chivito (baby goat). We spent four days there inspecting the result of our engineering efforts sprouting from the soil of the foothills of the Andes

Argentina wasn't through with us yet. A couple of weeks later it was Christmas Eve and we went out to a nearby restaurant for dinner. The place was busy but the service excellent, and we were soon enjoying a fine Christmas dinner. Before we had finished we noticed people were leaving in what seemed to a rush; our waiter came to our table and said something we didn't understand. Our young daughter, who was learning kitchen Spanish from our cook, translated, "He said there is a terrible storm coming and we should go home right away." As we left, flashes of lightening lit up the northern sky and distant thunder rumbled. A strong wind thrashed trees and whipped our coats, but we got home dry just before the rain began. That night we opened some shutters to watch. Sometimes the lightening was a continuous fire in the sky and the thunder was indistinguishable from the roaring of the wind. By noon of the next day, all was calm, the sky clear, and we ventured out to assess the damage in our area. It was a mess, with some tees uprooted and others stripped of foliage, and there was trash everywhere. We later learned that a hurricane had hit the area and was still venting its wrath to the south. In the port area, buildings had been stripped of corrugated roofing and siding, with the sheets flying off in all directions.

We celebrated a warm summer Christmas, wondering if our parents and friends in the States were having a cold winter one. Later, we learned that California had been subjected to drenching rains causing much damage and some loss of life.

There were things we enjoyed in Argentina. Buenos Aires with its wide avenue, Nuevo se Julio, the classical old opera house, the beautiful parks, and the riverfront area called La Boca with its colorful buildings were all places of interest and we took every opportunity to try and see all we could. Being out with friends to a nightclub was a new experience. We would arrive around nine p.m., sitting down to dinner by ten p.m. After dinner some of the patrons might gather at the piano and start a songfest. It didn't take long before everyone joined in and it would be two in the morning when people began leaving for home. I remember those times as warm and friendly events.

A rodeo differed from the ones we see in the States. No stalls, no chutes, and no fences, just a six-inch pole driven into the ground so that six or seven feet remained visible. There were no stands and no bleachers. Spectators formed a loose circle sixty feet in diameter, a few in autos, more on foot, and twenty or thirty on horseback. Each horse was beautifully caparisoned with carved bridles, reins, saddle, and stirrups, all decorated with silver. Some of the riders wore the typical baggy gaucho pants with shoes, belts, vests, and hats decorated with silver.

A blindfolded horse with a mounted rider was brought out by an attendant holding a strap attached to the bridle. Arriving at the post, he wrapped the strap several times around the post until it held the horse tight against the pole. Then he removed the blindfold and ran clear of the open circle. The strap unwound slowly until the horse was free. Bucking and snorting in a cloud of dust, the horse tried to unseat the rider. Sometimes he succeeded, sometimes not. I don't remember any prizes and there was no calf roping, bulldogging, or bull riding. Much shouting and cheering went on, and I guessed the riders had to be satisfied with that.

We made many friends in Argentina, and I arranged jobs for two of them back in Oakland. I am sad that both are no longer with us. We left Argentina in mid-1956. There was a lump in my throat as I waved goodbye to those who came to see us off. I recall a bigger lump when we came home into the beautiful Bay Area after several stops on the way. It was twilight as we approached and the bay was like a shining dark jewel.

Chapter Twenty-Two

The Big Projects

On the way home from Argentina, we stopped off at Santiago, Lima, and Panama. At the first two places we were met by relatives of men who had worked for me on the auto plant job. In each city, we were taken to places not on the tourist routes and saw things we could not have found on our own. In Panama City, on a tour of the old city, there was an almost palpable air of hostility as locals watched us go by. Out at the canal, the process of bringing a big ship through the locks and moving it along with the donkey engines fascinated us, and I recalled the failure of the French effort and the takeover by America to complete that tremendous program. This occurred during the presidency of Teddy Roosevelt, whose foreign policy was "Speak softly and carry a big stick." There are books describing the construction achievements in cutting a passage between the Atlantic and Pacific Oceans. Previously, the shipping route between New York and San Francisco was by way of the southern tip of South America, a cold, stormy, and often dangerous voyage. During work on the canal, many workers were stricken with fatal illnesses until a doctor finally found that the mosquito was the carrier and measures were taken to combat the problem.

The canal is in operation today, but is now owned by Panama as a result of a much-criticized handover to that country during the Carter administration. The cost to build the canal in both dollars and human lives was enormous, and it is hoped that great facility will never be closed to interocean traffic.

On a late afternoon in December of 1956 our plane came gliding into the Bay Area. A wide sweeping turn because of traffic gave us a view we would never forget. On the left, San Francisco stood in shadow; below, the Golden Gate Bridge, red color etched sharply against the blue waters below.

The Bay, a shimmering bed of jewels, cut by the white wake of a tanker heading back out to sea, slowly revolved below. Over Oakland, we tried to spot our house but couldn't find it. A final turn and the plane was headed for the airport runway. A rumble of landing gear and noise of reversing props told us we were home. Coming home is an emotional experience difficult to describe; someday you may know it.

LOOKING FOR A JOB AND A NEW HOME

In Argentina, I had been sharply critical of the fact we had not been notified that there was a bus that had been hired to take a number of the auto and Kaiser Engineers' children to school. Grandmother and I were nervous about the children being on their own, so Grandmother decided to walk Lori to school and Serin to the train where she took a ten-minute ride to school. In the afternoon there was another trip. Serin came home one day saying our manager's daughter had asked her why she wasn't taking the bus.

Angry that we had not been told of this, particularly because the unsettled conditions of the revolution made things risky for us, I stormed into the office and asked why we had not been told of the bus. I cannot recall the answer, I suppose because I was too angry, but from then on Serin and Lori rode the bus. Then there was the salary problem. Those of us from Oakland had agreed to take half of our salary in dollars, deposited in the States, and half in Pesos at an official exchange rate of sixteen to one. What the real rate (black market) was at that time, I didn't know. By the time the job ended, the real rate was forty-eight to one, and we were still being paid at sixteen to one regardless of our protests. As you might guess, this left us with fewer pesos each month to pay the steadily inflating cost of living. Angered by this, I stomped into our project manager's office and told him I would leave as soon as the engineering and construction specifications were complete, and that I would nominate one of my Argentine engineers to do the construction inspection. As it turned out, that was the right way to do it, but I didn't earn any brownie points by making that decision myself.

A final disturbing incident remained. In those days (1955), Peron, in order to provide top officials, including generals in the army, with a way to boost their earnings, issued import permits for items on which very high import duties had been assigned. A preferred item was a Cadillac costing the official around $3600, including shipping. In great demand, that vehicle could be sold for $18,000 US, which amounted to a tidy bunch of pesos in the then-current inflation, a neat little profit for the top dogs.

We were permitted to ship our private auto with our household goods with the proviso that the car would go with us when we left. My car was a 1955 Mercury four-door sedan, two-tone blue with beautiful white sidewall tires. One day on the way to lunch, I was approached by a well-dressed man who said he would like to buy my car. He would pay cash, either in black market Pesos or US dollars for a total of $11,000. I told him I would think about it, and he gave me a phone number to call when I had decided. Sorely tempted, I finally decided, in view of our agreement and the possibility of action against Kaiser, to decline. It was only after I had returned home that I learned our project manager had sold his car to someone in Buenos Aires.

Now the job search. When I arrived back at the office I had no assignment, no desk, not even a chair. Both top management people were out of town, and I knew I had to see one to find out if I still had a job or was fired. With nothing to do, I wandered around the four scattered buildings where Kaiser Engineers had offices, saying hello to the many people I knew and catching up on the latest scuttlebutt. The second week after my return, I joined a group going to lunch at the Bistro on Broadway and Grand. One of the bunch was Jay Irvin, who was working on the Jones & Laughlin Steel job near Pittsburgh, Pennsylvania. The work was under the general direction of Chet Case, but Jay had heard Chet talking about an aluminum and power plant for a company called St. Joseph Lead Company. Jay knew I had worked on the Chalmette aluminum plant and suggested it might be a good idea if I called Chet. I did so, and got my next assignment, project engineer for the newly awarded job.

I knew and respected Chet, who was, at that time, the head of the Industrial Minerals division. He was a fine engineer, rather courtly in manner, easy to work with. He had the habit of preparing memos, letters, and reports hand-written with pencils on paper, and he would hand them to his secretary for typing. She told me she was losing the ability to use shorthand. On the first occasion your grandmother and I had Chet and his wife to dinner, I recall she was a lovely, soft-spoken, impeccably dressed woman, but I will always remember the silk stockings she wore. They were a soft powder blue, the first I had ever seen!

ST. JOSEPH LEAD CO. POWER PLANT

This was my first job for a client other than a Kaiser company. As I write this I still feel the emotion of my memories of working with George Weaton, the man St. Joe Lead had assigned to oversee the project. A retired manager of the lead plant, George was given the responsibility for selecting an engineering firm, negotiating a contract, and monitoring the design and construction of the project, which was to be an aluminum plant and power plant. A strict taskmaster, technically sound, and interested in every detail, George (see illustration) was a joy to work with and I will always be grateful for the opportunity he gave me.

The mission was to build a power plant along with the aluminum facility so St. Joe Lead would not have to depend on Duquesne Light and Power, the local utility company. This meant installing a 1200-horsepower diesel electric generating unit to provide power for those items required to start the generation of steam to run the main turbine generator units. Even with the "self-starting" capability, we still had to maintain the possible connection to Duquesne.

The aluminum plant was to be located between the lead and power plants, and we prepared a contact for grading the entire area. Shortly after the clearing was completed, St. Joe decided not to go ahead with the aluminum plant at that time, but delay it until some future date. In spite of this, the power plant was still to be built to supply power to the zinc refinery. In Oakland, I was responsible for setting up a separate design group while at the jobsite. We assigned a construction manager and small staff to receive materials and equipment, monitor the schedule, inspect the work, and provide us with progress reports. All work was done by union personnel. As the job neared completion, we had three or four people from the design group at the site to identify work priorities. To organize this, I would prepare a list of work items each night for the agenda of the next day. This usually filled an eleven-by-seventeen sheet with connections to be made to each sensor, recorder, or controller, and to the indicators on the main control panel. This was a lot of work for me, but it greatly facilitated that final complex and detailed activity.

Of course, there were problems arising from design oversights or equipment manufacture, but it was always rewarding to have the hands-on experience to analyze the difficulty and then provide a solution to rectify it. That has always been a favorite part of the engineering profession for me. Here's a small example. The steam boilers were fired by coal, which was unloaded from barges tied up at our dock along the banks of the Ohio River. From there, a sloping conveyor ran up to a ninety-foot tower where it was dumped, forming a conical pile around the tower. We had been sweltering under a hot, oppressive sun for a week or more, which had been broken by a sudden violent thunderstorm bringing a cold rain and hail. I was about to run for cover when I heard a loud bang. Looking up, I saw coal spilling from the side of the conveyor and shouted for the operator to turn off the power. Climbing the walkway to the tower, I found that the conveyor had torn loose and was sitting precariously on a tower crossmember. I had the conveyor tied in place with wire rope and called Oakland Design to see what they had done. On the assumption that the tower was flexible enough to allow for temperature changes, no expansion joint had been designed. I drew up a joint, had it fabricated at the zinc plant, and our workers installed it to allow the conveyor frame to move with temperature changes. Our design group had forgotten that as coal piled around the tower it prevented any movement at the point at which the conveyor attached to the tower.

This was the beginning of my good fortune to work with the many fine people of Kaiser Engineers on major projects. These were the engineers, accountants, administrators, personnel, secretaries, and management team of a company that, at the time, was one of the foremost engineering/construction companies in the world.

As construction neared completion, I prepared a book containing specifications, operating characteristics, and maintenance and lubrication information for all items of equipment in the plant. This was a three-inch-thick book I entitled "Checkout, Acceptance, and Operating Manual." This turned out to be so successful that it became standard procedure for all my industrial projects thereafter.

George Weaton had been visiting Oakland every three or four weeks during the design phase, and as work began in the field he was a frequent visitor to the jobsite. On my trips to the job, I would sometimes have lunch with George or spend an evening at his home. With the project about 90 percent complete, I noticed George was not making his usual inspections, so I called and invited myself to his home one evening. Arriving, I was met by a woman in a nurse's uniform who said that George was in bed but wanted to see me. "Don't stay too long," she told me. I was shocked when I saw him, propped up by pillows, looking small and frail. He greeted me warmly and when we shook hands, the grip was still strong. He wanted to know how things were going and, when I told him we would be ready to roll the first turbine in about four days, he said, "You come get me and I'll show you guys how it's done."

The big day came and we brought George to the plant where he climbed the stairs to the turbine floor and then walked over to the high-pressure steam valve. He looked at the ten of us gathered near the low-pressure end of the turbine and began turning the valve wheel. Soon the turbine and generator were up to speed and George stood there with a huge smile on his face. I drove him home and, as I helped him from the car, he said, "Well, we did it, didn't we?" "No," I said, "You did it, George. Without you, there might not have been a plant." That was the last time I saw George. Back in Oakland I got a phone call telling me he had passed away ten days after the start-up, two and a half years from when I had first met him.

A final note. On the way home from Washington, D.C., where I had concluded studies and layouts for the rapid transit system, your grandmother, Lori, and I stopped by to visit the power plant. I wanted to renew my acquaintance with Bill McCullough, power plant manager, and show off the job to my family. After dinner, Bill took us out to see the plant. We spent two hours and Bill proudly showed every part of the facility. I had enjoyed working with Bill, and we often talked about classical music and hi-fi systems. On a couple of occasions, I babysat Bill's young daughter while he and his family attended some school affairs. Sometime in the ensuing years I lost track of Bill, and one of these days I will try and find him on the Internet.

Although the power plant was very successful and still runs to this day, the aluminum plant (for reasons I never knew) was never built. Even though this project cost only $30 million—nearly $200 million in today's dollars—it was the beginning of the big projects that I managed, and I consider this one of the most enjoyable parts of my engineering career. The total construction cost of the projects was $400 million, or $2 billion in present-day dollars. All this would have netted Kaiser Engineers about $100 million in today's fees. I give you these numbers because I am proud of my record.

George F. Wheaton 1953

Chapter Twenty-Three

1958–1961

This period was a busy one for me, and it included three projects for the East Bay Municipal Utility District and one for Lockheed Aircraft Company. Each of these projects involved a different technology, which made them more interesting to me.

EBMUD

EBMUD is the acronym for East Bay Municipal Utility District, and Briones (Breeoneez), a couple of miles northeast of Orinda, California, was to be an earth-fill dam creating a water reservoir for the Bay Area, supplied by way of the second Lafayette tunnel branching off the main line bringing Mokelumne river water down from the mountains. Because the reservoir was located above populated areas, the stability of the dam was of paramount importance. Accordingly, much foundation exploration was done. I recall one three-foot-diameter hole, sixty feet deep, with a lateral tunnel about thirty feet long. I descended this hole and with lights inspected for any sign of seismic faults. Nothing was found, but as I recall that descent, I wonder why I did not feel claustrophobic. Maybe I did but didn't dare show my fear. After smaller drill holes were completed and examined, it was determined the area was free from any seismic risk and we proceeded with design for the dam, spillway, and outlet works.

You may think of an earth-fill dam as a pile of dirt, but it is not. It is a cross-section of different materials carefully placed and compacted as the structure rises. Dam stability is calculated by a formula known as the Swedish slip circle, a complex formula made more difficult by the different materials in the cross-section. The manual calculation is a lengthy and laborious job, so, to save time, we turned to our newly formed computer department. At that time, the computer didn't have the capacity to do the calculation in one run, so we had to split the formula into two parts. Today you could do the job on your laptop.

After completion of the design and preparation of the drawings and specifications, we assisted EBMUD in the solicitation of bids for construction of the dam. A contract was awarded and soon the area was alive with earth-moving and compacting equipment.

SECOND LAFAYETTE TUNNEL

To deliver water to the Briones reservoir, a 17,000-foot tunnel was to be constructed beneath the East Bay hills. Much soils exploration was also carried out to identify the character of materials and to locate any seismic faults. That work, along with our design, provided the information from which a contractor could prepare an accurate bid. A variety of materials was found to exist along the more than three miles of the bore, including a rather large fault where the soils were fractured and wet. Most of the tunnel ran through rock and the contractor used a boring machine. As the machine advanced, material ground up by the big rotating head was passed back through a chute to a small electric railcar, where it was hauled out to the entrance and dumped. Some very hard rock was encountered and required blasting. This elicited complaints from residents forty feet above, but since no damage occurred, except some loss of sleep, it seemed people got used to the slight shaking.

I am reminded of the highway tunnels between Oakland and Orinda. Kaiser had won the contract for that work in the mid-thirties and, after encountering major difficulties, walked off the job, leaving it up to the bonding company to arrange for completion. I knew about the problems because a fraternity brother worked on a night shift. That was two years before I began my job at Coulee. So far as I know, it was the only job Kaiser did not finish.

23rd AVENUE RESERVOIR

This large reservoir just west of the Diamond district of Oakland was an uncovered and unlined water storage facility. Because of increasing pollution and also because leakage had resulted in loss of property above Diamond, EBMUD had decided to cover and line the reservoir. I was then living across the street from the reservoir and had noticed a sump pump in the basement discharging water and wondered why it ran so often. When I found that the reservoir was unlined I knew the reason.

My job on all three of these projects was to manage the soils investigation and design and preparation of specifications so that EBMUD could call for bids to construct each item. Thanks in large measure to our estimating and scheduling departments, we finished all three projects on schedule and within the budget. Our final work on the projects was to assist EBMUD in the inspection to assure compliance with specifications by the contractors.

I enjoyed all three of the jobs, and was assisted by Dick Ringwood and Fred Nielsen on design and by Harold Shandrew on the soils work. Joseph de Costa, manager of EBMUD, was professional, capable, and easy to work with, which made my job easier.

NOVA

In the early sixties, an aluminum sphere about the size of a soccer ball was blasted into an orbit around earth. Its beep-beep-beep announced that to the world that Russia had won the race into space. It was a wakeup call, jolting the United States out of its bed of complacency. Schools were urged to emphasize science. NASA became a lightning rod, attracting hundreds of astrophysicists and engineers. Major corporations were assigned space studies, and suddenly we were hell-bent for space hoping to beat Russia to the next punch. All that activity is what led to my assignment to Lockheed Aircraft to assist in studies they were doing on two space vehicles, Nova and Saturn. You probably never heard of Nova, but may be familiar with the exploits of Saturn. Nova was to be about 40 percent bigger than Saturn and, in the engineering room where I worked at Lockheed, the base of that monster was painted on the ceiling. The diameter of the circle was fifty feet!

My job was to develop a method of transporting Nova from the assembly building to the launch pad. After considering several methods, I settled on a floating system. A canal, sixty feet wide, would allow the vehicle to be moved with minimum power, and guide wheels at each corner would prevent tilting under wind loads. My recommendation was accepted by Lockheed, but NASA finally concluded that Saturn was to be the vehicle of choice and my great idea was history. The heavy loads that were required by the bigger Nova could be lifted by attaching boosters to Saturn. Transport to the launch pad would be by a track layer similar to a very large tractor, even though that would require a road bed fifteen feet in depth. I could not argue with that decision, but confess that I was disappointed. Thus ended my involvement in the race to space.

RAPID TRANSIT

In 1960, with Kaiser's fledgling rapid transit department busy with other projects, I was asked to move to Washington, D.C., where I would develop the layout of an underground transit system. I was to prepare estimates and schedules for the work and to assist in presentations to the areas to be served. My only qualification was that I had done much of the railroad layout in the shipyards in Richmond, and that background seemed to satisfy the agency charged with overall management of the project. I had an office in the building where Kaiser Industries people were lodged. Mine was in the core of the building, and around it spiraled a ramp leading to auto parking. To avoid being fumigated by exhaust gasses we had to keep our doors tightly closed. Even then, the morning and evening rush-hour gases leaked in upon us. In the cavernous space there were four drawing tables, a desk table and book cases for me, and a desk for my secretary, Marsha Weitz. The drawing tables were for engineers from Oakland who often came to help us with our work. There was one permanent engineer with us who had a better background than I in rail work. That was Wilbur Squire and he was a great help in our work.

For the first three months I was on single status and lived in a less-than-impressive hotel a couple of blocks from the famous Mayflower. When your grandmother and Lori joined me in September we stayed at the Hilton until we found a place to rent in Bethesda, Maryland, just outside the capital district line. We soon began a weekend tour of many historic sites and other places of interest. A comment at this point will be of interest to you, Ariel. Your mother, Lori, was thirteen at the time and her school offered her the kind of experiences she would not have gained elsewhere. She also went on our many weekend ventures, until one day she put her foot down and refused to go on another trip.

Of all the wonderful sights, the Lincoln Memorial will remain as the most impressive to me. One special visit remains vivid in my memory. It was late one night, and we were on our way home from hearing the National Symphony and Chorus present Handel's Messiah when we decided to stop for a look. We were bundled against the cold and walked the short distance to the memorial. We were alone; there was not a sound but our footsteps. Standing at the foot of the steps, without talking, we were held by the beauty of the monument. I remember reading excerpts from the great man's speeches carved on the walls. As we were about to leave a light drift of snow sifted down from the dark sky above. We lingered a while longer, reluctant to leave. When reaching home that night our emotional cups were filled to the brim.

I am angry that we celebrate the birthdays of two men in a meaningless President's Day. How many young people of today know who the two men are? I wonder if it is just a day off from work! Washington led a ragged army to victory over a vastly superior British and Hessian army to secure the freedom we all enjoy 226 years later. Lincoln prevented the fracture of our nation and took the first steps to abolish the inhuman practice of slavery. Do not both of these men deserve a separate place in our history?

Rock Creek Park meanders through the District of Columbia. It is a place where people can walk, have a picnic, sit quietly, or read a book. The year 1960 was the first white Christmas in thirty years in D.C. and our family's first white Christmas ever. While our turkey roasted in the oven we took a walk into a winter wonderland. Five minutes from our home, our footprints were the first in the foot-deep snow. Our voices were lost in the quiet, a bench and table were just white lumps in the snow, and, after making a few snowballs, it was time to return home and check the turkey. We walked back, leaving a new set of tracks in the snow. The memory of just the three of us alone in the beautiful white Rock Creek Park at Christmas brings a tear I cannot repress.

It was interesting to sit in on committee meetings and senate hearings, and to explain the system to the general public. It gave me a different perspective on how our government works. You may know that 1961 saw the ill-fated "Bay of Pigs" incident in which the United States embarrassed itself at the shores of Cuba. It was also the time when President Kennedy stopped Russia's shipment of missiles to Cuba. The atmosphere of the Capitol was electric. Siren-led official cars often were heard late at night. The feeling of all the tension while living in the middle of it is much different from that we experience out in California.

It was sad to leave D.C. that summer, but we looked forward to our return to the Bay Area. Before leaving this chapter, I must say that I left Washington a completed transit layout and an estimated cost of about $400 million with a schedule of up to five years, depending upon the desired rate of expenditure. In accordance with government procedures, final design of the system was divided among qualified firms around the country. Kaiser Engineers did final design of the Connecticut Avenue Station, and Bechtel was awarded construction management for the system. I cannot tell you what the final cost was because the program suffered delays, and escalation probably increased the cost by 50 percent.

I must add a comment here. In the beginning people came to this land to escape oppression and to seek new opportunities. It was a turbulent time and your forbears endured many hardships, including a fight for freedom marked by bloody footprints in the winter snow. Our nation grew by the migration of millions of people seeking that freedom. They still come today, and they still enrich our culture, but there is something missing; most do not know how the freedom and opportunity to earn a living, or even prosper, came to be. As I alluded to before, some among us want to rewrite history and I cannot understand their reasons. We all must strive to prevent this by talking to our friends and children, and by insisting that every institution in this country support that legacy. It is being diluted by the very mass of immigrants who are adding to our culture. To maintain our history we must first know it. Do you? If you would like a refresher, read the following: biographies of John Adams, George Washington, Benjamin Franklin, and Thomas Jefferson; and the book *The Hornet's Nest* by Jimmy Carter, a novel of revolutionary times. It is said that truth is stranger than fiction, and that is certainly true of all the above.

In closing I want to urge you, my granddaughters, to visit Washington, D.C., and surrounding areas. You will find much of interest there, and you will learn of the people and institutions that shaped this great country.

Chapter Twenty-Four

Ghana Aluminum

$\mathcal{B}$ack home from the rapid transit job in Washington, D.C., and having finished the Nova missile study for Lockheed, I wondered what my next assignment would be. (See illustration from about 1965.) I didn't have long to wait before being asked to join a group going to Ghana, a small country on the horn of Africa fronting on the sea, where the coast line runs east and west. It was an information-gathering trip for an aluminum plant to be built for Kaiser Aluminum Company, and I was to be engineering manager. There was time enough to do a bit of reading about the country where I was to be involved for the next three years.

I found that Ghana had declared its independence from England in 1961. A large river, the Volta, ran from the mountainous area in the north to a confluence with the sea. A dominant tribe was the Ashanti, whose wealth came from gold found in their part of the country; the principal language was Twi and there was no written text until the British used phonetic spelling. Two large palaces along the coast had been used to hold captives for the slave trade as far back as the 1400s.

Before going further I must note that Andy, who began as project manager, was transferred to another job after four months and I then took over the manager's job in addition to the position I was originally assigned. I have thus considered Ghana Aluminum as my project.

It was a beautiful morning as we boarded the United Flight to New York, there to transfer to Pan Am, which would fly us five thousand miles to our destination by the next day at noon. With me on that first trip were Andy Anderson, project manager, Bill Smith, design engineer, and Jack O'Neal, estimator. In 1963, for a flight of that duration, we flew first class.

That meant fancy big menus, fine food with cocktails and French wine, all on the house. Such were the good old days!

Pan Am lifted us out of New York as the sun was setting in the west. We met the sun coming up over Dakar, where we landed for refueling. From there we headed south for another refueling stop in Liberia, then a quiet peaceful country but now as I write this torn by revolution. After deplaning to stretch our legs and have a big glass of orange juice, we reboarded for the last leg of the long flight. On the approach to Liberia airport I noticed large circular patches in the forest where there was no growth. I later learned the people planted their crops in these circles. Not having equipment to plough, they cut down everything and burned it. When cooled, the ash-fertilized soil was perfect for the planted seeds.

We were descending again and I could see a city below. This was Accra, Ghana, a city I would see many times over the next four years. Met by several government officials, we were taken to the Ambassador Hotel in Accra. They said we should rest until tomorrow morning when they would come by to pick us up at nine a.m.

This was 1963, three years after Ghana had declared independence from Britain, and the transfer of management in the government offices was still causing much confusion. As a result, there was some difficulty finding our way to the sources of the information we needed to begin design of the project. We received a great deal of help from Parkindon/Hiward, the British firm with a contract to construct a harbor, warehouses, docks, and unloading facilities at Tema, a small fishing village that was to see major changes in the ensuing years. This was where Kaiser Aluminum intended to build an aluminum plant. I will always remember those meetings with P/H because they unfailingly began with a service of tea laced with milk and sugar, English style. To further set the stage for this chapter it is useful to begin with the negotiations between Edgar Kaiser and Kwame Nkruma, president of Ghana. Edgar had secured a contract to design and construct a dam and powerhouse on the Volta River at a place called Acosombo. Since the powerhouse would provide more power than Ghana needed, and because Kaiser Aluminum wanted more production, a smelter was agreed upon. It would use a large part of the excess power and would provide 450 jobs and tax benefits for Ghana. Financing was by Ex-Im Bank, and Reynolds Aluminum was a 10 percent partner.

That first visit lasted a month and we were able to accomplish all we needed to proceed with the project. The Ghanaian people were friendly and anxious to cooperate. There was also a little time to explore a bit outside Accra and Tema. It was exciting to find ourselves dropped into a different culture, and we did our best to learn the ways of the Ghanaian people.

I think it will be interesting for you to know a bit about how aluminum is produced, so I will pause here for a brief description of the process. The noncorrosive, lightweight, easy-to-work material is everywhere around you and you encounter it every day.

The process begins with the mining of bauxite, a reddish ore found in many places, which is then crushed and delivered to a plant. There it is cooked in a chemical process from which it emerges as white granular material known as aluminum oxide. The oxide is then delivered to a reduction plant (aluminum plant) where the final process takes place to produce pure aluminum.

This next step is accomplished in reduction cells known as pots. A pot is a steel tub about twenty-five by fifteen by two feet lined with a carbon material called a cathode. Above the pot is an insulated structure holding several anodes, all of which penetrate the bath of oxide, and a catalyst. As many as fifty pots are placed end-to-end in a building known as a pot room. Two such buildings side by side are a potline. A plant may have as many as four or eight potlines. Across the head of the potlines are the rectifier rooms, where incoming AC power is converted to direct current at 150,000 amps. This is delivered to the first pot superstructure where it passes to the pot cathode from which it passes to the next superstructure, and so on to the end of the building where it crosses over to the second room pots and back to the rectifiers. To give you an idea of the power consumed, consider the following:

Each pot has a voltage drop of 5.
Each pot consumes 5 x 150,000 = 750,000 watts.
That is enough to power 7,500 100-watt light bulbs or to heat 750 electric clothes irons.
For a single potline, multiply all the above by 100!

Other buildings complete a plant. There is the carbon plant where anodes are made, and a baking furnace where they are baked to eliminate the volatiles. A metal service building casts the molten aluminum into pigs, sows, and ingots for delivery to customers. An effluent system eliminates pollutant materials, and storage structures to receive raw materials complete the basic plant.

Now I would like to explain some of the details of the project. It was known as VALCO (Volta Aluminum Company), and we initiated several new procedures for project control. Although I had used a computer scheduling program in a study of the California water program, this job would be the company's first application to a large project and became the standard for all programs after. This scheduling method was first developed by DuPont in the early 1960s and was called CRITICAL PATH. It is now available from Microsoft. We called it PRESIDENT DIAGRAMMING. It enabled us to show much more detail than the old bar chart system, and we could print out a report from the computer at any time. This afforded us the opportunity to develop a purchasing program we called PSSR, for purchasing schedule and status report. I sketched out a hand-illustrated version of what I wanted and our scheduling group prepared a computer program. From the schedule we determined arrival at job site time for all items of material and equipment. Backing up from that date, we applied estimated times for shipping, manufacturing, and placing a purchasing order to the date the specifications had to be completed. When an actual purchase order was placed, we entered the supplier's schedule for the item, and we then had a control document. This later became a standard for all jobs thereafter.

Company practice had been to prepare a document called SCOPE OF WORK within two or three weeks of project initiation and then, using that information, develop a schedule and estimate of cost. I felt this was a flawed method for large projects, and I suggested we should prepare a Project Criteria that would provide enough information to develop a control estimate and schedule. I said it would take four months and Kaiser Aluminum agreed. Once completed and approved by Kaiser Aluminum, the document enabled us to prepare a good estimate and schedule. Any additions or deletions from the Criteria had to be approved by Kaiser Aluminum. This gave us all the tools we needed to effect complete control of the job. I am proud of the fact that we completed a complex job in Africa on schedule and within budget.

Before finishing this tale, I want to tell you a few of the things we built and a story or two of our experiences.

Edgar Kaiser had decreed that we must provide a small hospital, to be ready by the time the main contingent of personnel got to the jobsite. By using prefabricated building elements we were able to have a twenty-bed facility complete with X-ray, operating, recovery, examining, and waiting rooms. Even an ambulance was provided. I recall that the wife of our labor relations manager was an early patient when she had her first child.

To provide entertainment for our people we built a clubhouse, tennis court, and swimming pool. There was a movie projection room, a kitchen, and a large open but covered dining area. There were people from many nations on our construction bunch, and there would occasionally be an international dinner. I happened to be at the job when one of those feasts was put on and what a wonderful event it was. Each group wore traditional dress and prepared a favorite country dish.

We built bachelors' quarters for those men arriving without families, and for the first few trips I stayed there. A mess hall across the street provided good meals. The quarters were rather primitive, with a bedroom, tiny living room, and mini kitchen. For some unknown reason there was a bathtub next to the kitchen, but the toilet was accessed by going out the front door and walking outside. One night after dinner I needed to use the toilet. It was raining, so to avoid getting my clothes wet I went out in my underwear. I felt a soft cushion under my feet and I wondered what it was. It was winged ants, crawling on my feet and squishing between my toes. I hurried through the mess and was able to wash one foot at a time in the toilet. Then I still had to go back through the mess to get inside. I ran back, sat on the step, and in the rain washed my feet as much as possible. Finally, I sat on the bathtub and washed the rest of the ants down the drain. The bachelors' quarters had not finished with me yet. I was in a rush to grab a shower and get dressed to catch the plane home. I was thoroughly soaped when the water shut off. Now what do I do? Put my clothes on over the soap? Then I remembered. We always had bottled water in the refrigerator! There was barely enough to rinse off in that freezing water. I caught my flight with only moments to spare.

To obtain aggregate for concrete we had to go twenty miles inland to a rock quarry. We had excavating equipment and trucks to haul the aggregate to the jobsite. I did not see this, but was told that a group of chimpanzees came out of the surrounding forest around two-thirty each afternoon and assembled along a ridge three hundred feet from the quarry. Thirty or forty of the animals would sit there watching intently as the machines went about their noisy business. An hour or so later they would all rise as if on signal and melt back into the forest. When I heard the story I couldn't help wondering what the chimps were thinking as they watched the noisy monsters chewing up all that rock, especially since the stuff was not good to eat.

Even though the following incident happened at the Akosombo Dam, it is worth relating here as an example of communication problems between different cultures. Our engineers had placed stakes in the reservoir area above the dam. This is done to clear any brush, trees, and debris that might be swept into the turbines of the powerhouse. The surveyors took pains to seek out the tribes living in the area to explain that the water in the reservoir would rise to the level indicated by the stakes. Some time later, it was found that many of the stakes had been moved, and always to a lower position. When quizzed, the answer was, "You told us the water would come to the stakes. We did not want to lose so much of our land, so we moved the stakes lower so the water would stop there." Very logical.

Our construction superintendent, George Humphrey, and his wife, Beverly, brought along their youngest daughter, Cindy. In the States, Cindy had done a great deal of horseback riding and wanted to have a horse in Ghana. Somehow George managed to find a good-looking animal and Cindy was able to resume her riding. One day the horse came up lame. No veterinarian was available so George sought help from the doctor managing the hospital we had built. The horse was reluctant to be examined and the doctor decided he must administer a sedative. The doctor, not familiar with animal medicine, had to make a judgment as to the size of the shot. With George holding the horse Doc administered the sedative. Within minutes the horse quieted and stood still. Everyone heaved a sigh of relief, but within five minutes the horse began to shake and shortly fell to the ground. To everyone's astonishment the poor animal was dead. For some time after the unfortunate doctor was introduced as, "This is our horse doctor."

In 1964, the Volta River went on a rampage, overflowed its banks, and wiped out villages and settlements with its raging waters. One of our people, an architect, had been working for the Ghana government for about a year before the flood and was called upon to assist in the design of housing to resettle the displaced people. She was out selecting building sites when she fell and suffered a severe ankle sprain. Her transportation had left, expecting to return later that day. Unable to walk and in obvious pain, she had need of medical help. Her party had no radio and a telephone was miles away. The solution? The language of the drum! Over forty-five miles from Accra the drums, by relay, communicated the message, and a helicopter was dispatched to the scene and returned the woman to a hospital for treatment. I have been at a tribal drumming celebration and am convinced that the sounds can be read if you know what to listen for. I recall the drum event our driver took two of us to see and hear way out in the bush. There were drums of all sizes, from a big twenty-foot monster to a tiny little finger-activated thing. I will never forget that evening. We fell under the spell of the sounds. We could feel the sound of the bigger drums, and the smaller ones made the hair stand up on the back of our necks.

A couple of experiences are worth describing. The first was the revolution ousting the president of Ghana, Kwame Nkruma. I was on my way into Accra one day when I heard several loud reports. My driver said something I didn't hear, and as we rounded a turn in the street we came upon a crowd of about fifty people shouting, waving arms, and pointing at what I knew was the gate to Nkruma's residence compound. As we slowly made our way through the crowd I saw the object of the excitement, several blackened holes in the gate structure. Just up ahead several uniformed individuals were hauling a small, wheeled canon around the building to our left, which I later learned was a police barracks. The driver seemed unconcerned and we drove on into the city where I purchased a few gifts to take home on a flight scheduled to depart three days later. Accra was calm, but when I got back to the job site there was excitement over the news that Jerry Rawlings, a lieutenant in the Air Force, had seized control of the government as Nkruma fled to safety in the adjacent country. Even with that news our job went on without interruption.

As I left the airport building to board the plane I was startled to see a line of soldiers behind sandbags, obviously there to prevent any unauthorized departures. I tried what I hoped was a friendly smile, but it was met with impassive stares. I walked though the narrow opening in a barricade of sand bags and ascended the stairs to the plane, the smile replaced by a feeling of relief. This little performance was repeated the next three or four times I went to the job, but finally there appeared to be no further concern about unauthorized arrivals or departures. Since 2005, when Rawlings was voted out of office, Ghana has been relatively stable although suffering a rather fragile economy, made worse by the closing of the aluminum plant we hoped would be the start of better times.

Russia dealt Ghana a bad hand in 1964, beginning with a gift of three Ilyushin commercial planes. I believe this was in partial payment for a year's cocoa crop. Russia then dumped the entire crop on the market, depressing the price for some time. Adding insult to injury, no spare parts were supplied with the planes, so it became necessary to cannibalize one plane for spare parts. By the time I left in 1967, only one plane was flyable and it was on its last legs. Russia had one more card to play, the tractor deal. I am not sure whether this was a purchase or a gift, because Nkruma was a communist fellow traveler. I saw some of the tractors being unloaded at the port but was not sure now many were finally delivered; maybe twenty or thirty. I heard the things were to be used as ditch diggers for agricultural use. There was a large blade on the front of each and I recognized it as a snow plough, not very useful in Ghana, I thought. At the bottom of each blade a triangular attachment was welded on, obviously an afterthought. That was the ditching device! Each tractor had a windowed cab with a door entry. Only later did I learn that the cab was heated with a closed system from the exhaust, and in the tropical ambiance of Ghana, nearly roasted the driver. Some commissar in Russia had overproduced snow ploughs so there was a surplus to give away; the people of Ghana didn't deserve that!

Such a wonderful job, so many fine people in our construction crew, and such a great opportunity to get to know the friendly and helpful people of Ghana. It would take a small book to recount all the experiences.

Bill Ball 1965

Chapter Twenty-Five

A Flurry of Jobs

ALGERIA 1972—1975

*A*l Garcia, with Kaiser Aluminum, along with Don Montez and I, from Kaiser Engineers, were on our way to Algeria, following up on an inquiry made to Kaiser Aluminum expressing that Algeria hoped to build interest in Kaiser Aluminum technology for an aluminum plant. We knew there had been some unrest in the country, but at the moment all seemed quiet.

Algeria had been a French colony, but in the period when other African countries were achieving independence the French pulled out, leaving turbulence and some violence in their wake. It was some time before quiet returned, and still little disturbances popped up now and then.

Reservations had been made for us at a hotel in the capital, and although the place had seen better days the service and food were very good, even the often-served couscous.

Meetings were held at a conference room in a government building for the most part, but there were other offices where we met with different government department personnel. In all the meetings we noted the presence of a young woman taking notes, and in most cases monitoring the discussions. She proved to be bright and knowledgeable, and we soon came to respect her deft handling of the meetings.

We entertained on several occasions, always with the help of the young woman, and as the meetings were concluded we were in turn entertained at a resort on the shores of the Mediterranean. The resort was deserted, except for service personnel, and we assumed vacation season was over, or had not begun. We sat under palms in a beautiful garden overlooking the sea as we sipped tall glasses of delicious juice. At dinner, only the six of us occupied the big dining room, and I recall feeling a bit guilty about the whole affair.

Returning to Algiers, we spent the night and in the morning were out at the airport for the flight home. This was my first experience with airport security. About one hundred passengers lined up, and each was questioned while another person carefully examined the passport. No body search was carried out and we handed in our luggage as we were cleared. After a wait of half an hour, everyone was ushered out the gate where a line of luggage waited. We each identified our bags, saw them loaded onto a baggage cart, and then were permitted to board the plane. Arriving in Paris at two a.m., we spent the night before catching Pan Am for home out of DeGaulle Airport at ten a.m.

Three weeks after we left, violent uprisings took place in Algeria, and we finally received notice the aluminum program had been canceled.

THE AFRICAN RAILWAY

Our company heard of a plan to build a railway from the copper mines in Zambia (the old North Rhodesia) to the port of Dar es Salaam in Tanzania. Zambia was concerned that the present route down through South Rhodesia could be blocked, thus closing off access to an outlet port. Dick Ringwood and I were assigned to job of selecting a route and preparing preliminary schedules and estimates. If possible, we would submit proposals to both Kenneth Kaenda, president of Zambia, and Julius Nyrerre, president of Tanzania. I chose to begin in Nairobi, Kenya, where there was a British Railway office I had contacted to arrange a meeting.

We stayed at a fine hotel where the attached restaurant was the Thorn Tree, mentioned in a Hemingway novel. I remember the first dinner we had there. I was perusing a menu when a waiter came over and, in very good Oxford English, asked if we would like to have a cocktail as a starter. I looked up and was startled to see a somewhat elderly man with great dangling earlobes that were no doubt the result of having the ears pierced for the insertion of circular wooden disks. Either the waiter only wore the disks on special occasions or he had given up the practice altogether. I never had the courage to ask.

There were other places to eat, and one day we noticed an ad for a Chinese restaurant nearby. Odd, we thought, but why not give it a try? Two nights later we did and found the dinner to be the best we had ever tasted. Quizzing our hotel clerk we found out why. On the floor above the restaurant was the headquarters of the Kenya Chinese communist party; that explained what we thought was an unusual number of Chinese when we had dinner there! We were to encounter the Chinese once more before we departed for home.

British railway was helpful, offering us maps and other information on the possible routes. To get a better look at the country, I rented a plane with a Plexiglas window in the belly through which I was able to photograph many points of interest. Our pilot was a Turk who had ferried planes to Africa during World War II. He was an excellent pilot, and we soon felt comfortable with him at the controls. I recall a landing field where we refueled twice. Each time as we approached, a beat-up old fire truck raced alongside until we came to a stop. When I asked why they did this the pilot replied, "Not many planes land here, and it gives them a little excitement to relieve the boredom."

We prepared a route map, schedule, and preliminary estimate of cost, working from the hotel in Nairobi, and arranged dates to meet with the presidents of the two countries involved. We flew to Lusaka, Zambia, where we met Kenneth Kahunda at ten in the evening. Our reception was very cordial, lasting two hours, during which the president asked pertinent questions about the project. We left at midnight and wondered if the president always worked that late.

The next day we flew to Mombassa, where we would wait two days before our meeting with Julius Nyerere of Tanzania. I must admit that our short stay was deluxe R & R. We were lodged in a comfortable cabin fifty feet from the seashore, with bathing trunks for a dip in the gentle surf; lobster three times a day if we chose; beer, coffee, or fruit juice at a moment's notice all day! We had to leave all this for our meeting in Dar es Salaam.

Again we were greeted cordially and given ample time to present our program. Nyerere was dressed in what we used to call a "Mouse Suit," a simple gray without ornamentation such as that worn by Mao Tse-Tung, the Chinese communist leader. He was courteous, asked many questions, and, we thought, expressed great interest in our program. As we were leaving, Nyerere asked if we would step into a side office for a few minutes. He explained that a Chinese deputation was on the way down the hall and he thought it better if we did not encounter each other in the hall. I knew they were Red Chinese, and I had a sinking feeling that our efforts would prove to have been in vain. My hunch was right. The letters my company received thanked us for our interest, but the job had been awarded to "others." Our program was a three-and-a-half-year schedule using local workmen supervised by thirty Americans. The estimate was $125 million including American and European rolling stock. The last I heard of the job was that the Chinese proposal was for a five-year schedule importing eight to ten thousand Chinese workers. The information was secondhand, so I am unable to verify the numbers.

This was a rare and exciting experience during which we saw a great deal of Africa, flying over much of the Stanley/Livingston trail. We spent a night at the little village at the tip of Lake Nyasa where Stanley uttered the oft-quoted phrase, "Dr. Livingston, I presume."

I cannot leave this tale without paying my respects to the two presidents I met. Both were devoted to improving the economy of their country and the quality of life for their people.

MANAGER—ALUMINUM SMELTERS

Not long after the Southwire job I was appointed manager of Aluminum Smelter Division, a job involving marketing, preliminary studies, and proposal preparation. Probably one of the most frustrating experiences I ever had was that ALUMAX job. A subsidiary of AMAX, the well-known mining and minerals company, ALUMAX intended to build an aluminum plant in Puerto Rico and had arranged with Kaiser Aluminum to utilize the same technology as that used for Southwire. We were automatically involved and began with visits to the proposed jobsite followed by plant layouts, estimates of cost, and schedule. We were told that soils investigation had been done but, just to be sure, we did some of our own. To everyone's surprise it was found that a seismic fault ran though the site. After much lamentation and finger pointing, the location was abandoned.

Next stop? Astoria, Oregon! More estimates, schedules, and this time we did the soils work. I was asked to assist in presenting the program to local interests. In one session the question of pollution was raised. Grandmother and I had stopped at a big campground near Astoria some years before and had seen many campfires pouring smoke and other pollutants into the air. I explained that the aluminum plant would not discharge anything like the amount the campground did, and in addition the plant would help the economy. One of the biggest enterprises, the fishing industry, was suffering a decline, which would be offset by the employment of four hundred people in the new plant. After five months ALUMAX gave up. No matter what advantages might have accrued, the environmental group had made up its mind they just didn't want an aluminum plant in the Astoria area. With such resistance the company pulled its skirts out of the mud of Astoria and moved east along the Columbia River to a site near Pendleton.

During the hopscotching, ALUMAX questioned our ability to handle the construction. To convince them we had no concerns, we took several of their people to Cleveland where we were building a nuclear power plant. After a full day of touring the job and talking with our construction manager there, we felt they were convinced we could do the work. On the way home we talked about timing to assemble our design group and other details. Arriving back in Oakland we were convinced the job was an immediate go. How wrong we were!

Someone in the multiplayer organization of ALUMAX had been talking with ALCOA, the largest aluminum company in the States, and had been convinced that ALCOA technology was superior to that of Kaiser Aluminum. We were informed that the ALCOA technology would be used and, because ALCOA did not want any information leaking back to Kaiser Aluminum through Kaiser Engineers, Bechtel would do design and construction. Devastated, we had to acknowledge that the job would be done well by the new team. A final site change relocated the plant to the southeast at a place I did not choose to remember. ALUMAX spent $4.5 million following a moving target before finally building a plant. The only satisfaction we got from all this was a modest profit and four hundred sheets of drawing paper with borders and title block. Some of that paper I held onto until I used it in 1999 to draw the plans for your hope chests.

I cannot leave this tale without mentioning the deep personal loss to the family of the man designated to be the plant manager for the new facility. Whether it was the frustration of moves from one place to another, or being away from his family for long periods, I can't say, but whatever the reason for the suicide of James Howarth, I believe there is one whose conscience must bother him.

PERMANENTE CEMENT

Arnold Kackman, manager of our Cement division, was sent to Canada to repair some of the holes Edgar Kaiser Jr. had rent in a project he was managing. Arnold, a fine engineer with considerable background in similar operations, had to leave his post in the cement group and I was asked to pinch hit for hum. Shortly after I took over, problems arose. A member of Permanente had supervised soils exploration and awarded a contract to a Japanese company to furnish all the machinery and equipment for a cement plant to be built in Indonesia.

As Kaiser Engineers began construction, it was found that there were underground caverns of various sizes around the site as a result of water seepage dissolving deposits of limestone. Many of the foundations for structures fell in these locations, and we had to quickly design a beam straddling the caverns so we would have a support for a building corner or equipment pad. This added considerable cost to the job.

The Japanese company had not been given a schedule for delivery of equipment to suit the priority of construction, and it was necessary to arrange a proper schedule for the machinery. This took a bit of negotiation and resulted in two trips to our office in Hiroshima. You may remember that city was the target of the first atomic bomb dropped on Japan. Although most of the city had been rebuilt, the familiar skeleton of a dome remained. Not far from the office was a memorial park where lawns, some twisted steel, remnants of the blast, and a building in which photos depicting the awful destruction of buildings and the cruel effect of radiation on the human body, scenes I found difficult to look at. Just outside the building was the stone step with an image of a body imprinted by the maelstrom of heat and radiation from the bomb called FAT BOY.

I saw a group of twenty children, about ten or twelve years of age, being escorted around the park by a young woman I took to be a teacher. I was later told tours were a regular thing and the children are told something like, "We must all see what happens when the warlords control our country. We must never let it happen again." If there was any indictment of the United States I could not tell.

On my first visit I had noticed there was a bit of homesickness among our staff and their wives, so on my second trip we had a gala dinner party at a fine restaurant. There was koto music and a little kabuki play. We sat, legs crossed, at a low table and watched our repast being prepared on several charcoal braziers. We talked about what was going on back home, and particularly at Kaiser. I still remember that get-together because it gave everyone a feeling of contact with the home office, something always welcomed on overseas assignments. The determination of the Hiroshima group to complete the project without further problems was rewarded by a letter of thanks from the client, Permanente Cement.

RUSSIA

In 1975, as a result of exchanged communications between Gene Trefethen and a well-placed Russian diplomat, both Kaiser Engineers and Kaiser Aluminum were invited to Moscow for discussions of the Russian Aluminum industry. There was an additional reason for the invitation: Gene Trefethen, highest-ranking officer and most trusted director of Kaiser Industries, had established a successful wine business in the Napa area. One of his wines, a chardonnay, won first prize in the year's competition in which the best of French wines were exhibited. Gene had presented a case of the wine to a Russian diplomat, and the rapport between the two was obvious at the meetings in Moscow.

Our mission was to meet with representatives of the Russian aluminum industry to address two subjects: pollution from antiquated reduction plants near Lake Baikal and new technology in the production of alumina, the feed stock for the reduction process. You may not know that Baikal at one time represented 10 percent of the entire world's fresh water. It was now becoming a cesspool from pollution, mainly from the nearby aluminum plants built using the outdated Soderberg technology.

In Moscow, we were assigned rooms on the sixth floor of the Intourist Hotel. From my corner room I looked into the Kremlin and at the large building where Lipizzaner horses were once trained for performances. Directly out front was the structure housing the body of Lenin, hero of the 1917 revolution bringing communism to Russia. It was partly visible, but I could see people climbing the stairs and walking across the viewing platform where lay the body of their hero. Before me lay the vast expanse of Red Square, where a month ago on May Day I had seen, on television, the massive display of missiles, tanks, and troops. This day it was quiet. Beyond the square sat the ornate St. Basil's church, now a museum in atheist Russia. To the right of St. Basil's was the huge double-paneled gate into the Kremlin. Left of the square was the monster Gum Department Store with the big half-cylinder glass-paned roof. Inside, a center aisle ran the length of the building and provided light to the interior. On either side of the central passage, four floors of shops could be seen. Some appeared empty and the rest were sparsely supplied.

A tourist guide was assigned to us. She was an attractive young woman speaking good English, and she told us she was studying to be an opera singer. She took us to the space exhibit where we saw a model of Sputnik, the little soccer ball-sized space traveler that, with its beeping signal, had awakened America to the fact that Russia had beat us into space. Other space exhibits were on display and I saw they were equipped with old vacuum tube electronics. We had long since developed miniature transistor electronics. One interesting side trip was to the Trechikov Gallery, once a very large private residence, now the repository of a collection of fine paintings, mostly oils and all well done by artists I didn't know. I guessed there were around four hundred, and, strangely, one-third were clearly religious scenes. How this had survived a half mile from the Kremlin could only be explained by assuming that Russia appreciated good art no matter what the subject. That the gallery was well known became evident by the number of people in attendance. We exited through the last room. There we came face-to-face with the ubiquitous, twice life-size, heroic figure, arms upraised, clutching the famous hammer and sickle.

Our deputation split into two groups, one traveling out to Siberia for a look at the aluminum plants and the other going to Leningrad to meet with the alumina and reduction specialists. I was fortunate to be part of the three-man party for the meetings in that old city built by Peter the Great to create a warm-water port and a large winter palace. After the fall of communism, the city reverted to its original name of Petrograd. Our hosts had read everything available on the manufacture of aluminum, even the several articles I had written on the subject. We were impressed by the knowledge and desire of the Russian engineers to learn all they could about the business. The meetings, conducted in a conference room at the Aluminum Institute, were cordial, and we came away convinced the engineers were hoping to work with us on the projects.

During the time in Leningrad we were taken to the ballet, shown the points of interest in the city, and, as icing on the cake, were treated to a lengthy tour of the famed Hermitage Museum. Even knowing that many of the paintings on exhibit had been plundered when the Russians occupied Germany as the war ended, I found the magnitude of the museum nearly overwhelming. Upon entering, we saw a pair of beautiful curved stairs leading to the floor above. Massive doors opened to a great reception hall, where four huge chandeliers caught our eyes. We learned that the chandeliers had been taken down, disassembled, and packed along with most of the exhibits for underground storage where all would be secure from the German onslaught. Such an enormous task, and now all had been reassembled as though nothing had ever happened. Even a bronze statue of a man on horseback had been safely stored. About thirty feet high and nearly the same in length, it must have required a great effort to move underground, but there it stood outside on its granite pedestal as if it had never been moved!

Germany had laid siege to Leningrad in World War II. The siege lasted for nine months and the winter of 1943-1944 found the people without food and fuel. Heroic efforts were made to relieve the suffering, but crossing frozen water and tramping through foot-deep snow proved too difficult for those who made the attempt. Thousands died during that terrible time, and the dead as well as the survivors are memorialized in a cemetery just outside the city. Upon approaching, one is reminded of a county fair in the States. There are vendors offering food, dink, and souvenirs. Entry is through a large, ornate gate. Once inside, one sees a large reflecting pool with a tile bottom so level that only an inch and a half of water is needed to cover it. Around the pool four soldiers march in a stiff slow cadence. Each soldier is six foot four, and the marching goes on in shifts twenty-four hours a day. Beyond the pool lie the graves, simple, continuous mounds at right angles to a central walkway that leads to a memorial statue about seven hundred feet away. Along the walk speakers play a funeral dirge, a sort of macabre touch, I thought.

Upon the return to Moscow of our two parties from Leningrad and Siberia, we were invited to two dinners. The first was a general discussion of our impressions relating to the cost and schedule for the overall project ($3 billion and four to five years). The second dinner, a long and friendly affair with many vodka toasts, celebrated the signing of a protocol agreement for the job. We managed to walk away from those banquets, having been forewarned that many vodka toasts would be offered. While our Russian friends bolted the full shot glass we sipped ours, making a single filling last through several toasts.

At the preliminary meetings in London, Gene Trefethen had informed us that the assistant to Kaiser Engineers' general manager would probably be assigned as manager of the Russian project. At the conclusion of the last dinner the Russians asked who would be the manager for the project. Gene replied, saying he would assign a highly qualified, experienced person and would send a photograph and resume when we received notice to proceed. The other Kaiser Engineers person and I looked at each other, wondering what had changed Gene's mind.

About two weeks after our return, a memo was circulated announcing the retirement of that original designee. Word got out later that he had imbibed too much vodka on the way to Siberia and, with a loose tongue, said things better left unsaid. That left the two of us wondering who might get tagged for the manager's job. A month later we learned to our chagrin (relief?) that some commissar had decided it would not be appropriate to have a bunch of capitalists contaminating the pristine world of communism.

After the big dinner it was time to leave, and none of us took the same route home. I chose to spend a few days in Switzerland at the Dolder Grande Hotel, a beautiful old nineteenth-century hotel I had stayed in before. I flew from Moscow to Kiev, where my luggage was subjected to a complete search including checking for a false bottom. I had to hand over my passport and it was inspected for what seemed like an hour. The only word I understood was Amerikaner, to which I simply nodded. After that hand signals directed me and not a one of the officials permitted a smile to ease my way through the system. After retrieving my passport and repacking my suitcase I was waved to the waiting plane, relieved to be on my way!

Arriving at the hotel I was escorted to a big, high-ceilinged room where I slept until nine the next morning. Having ordered breakfast to be sent to my room, I was soon sitting at a beautifully done tray with two bright flowers in a small vase. It was a relief to note that neither of the poached eggs had a baby chick as they had in Moscow. After four days at the lovely old establishment I departed for home, much the better for the little R&R.

Chapter Twenty-Six

National - Southwire

In February of 1968, Southwire, a wire manufacturing company in Carrollton, Georgia, had secured the rights to build an aluminum plant utilizing the technology developed by Kaiser Aluminum for the Ghana plant. There was a proviso that Kaiser Engineers must do the design and construction management. Since Southwire wanted to have the plant built with nonunion labor, and was negotiating an open-shop contract with Daniel Construction Company, Kaiser Engineers could not do direct construction. The reason for this was that all Kaiser companies operated under union contracts, and for us to hire nonunion workers would create a political firestorm. Now it was in May of 1968 that I arrived in Carrollton with Vic Cole, vice president for industrial projects, to negotiate a contract for engineering and construction management for the plant to be built in Hawesville, Kentucky, a small town twenty miles from Owensboro, a city I was to later learn was the proud possessor of the world's largest sassafras tree, and home of some of the largest bourbon liquor distilleries and aging warehouses in the United States.

We stayed that night at a motel, and by eight the next morning arrived at the offices of Southwire Company where we were met by Roy Richards, owner of Southwire. Cornell Maier, president of Kaiser Aluminum, had briefed us on a bit of Richards' background, and since I was to be dealing with Roy for the next two and a half years it is appropriate to tell you something of the man.

Fresh out of college, without either experience or capital, Roy Richards somehow managed to secure a contract to string power lines on a part of a new grid system. Short of cash but needing something to haul supplies, he bought a truck chassis, nothing but wheels, frame, and engine. Roy built a bed with sideboards and replaced the single seat with a wooden one for two people. The vehicle served for several years and the business prospered. One day, it occurred to Roy that he was paying the wire manufacturer a substantial profit, and that could be avoided if he built his own wire plant. From that idea Southwire was born. Starting small, the business grew to its present large, modern facility.

Roy was still not satisfied. He was paying the suppliers of aluminum and copper a profit, and that could be avoided if he produced his own raw materials. Copper was a tough nut to crack, but Southwire could build an aluminum plant and that was what brought Vic and me to Carrollton this bright May morning. How National Steel Company of Pittsburgh came to form a partnership we did not know, but since Roy Richards had authority to sign our contract we didn't care.

After a cordial greeting we were offered coffee or tea and then the meeting got down to business. When Vic and I compared notes on the way home we decided we had gone through the most intense grilling ever. At lunch, sandwiches were brought in from a small kitchen behind Roy's office. By six p.m., we were getting hungry when Roy suggested we break for dinner. What a welcome suggestion! We thought, "Now for a relaxing time at a good restaurant and a good juicy steak." Roy punched a button on his desk and someone appeared from the little kitchen. We had a choice, beef or fish. To our great disappointment, the person was taking our order for frozen dinners and we could have coffee or tea! Roy informed us that if there were any more questions after dinner we could wind up things and then repair to our motel. He then invited us to an escorted tour of the wire plant the next morning. I must say, we were impressed with the efficient layout and operation of the wire plant and it was plain to see Roy was proud of what he had done. The tour was completed about noon, we had lunch, this time at a local restaurant, and we picked up the tab.

Fortunately we had booked a late afternoon flight home from Atlanta and had plenty of time to make a leisurely drive to the airport. We carried with us a signed contract for the job. My first job was to mobilize a task force to design the plant, but there was something else I felt needed attention. Southwire had prepared an estimate of cost and construction schedule for the project, and had already arranged financing by a bond issue floated by the county in which the plant was to be built. During our first negotiations, I felt that both cost and schedule needed review. When I finally got around to this task, I found that there would be enough money to build a plant about a third larger than Southwire had anticipated, and even with the larger plant we could shave a year off the schedule. This time saving would result in a corresponding saving of $1.5 million in interest. Roy, in a letter to Kaiser Engineers, expressed his thanks for this study that not only saved money but permitted a larger plant than anticipated.

AT THE JOBSITE

I will interrupt to tell you about the motel where we stayed in Owensboro, Kentucky. There was no place to stay in Hawesville until after the plant was completed. On our first few visits to the job we stayed at Gabe's motel in Hawesville, a seven-story, circular structure. Adjacent stood a forty-foot plaster sculpture of Gabe himself, in full living color, arm upraised in welcome as he slowly and majestically rotated. We later moved to a more conventional motel where the dining was better, and because Gabe insisted on serving red wine chilled and white at room temperature.

Roy Richards had negotiated a contract with Daniel Construction of South Carolina to do all construction with open shop labor. When Daniel was moving trailers to the site to serve as offices, they were met by a group of angry union people from across the Ohio River. This attempt at intimidation failed, but shortly after the trailers were in place rifle shots were directed at the units from an unknown location. Fortunately no one was injured, but the incident prompted the Governor of Kentucky to issue a stern warning that further incidents would be met with retaliation from the state's National Guard. After that there were no more attempts to disrupt the work for the remainder of the job. Even when we awarded a contract to Butler Buildings for the prefabricated offices using union crews for installation, no problems arose. Strangely, even with union and nonunion men working virtually next to each other, calm reigned. I wondered about this, but concluded that it only took a single agitator to kindle a flame of disruption.

Kaiser Engineers assigned eight personnel to the job and all did a fine job for us, gaining the respect of both Daniel and Southwire. Jim Miller as the head of this group did a superb job of providing me with clear, concise reports. Jim was alone with his several children when I visited the job a few days before Thanksgiving. Jo, his wife, was on her way home from Tibet after climbing to base camp on Mt. Everest. I still remember my first visit to Jim's home. He opened the door and as I stepped in I saw the children, all five of them, lined up on the stairs waiting for us. On subsequent trips I would bring each one some little thing I bought at the Chicago airport. For Jo I would get a box of Fannie May chocolates, and she often treated me to a great home-cooked dinner.

Near the end of the job Jim was reassigned to the labor-plagued Noranda project in New Madrid, Missouri. At that point, Rick Larsen took over Jim's position and did a fine job for us. I still correspond with both Jim and Rick.

The job, completed on schedule and within the budget, was a success except for one major mistake. You may have noticed that the chapter heading was National-Southwire. As I mentioned, Roy Richards had negotiated a partnership with National Steel Company, and National representatives were looking at everything we did, but after several months they withdrew their watchdogs and left us alone, apparently satisfied we knew what we were doing.

It was not until a decision had to be made on the method of pollution control that National descended upon us once more. ALCOA, the largest producer of aluminum in the world, had recently invented a method of handling plant effluent called Fluid Bed, which collected more than 99 percent of the material that polluted the landscape, and then made the system available to the aluminum industry. I strongly recommended this system, but National's environmental chief insisted on using the wet system in which water spray was introduced in the last three hundred feet of the ducts before discharging into a five-hundred-foot chimney. One other factor entered the picture now. Southwire had often tried to negotiate lower prices on items we were purchasing, and on the wet system we reluctantly drew up a contract in which they had managed to "save" around $250,000. I was concerned that the supplier could only offer this savings by reducing material and labor from the lining of the ducts. I worried this might result in serious corrosion problems. Unfortunately I was right, and the repair cost a great deal more than was saved, and while it lasted released much pollution into the atmosphere.

There was a gala plant dedication. Two top-level managers from Kaiser Engineers flew in, fluffed their feathers, and made great speeches. Your grandmother and I had come in two days earlier. The last leg of our flight was in a small single-engine plane, affording us a beautiful view of the countryside and then of the plant as we landed at the adjacent airport. Following the dedication, we took a few days to tour the bluegrass country, finally visiting the famous racetrack in Louisville, Kentucky, before return-ing to Oakland.

I maintained contact with Roy Richards by notes on our Christmas cards and he responded with photos of his family and notes on his holiday cards. Sadly this ended with Roy's death in 1995. I admired him.

Three people stand out clearly in my memory of the project: Roy Richards, Gary Satterwhite, and Chap Chandler. I have told you something of Roy, but I should add one more item. Roy was photographed by Karsch of Ottawa, a well-known portrait artist who was noted for limiting his work to important figures. You may have seen the portrait of the famous wartime leader Winston Churchill. It is regarded as a work of art, and the best ever taken of Churchill. Roy sat for a portrait by Karsch and it was a beautiful shot. I have a copy somewhere in the pile of memorabilia.

Gary was introduced as the intended manager of the plant we were to build. I remember thinking, "This kid is too young; that job requires some-one with years of experience, and this guy does not look more than twenty-five." I needn't have worried. Gary did a fine job, helping us along the way and managing a smooth startup.

Chap, introduced as our principal contact and Southwire's monitor on the project, was a delight to work with. He was always helpful, making my job so much easier. I had many great times with Chap at the jobsite, at meetings in Carrollton, and on trips to suppliers.

Many other people contributed to the success of the job, and I wish I could gather them at a giant party so I could thank them all.

Chapter Twenty-Seven

Return to Ghana

Returning from the Russian trip in late June of 1975, I found a full inbox and a spindle of telephone messages. Among the latter was a call from Kaiser's Vice President-Africa asking me to call ASAP. Almost certain what this was about, I recalled a discussion the VP and I had back in January concerning selection of a project manager for the addition that Kaiser Aluminum was planning to make to the Ghana plant. The VP had someone in mind and wanted my opinion of the choice. Having employed the candidate on the original Ghana job, I felt I had a good knowledge of his performance.

I clearly recall my comments. I said he had a good knowledge of the process but often got bogged down in details that distracted his attention from other tasks. He also had a prickly personality, likely to lead to friction with the client. When I talked with the VP this time he had the grace to say, "You were right, Kaiser Aluminum is unhappy and wants the guy off the job. We've got to do something right now."

I knew what was coming before he asked me to take a look here, and then see what's going on at the job. I didn't want to get involved as a cleanup boy, but as I thought about it I realized I had put too much into the original project to see it end in an acrimonious finale, so I agreed, but with the proviso that my wife would go along whenever I felt it necessary to go to the job.

That was the beginning of three trips to Ghana, each a month in duration. Each time we returned we took two or three weeks touring places like England, France, Switzerland, Spain, and Italy. Grandmother loved every minute of these trips, especially the times in Ghana when we explored the country every weekend. There were drives to Akosombo Dam, where we enjoyed an escorted tour through the entire facility. One time we hiked to the falls near the Togo border where fruit bats nested in the trees above. Clapping hands resulted in the rising of a great cloud of these rather large creatures, only to have them settle back down when quiet returned.

One time we drove to Cape Coast Castle, forty miles west of Accra (remember that the coast runs east and west in this part of Africa). The structure had a five-hundred-year history, including a reputed visit from Columbus. A three-story structure surrounded a parade ground for military troops who had been bivouacked on the ground floor at either side. Officers occupied the quarters on the second floor. We were told that Columbus had stopped at the castle on one of his voyages nearly five hundred years ago. A terrible part of the castle's history has to do with the inhuman business of slavery. White people from Europe bribed African chiefs to round up men, women, and even children, often ripping families apart to be herded to the dungeon of the castle. We saw that dungeon. Dark, dank, with little light, it must have been terrifying to sit there waiting for a fate they could not have imagined.

One final story remains. A man and wife had been imprisoned on the third floor of the building. An open walkway connected the two apartments. As a further punishment the jailers erected a barrier to block the interconnection, thus separating the lovers. They could see and talk to each other but were destined to remain forever separated. A cruel penalty, we thought.

After the castle visit, we took the lunches we had prepared and walked to what appeared to be a resort area where there were benches under a grove of palm trees. From there we could see a pleasant natural harbor with a variety of boats drawn up on the curve of a sandy beach. I remember wondering if Columbus might have anchored the Santa Maria there on one of his voyages of exploration.

Other explorations of Ghana and our several trips home through Europe blurred memories of the dungeon, but as I write about it thirty years later I am reminded again of how many shackled and chained people were incarcerated there waiting to be loaded onto filthy, rat-infested ships to be sailed off to an unknown fate.

Although I put in long hours at the job, many of the people I knew on the original project were back on this latest one, and it was good to see old friends again. As usual, everyone wanted to know what was going on at home. The best way to find out was to put on a little party. Grandmother and I enjoyed the social whirl but tried to wind things up before midnight to get a little sleep before the start of the next day.

As I said, we had wonderful trips home, but one we remembered for a long time. We had booked a flight on Swiss Air to Zurich. It was a beautiful, clear day as we came in over the Alps through a cerulean, nearly cloudless sky. What clouds there were seemed anchored to the tallest peaks, making the whole scene like a painting from a fairy tale. We stayed at a small hotel and I took Grandmother for cocktails at the Dolder Grande Hotel just for old times' sake. (Remember my return from Russia?) After cocktails we had a superb dinner at a small restaurant across the lake. After a day of wandering the city, looking in windows loaded with mouth-watering pastries and chocolates, we booked a bus trip into the Alps for the next day.

The bus took us through rolling, verdant country looking as if it had just been newly swept. Arriving at a small town perched on the hills, we bought a ticket on the cable way. Even at eleven in the morning the air was chilly. That was no problem, since each car was equipped with a big rubber-faced blanket that can be zipped around two people. On the way, we heard the distant, soft sounds of cowbells and could see the cattle ahead. As we passed overhead, the separate musical sound of the bells became a lovely harmony, fading away slowly as we left them behind. Five minutes from the top, snow began to fall, but we were snug in the big blanket. Our car slid into a dock in the enclosed building and we climbed out to look at the view. What a panorama greeted us! Mountains seemed to go on forever and we sat enthralled. Finally it was time to have lunch and get back to our bus. That night we talked about what a beautiful day it had been and gave thanks for the opportunity. Next morning we caught the plane to London where we would spend three days before flying home.

Yes, the Bay Area was as beautiful as ever, with a low fog sneaking under the Golden Gate Bridge. Grandmother and I were always enchanted by the view as the plane, jets muted, moved over the East Bay hills offering us the sight of waters, bridges, and cities. Flaps extending, landing gear lowering, and the thump of wheels on the runway told us we were home again. Finally, after three trips, each time taking a different route home, the job was fished and our client was once more happy.

On our last trip to Ghana, Beverley Humphrey took us on a short ride to a picnic area where the Volta River emptied into the ocean. There was a shop where we could buy a few things, including beer and Fanta. Everyone brought along their own lunches, which we enjoyed in a shaded area under a trellised spot near the riverside. As we sat eating our lunches and chatting, we became aware of a sound no one could identify. Rhythmic, it seemed to come from upriver and was growing louder. Watching, we saw a canoe, a big one; we all thought it might be a war canoe and were a bit uneasy about it. As it grew closer we counted eight oarsmen who were the source of the chanting. Behind them sat five white women with Ghanaian clothing draped over their shoulders, chanting in unison with the oarsmen. At the stern was a young white man wearing a bright Hawaiian shirt and white shorts, banging away on a native drum. I recognized him as a member of our field engineering crew. He was an Italian, known around the job for his happy-go-lucky personality. I never knew how he managed to engage the canoe and crew, but I did learn that the young women were flight attendants from an Al Italia plane. Our friend entertained his countrywomen in a way they would not soon forget!

Now is a good time to take a look at the projects depicted in the illustrations at the end of this chapter. These are projects I worked on during my career with Kaiser; some I managed start to finish.

With 1975 drawing to a close, things were afoot and destined to have a major impact on Kaiser Engineers. Though it was not generally known, concern was brewing over the disparity between the market price and book value of Kaiser Industries stock. This issue was to affect the entire industrial empire of Henry Kaiser and his son, Edgar. More importantly, to me, would be the impact on Kaiser Engineers. I will address the subject in the chapter to follow, Year of the Falling Sky.

Chalmette Aluminum Plant, Louisiana, on the banks of the Mississippi

Valco Aluminum Plant, Ghana, Africa

Akosombo Hydro Project, Ghana, providing power for Valco

Nordberg gas generators erected to power Chalmette Aluminum

National Southwire Smelter, Kentucky

P.T. Semen Cibinong cement plant, Indonesia

El Sobrante Outlet Works, San Pablo Reservoir, EBMUD

Industrias Kaiser Argentina integrated automobile plant,
Cordoba, Argentina

Chapter Twenty-Eight

'76, Year of the Falling Sky

*B*usy with a big backlog of work, most of us were not aware that a piece of sky was about to fall upon us. Just when the first cracks appeared is difficult to pinpoint, but as I look back from the perspective of twenty-nine years, I believe the first evidence, although most of us didn't realize it, began to emerge after Henry Kaiser turned over control of the then-flourishing empire to his son, Edgar. From that time, events led to the eventual liquidation of Kaiser Industries. Whether this was the result of action by the Securities Exchange Commission or the Kaiser family was the subject for debate. I have always felt that, while the SEC desired the change, the Kaiser family did too. A five-fold increase in their financial position would have been too great to resist, though perhaps it was not prudent.

To give you a bit of background leading to the liquidation, I must take you back to a decision destined to stir up a dust storm in the quiet halls of Kaiser Industries. This came about when the banks handling financial matters for Industries urgently suggested that Edgar should seek a strong manager to take over as CEO. Whether Edgar or the banks made the choice was not clear, but William Rush arrived in town with a large broom. He intended to make sweeping changes in Industries, and his first move was to centralize the departments of personnel, accounting, marketing, and services of the several wholly owned subsidiaries of Industries. Kaiser Engineers was one of the groups, and I recall the heartburn this move gave us. Some time after the consolidation, rumors began circulating about opposition to Rush's management style. The underground whispered that Edgar's second wife, Nina, his former secretary, was the focal point of the revolt. Of course, those of us in the trenches could not know, but soon word got out that the new CEO had resigned. He took with him a tidy departure sum (a "golden parachute") as he returned to his origins, the steel industry. It was later learned that William Rush died from an inoperable brain tumor. I have wondered if the onset of that malady played a part in his resignation.

The next piece of sky was about to fall. We heard that the liquidation of Kaiser Industries was to take place and that the process would include the sale of the wholly owned subsidiaries. That got our attention because it meant we, Kaiser Engineers, would be on the auction block. We wondered who might buy us and what changes could be expected. The idea of an employee's stock ownership plan, ESOP, surfaced. Lawyers were contacted to discus how such a program could be implemented and financed. It all looked perfect; we had a very good management team, a large backlog of work, and an experienced, capable staff of engineers and construction personnel to carry out the work. A great idea, we thought, until a bucket of cold water quenched the fires of our enthusiasm. Edgar Kaiser was negotiating with a potential buyer and wanted no extraneous activities to affect, or interrupt, the talks.

Raymond International was the new owner of Kaiser Engineers for $30 million. I think we all felt a little chill as we emerged from beneath the umbrella of the Kaiser organization, but most of us knew Raymond as the fine old construction company whose founder had invented the Raymond Concrete Pile, used on foundations worldwide. What we did not know was that our new owner was not the company we had known. Changes were about to take place, changes we could not have imagined. There was more loose sky overhead, but we were too busy to notice.

I have always regarded 1976 as the year of events that would affect the lives of many people. Kaiser Industries was gone, Kaiser Engineers became a subsidiary of Raymond International, and a top Raymond executive moved to the Kaiser Center to coordinate details of the acquisition. In addition, we had a heavy backlog of work on the books, enough to keep us busy for at least three years. A rosy future, we thought.

I was busy with several projects as well as with the marketing effort. I had also begun the task of preparing a book of procedures governing the activities of Kaiser Engineers. This turned out to be more of a job than anticipated, particularly when sandwiched in with my other work. I was beginning to see daylight ahead when the big retirement hit the fan. Four division vice presidents reached the magic age at the same time in mid-1977, and all elected to take the big step into retirement. I will always believe that they saw things the rest of us either missed or could not have known. As might be expected, a shuffling of personnel followed as the vacancies were filled. The office of vice president and chief engineer remained open, and I was asked to fill it. Not expecting this, I was confronted with a tough decision. For the past twenty-four years I had been involved with the planning and building of industrial projects. I knew I would miss the joy of taking a dream and turning it into a big, beautiful production facility. I would particularly miss contact with the many wonderful clients. On the other hand my engineering career had begun in the engineering office with lowly draftsman's work and had worked up to the design of machinery and equipment. Permit me a moment of bragging: I made very good drawings and was good at design. I loved the work, but knew I would not be doing it as chief engineer. I would, however, be directing the people who did. I had a choice to make, but which was the right one?

That night at home, your grandmother and I explored the pros and cons of my choices. It was midnight when we arrived at an agreed decision. I would accept the chief engineer's position!

The next few weeks were a blur of activity. Handing over work I had been doing to others, and obtaining engineering licenses in states where we were doing work, took much of my time. The licensing was aided by the fact I had both civil and mechanical licenses in California, a state with very strict requirements. This made it possible to obtain licenses in other states by reciprocal agreement. In others it was necessary to submit experience records or to sit for verbal interrogations. Next there were visits to our various offices around the country to meet with the Raymond engineering team to discuss cooperation and coordination. I had to become familiar with computer applications to engineering scheduling and design calculations, as well as with the growing practice of producing drawings by computer. Here we needed new software to replace the outdated automatic drafting machine. After these preliminaries, I could catch my breath and get out where the work was being done. In my division nearly seven hundred people were at work, and it was good to get around to the scattered drawing and design groups. I could say hello to the many friends I had associated with over the years and meet the new employees. I was proud to be a small part of that group of fine engineers and architects, and it is important that I tell you they were some of the finest in the country. They were the ones who turned Henry Kaiser's many dreams into reality.

We were busy. Integration of Kaiser Engineers into Raymond seemed destined for success. Calm returned after the recent perturbations, and the talk around the coffee machine and water cooler was optimistic about the future. None of us saw the crack beginning to widen in the sky above.

No doubt there will be other versions of those days of 1976, but how they affected me is still very clear in my mind because it marked the beginning of the end of what we all had regarded as a big family association. As I look around at the industry today, I find that the loyalty we felt for Kaiser and that which the company felt toward us is gone. There is a feeling that most employees want to retire as early as possible to "get out of the rat race." I am happy to have had nearly forty-three years with what was a great company!

Another element began to assert itself, and clients were beginning to see this as competition. Perhaps it was because we had begun as an engineering service group for Henry's new industries. Henry and his various managers expected full service from the engineers, and Kaiser Engineers was structured to deliver it. In the beginning our chief engineer was also chief engineer of Henry's new companies. We were expected to do everything to get each company into full production. As a result, we did much of want other companies do for themselves. For a time after we began to do jobs for outside companies; our clients appreciated this approach, which was known as "turnkey."

At some point, companies began to think they could save more by employing people to do some of the work on a new project. They could buy materials and equipment, let contracts, initiate project controls, and do other things we normally did. The engineer had only to prepare drawings and specifications and then provide some level of construction inspection. This meant an engineer should cut his fee and charge a lower overhead percentage.

We continued to do our turnkey work, but we had to cut fees and pare our overhead as a result of the changes affecting the engineering business. I have always maintained that the companies following the foregoing practice could point with pride at how they had saved on engineering costs while they buried a substantial cost in their own payroll.

I will close this chapter by noting the effect of politics. Some engineering firms have managed to place a high executive in responsible government positions, while others have put high ranking government officials on their payroll after the official retired from government service. The Kaisers never did that. Was it a mistake? We'll never know; the die was probably cast well before the year of the falling sky.

Chapter Twenty-Nine

Chief Engineer

The decision to accept the position of vice president and chief engineer, made with the help of your grandmother, was communicated to the president of Kaiser Engineers, James McCloud, first thing next morning, and I began preparations for the move to my new office. This would be the seventh since 1950, and would be the next to last. It was located in the new Ordway Building, named after A. B. Ordway, Henry Kaiser's first, most respected, and longest-term employee. Just across the street was the Kaiser Center. A passageway above the street connected the two facilities.

I will interrupt this tale for a moment to tell you a story from the early days of Ord and Henry. They had boarded a train after submitting a bid for a new job, and as it gathered speed Henry suddenly remembered they had forgotten something. Whatever it was, it was important enough for the two men to jump from the moving train and, in spite of skinned hands and knees, they ran back to attend to the problem. They were much younger in those days, but it is an example of a determination to succeed. Ord, as we all called him, was a warm, friendly, and unpretentious man, much respected by everyone.

My new quarters in a spacious corner office gave me a view of Lake Merritt and, in the opposite direction, a bit of San Francisco. Except for a secretary, who had left with my predecessor, a ready-made staff awaited me. They were a fine group of people and deserve a few words of description, which, I hope, will give you a picture of our engineering office.

More than seven hundred engineers were at that time working in several locations, including Chicago, Pittsburgh, Sydney, Australia, London, and Oakland, California. The offices outside Oakland were under the

general supervision of the respective local managers, reporting monthly to
Oakland. In my office were ten people with whom I had daily contact. This
included six discipline chiefs whose duties included maintenance of up-to-
date procedures and methods, consultation on difficult problems, and personnel review and performance evaluation. The six represented the Civil,
Mechanical, Structural, Electrical, Piping, and Architectural disciplines,
and were the most capable and experienced in the company. I came to
respect them all. Now, years later, I still enjoy lunches with the retirement
group that we call the Dinosaurs, including four of the members from the
old discipline chief bunch.

There was a routine of weekly meetings, schedule reviews, monthly
progress reports, three-year forecasts, and management meetings. At lunch
on the top floor of the Kaiser Center, where I had been a member since
1972, there was the opportunity to chat with managers of other divisions
within our company as well as with members of other Kaiser companies. I
remember it fondly for the excellent food, great views of both Oakland and
San Francisco, and the lively exchange of ideas and information. For a long
time I hung onto a binder containing photos and a brief bios of each member of the executive dinning room. It may still be in the pile of memorabilia.

From time to time I was called upon to assist in presentations to
potential clients, and I enjoyed the opportunity to stay in touch with various
project groups. Now time was slipping quickly by, and, almost before I
knew it, we were into 1979. Work had been going smoothly, but a little
undercurrent of unrest began to stir the waters. It was not long before I
learned from a member of our marketing department that meetings between
the second in command at Raymond and one of our vice presidents were
taking place in San Francisco without the knowledge of our management.
I never knew why I was informed of this, and have often wondered about it.
There was a risk in babbling about clandestine meetings, and I guessed a
few others had been informed. I remained mum, but I was sure somewhere
a tongue would wag. I turned sixty-four in June and still the waters had not
been ruffled, although the storm was gathering strength. Perhaps a signal
light blinked and I chose to ignore it. As I try to remember now, there must
have been a twinge of premonition, but I can't be certain.

In early July a memo came down from management asking all vice
presidents to consider the possible workload in the next two to three years
and prepare a list of personnel we could let go, those we would like to
retain, and those who were essential to the company's future. A difficult

task; I finally completed it by numbers rather than by names because I felt that changes in assignments could shift names from one category to another. I sat back and awaited my turn in the bucket, and it was not long in coming. I was thinking about what other VPs might be saying when the Raymond representative walked into my office. We exchanged pleasantries and then got down to the business at hand. It was not the business I had expected.

Our meeting opened with what I thought was an attempt at humor. "What do you think would happen if Mr. Management 'C' were to leave the company?" Thinking to answer in kind, I said, "I guess it's the same as if any of us left. Like pulling a finger out of a bucket of water; the hole is quickly filled!" The quiz continued; did I think Mr. "W" in accounting was trying to build an empire? Did I think Mr. "S" in personnel was not competent to handle the job? Realizing this was no fun and games, I felt a rising anger and said, "Your questions are not appropriate, and I will not dignify them with answers." The discussion ended with a curt nod and a baleful glare.

For long moments I stared at the wall, thoughts chasing each other around my brain as I tried to sort out what I had just heard. I finally concluded something was going on that I didn't like, and I'd better nose around to see if I could find out what it was. Talking with other VPs revealed that they were as puzzled as I. We didn't have long to wait. A few days later all the interviews appeared in a memo, copied to both Raymond and Kaiser Management. A little sleuthing revealed that one interviewee had been sharply critical of our management. With a bit more nosing, it was found that the critic was none other than the VP that had been attending the clandestine meetings in San Francisco. A dirty game of intrigue, we all thought. A week later, that person showed up in my office and asked if he could sit for a while and cool off. I said "Sure, cool off from what? How about a Coke?" Sipping the drink, he told me he had just come from a hot session with "those guys on eighteen" (KE management offices). Finally, after a "thanks," he left. No one was surprised when a memo circulated announcing his transfer to the Sydney office.

I have never been sure whether the move to Sydney was volunteered or ordered. It was later when I was in Sydney that I picked up a few more pieces of the puzzle. Talking with some of our people in that office, I learned that top brass visitors only came from Raymond; no one from Oakland showed up. I was told that the Raymond executive had been lavishly

entertained each of the two times he was in Australia and have always wondered why our brass never deigned to visit. Whatever the reason, it was not
long before another piece of the puzzle came plummeting into our in-trays.
It hit all of us by surprise because it was the announcement of the return of
the transferred (banished?) VP, now with the title executive vice president.
That title had never before been used, and it became the subject of much
speculation in the ranks. The full import of it was yet to come!

Meanwhile I was growing increasingly uneasy as I watched the gathering storm clouds. It seemed the ground beneath our feet was getting
shaky, and for the first time RETIREMENT entered my thoughts. Because
of my years of service I had the option of taking my retirement money in a
lump sum and, in addition, a fair sum had accumulated in a separate savings
account. Would that be jeopardized if things came unglued? Would I miss
the contact with friends and associates I had worked with for nearly forty
years? What would it be like to wake up in the morning and not have a job?
What about medical coverage? Would it continue for life as the fine print
said? There were so many other questions. Finally, I enlisted the aid of my
best advisor, your grandmother, and we sifted pros and cons. Pros won and
the next day I prepared a letter of resignation. It was around the middle of
December. My secretary typed and folded the letter in an envelope and
handed it to me with a questioning look. I told her she might like to stay on
but if not I had already done a little checking and there was a spot open if
she wanted to move.

With the letter in hand I went down to the bridge connecting Ordway
Building to the Kaiser Center. As I crossed, it occurred to me that in a couple of weeks I would be walking the bridge for the last time. A sobering
thought! Forty-one years of work coming to an end on New Year's Eve.
Would it be like switching off a bright light and stepping into a black hole?
I cannot describe the emotions I felt that day. Perhaps you two will experience them one day as you retire, and will remember.

On the eighteenth floor of the Kaiser Center I found that the president,
James McCloud, would not be back from a trip until next week. I stepped
over to Vic Cole's office only to find that he, too, was out but was expected
back around three. Handing the secretary the letter, I returned to my office
feeling a bit deflated. Shortly after five Vic called. He wanted to talk to me,
but, because of previously scheduled meetings, suggested lunch in the
executive dining room the next day.

At lunch Vic said he was sorry to see me leave but thought he understood. I was surprised he knew that Fluor, the big Southern California engineering company, had approached me asking if I would be interested in joining that firm to help set up an aluminum division. Although headquartered in Southern California, Fluor had a large office in Redwood City where the aluminum branch would be located. A meeting with the president of Fluor in Southern California led me to seriously consider the job, even though it meant Grandmother and I would move to Redwood City for at least four years. Near the end of our lunch meeting Vic offered me a contract as a consultant. I was grateful for this opportunity and accepted. Later I called Fluor to thank them for the offer and to give them the name of a person whom I felt would be interested in the job. This was the individual investigating the possibility of an ESOP, as you will recall I mentioned before. He got the job.

As the year ended, I cleaned out my office and moved to a new one in the Kaiser Center. This was to be the final office move of my years with Kaiser. There I would spend the next three years on a variety of work. My schedule was at least three days a week, but it often required four and five days. On the several trips overseas it was seven days. What was important is that the consulting was a transition from a job to full-time retirement. I received my retirement and savings monies in cash and put both in a rollover. Maybe what was more important was that I felt I was still a part of the great company I had gone to work for forty-one years ago, at a time when we were all part of a family we felt loyalty toward as the company did for us. Today that loyalty no longer exists, and employees no longer feel confidant they will have any kind of job security. How fortunate I was to work in those better times and to choose my own time to retire! Now there was a consulting job to do.

There are many ways to look at retirement. What do you do when, waking in the morning, there is no job waiting? Some are terrified of an uncertain future, and others are depressed by the feeling they are being thrown into the discard pile. Will you lose contact with all the people you've worked with over the years? What will it be like to sit in a rocking chair watching birds at the feeder?

Fortunately, I had none of those concerns. As a consultant, I could still make a contribution as well as maintain contact with people I had known and respected for many years. Even as I heard the sound of thunder in the distance I looked forward to a new adventure, and I was still in the business I loved. Without knowing the future, I was anxious to see what I could make of it.

Chapter Thirty

Consultant

*T*here is a definition of the title of this chapter that you should know. *A consultant is anyone fifty or more miles from home.* Obviously, I did not qualify under that definition, living only six miles from my office in the Kaiser Center. On the other hand, the business card prepared for me read "Consultant," so I will use that title even though much of what I did in the next three years was a continuation of work I had previously been doing. In addition, the three day-a-week job gave Grandmother and me long weekends, many of which were spent at the mountain house east of Jackson, California. We could also manage to drive to Ashland, Oregon, see some plays, and still have time to spend a night at Gold Beach on the Oregon coast before the drive home.

A beginning of what are known as "The Golden Years?" Not just yet! There was soon enough work to take five days a week. There was the project management manual I had started two years ago and requests to help with proposals and presentations. A trip to Sydney to assist with estimates, schedules, and a proposal for a plant in Brisbane took two weeks, and upon my return there were other tasks requiring attention. I finally completed work on the project manual, including a five-part video program. In the next year and a half I presented the video to our US offices, as well as in Perth and Sydney in Australia. Grandmother went along on all the trips, which were seven in number. On three projects I organized and made presentations, and we were lucky enough to land all of them. The last one was a large aluminum plant to be built in Australia for the Canadian aluminum company ALCAN. I recall a phone call from the person I had recommended to Fluor. He was then heading their aluminum division and wanted me to know that Fluor expected to get a go-ahead on the job sometime next week. Two days later we were asked to meet in Montreal to sign a contract. I never called my friend back.

We had completed preliminary layouts, estimates, and schedules, and obtained approval from ALCAN before transferring key people to Sydney. Four were in Sydney and two were on the way when we got notice to stop work. The great aluminum balloon of the sixties and seventies had burst!

With the reverberations from the aluminum crash still echoing down the hallways, other things began to happen. Both the president and number two man of Kaiser Engineers were retiring! Both were highly regarded managers, well liked, and each had been nearly forty years with Kaiser. That was not all. The man whom Raymond had named executive vice president would be the new president! Now events began to follow in rapid sequence.

Raymond, alarmed by a suspected takeover, quickly formed an E.S.O.P., urging employees to invest their savings in the stock to finance his plan. About this time, the business of engineering was changing. Work became tough to get and fees and overhead markups had to be cut to remain competitive, thus reducing profits. In the midst of this swirl of problems, something unethical or illegal took place and Kaiser Engineers was once again up for sale. I cannot tell you the details of the fiasco. Suffice it to say that it was the beginning of the end for the Kaiser Engineers I knew. Even today there remains an enduring dislike for the Raymond management and the then-president of Kaiser Engineers. I had to watch all these events unfold from my comfortable position of having already retired, and it was not pleasant.

Kaiser Engineers was purchased by ICF, a firm specializing in hazardous waste cleanup. It was not a good match and it was not long before Kaiser was once more up for sale. By this time the division's debt had risen to around $60 million, impossible to manage. Banks holding the notes concluded that no one would buy the company with such debt and decided to reduce it by more than half, thus facilitating the final sale.

I was busy during all this flap, but it had become apparent that a great belt-tightening would have to occur. I was prepared when I got a call telling me the company could no longer hire outside consultants. I spent a half a day saying goodbye to friends and associates. Walking over the bridge between buildings I remember thinking it was truly the last time. I was now absolutely, completely, 100 percent retired and I knew I could handle it!

On a cold, wet day at the end of 1982, I called Grandmother, asking her to come pick me up because I had returned the credit card, building pass, and keys to the company car. "I'm on my way," was her quick response. "Now we'll have plenty of time for ourselves." The ride home was a happy one and, in spite of the rain, we stopped for a bottle of champagne on the way. Dinner that night was a festive affair as we drank toasts to ourselves and to the future.

I would like to tell you things improved for Kaiser Engineers but, sadly, they did not; they worsened. The Raymond E.S.O.P. failed; some cried foul play. Many of my friends lost money when the stock plummeted, and a great anger swept through the company. The executive vice president became president, and a flood of terminations were handed out. They were not gracefully handled. The new president left after the third sale, and without the reputed golden parachute. Many were not sorry to see that happen. The name Kaiser is no longer associated with Engineers, Gypsum, Cement, Aluminum, Steel, Sand and Gravel, and Aircraft and Electronics. All that remains is the Kaiser Permanente Health Foundation. Perhaps that, alone, is a fitting tribute to Henry Kaiser.

I still feel a deep sense of loss for the great company I worked with for so many years. There will probably never be another quite like it.

Chapter Thirty-One

1982-2005

These years held many rewards for your grandmother and me. It was a time of complete freedom for us; freedom to do what we wanted whenever a mood struck. As I sit at the word processor today, so many memories run through my mind that it is difficult to select those to fill the final pages of *Tales*. Except for four significant events, these twenty-three years can be called by the time-worn phrase "The Golden Years."

I have given much thought to how I should finish this story. There were two ways to do it. Would it be better to interrupt the narrative as each of the events occurred, or should I describe them all in succession before getting on with the more pleasant conclusion? After my computer cycles through screen saver and screen shutdown I am still not sure, but have chosen to relate the four critical events up front.

THE KNEES.

In 1984, at age sixty-nine, my right knee was giving me fits. Climbing stairs was a problem. Cortisone shots helped, but only for a week. Finally, the doctor said only an operation would solve the problem. After a period of ingesting iron pills and storing two units of my own blood, I was ready. A fourteen-inch incision gave the surgeon access to the knee joint where a new steel ball-and-socket joint was installed. A week in the hospital followed, where a machine, strapped to the leg, continually moved the joint. That was followed by another week of physical therapy, and then I was home on crutches with a set of exercises to do for the next six weeks. The exercises fell under the category of "If it doesn't hurt, it doesn't help."

Two years later the left knee failed and it was, as Yogi Berra says, déjà vu all over again. That the joints are still working today, twenty years later, is proof that the post-surgery exercises are important. What I could no longer manage were the long hikes we had enjoyed in the past. In the mountains, we took short walks into the forest and to a picnic site, but no longer was I the ten-mile hiker of the past. I was down in the dumps, grumbling about my fate, when Grandmother said, "Don't get upset, we've still got a thousand things to keep us busy." She was right, as usual!

We took many car trips to visit friends, and we enjoyed the Symphony and other events. We spent time visiting Lori and family in Texas, Colorado, and Chicago, and we celebrated holidays and birthdays with family, at home in Oakland and in the mountains. We took relaxing trips to Oregon and Carmel. I know you granddaughters have many memories of time we spent on vacations with each of you.

After a couple of additions to our mountain home twenty miles east of Jackson, I found myself with a lot of work to do. Now I had a workshop and a darkroom, both with finishing work to do. In the shop, I built work benches and installed a professional craftsman's table. In the darkroom, the best one I ever had, I built cabinets, work counters, a sink, and a ventilating system.

During all this time, Grandmother was having a wonderful time making strawberry jam from berries we bought at a roadside stand, and making crabapple jelly from the fruit of a tree we had planted a few years before. She also put up pickled crabapples, reserved for the Thanksgiving feast we enjoyed each year.

The knees still work, although they ache a bit when the weather turns cold in winter. They will last as long as I need them, I think.

HEART ATTACK, DECEMBER 2000

The weather man had predicted a cold snap in the Sierras and I had not done any winterizing at the mountain house. I usually had the job done by Thanksgiving, and here it was mid December with no winter protection. I can't recall why I had delayed, but now there was no time to waste. A quick job of packing and we were on the way. Arriving too late to start work, we had dinner and went off to bed. With a window half open, we heard wind brushing through the trees and felt the chill. I knew there was no time to waste!

Next morning it was clear the weather prediction had been correct. An outside thermometer read 36°, and the blowing wind made it feel colder. Without stopping for lunch, the job was finished by four that afternoon and I went upstairs to rest and warm up by the fire Grandmother had built.

Soon I began to feel a pressure in my chest. It was as if a giant hand was squeezing me. I recall saying something about not feeling all that great. Without another word Grandmother called a paramedic ambulance. After a preliminary check I was driven to the Jackson hospital for more tests. From there I was taken to Sacramento, where a doctor skilled in the procedure I needed was a resident surgeon. I still remember the awful dreams I experienced while under the anesthesia. Everyone was lying to me and wanted to do something I didn't want. I don't recall what it was, but I fought desperately. Awakening from the anesthesia, I found my arms and legs taped to the gurney. You will remember that, Vanessa. You were one of those I could not trust!

I will always be grateful for the immediate support of my family. Vanessa came in from San Francisco, Lori flew in from Chicago, and Serin hurried back from a vacation in Arizona. I am certain that played a major part in a quick recovery. Even though some parts of the affair are lost in the kaleidoscope of those days, I knew your grandmother was with me every minute. She didn't flutter about; she was just there as I knew she would be. When I think about it today, there is a lump in my throat and I wish I could hold her and thank her again for the love and devotion.

Heeding the doctor's advice, I began an exercise program. This included a bending and stretching session before breakfast and, after breakfast had settled, a mile walk, rain or shine. Before bed I did more bending and stretching. With this regimen it was not long before I felt fit again.

SALE OF 6423 ASCOT DRIVE.

In 1940, Grandmother and I lived in a rented home on Fruitvale Avenue, two blocks north of McArthur Boulevard in Oakland. Your mother, Serin, was born while we were there, Vanessa. From there we moved to Ardley Avenue where we were living when your mother, Lori, joined our family, Ariel. Seven years later all of us were on the way to Argentina, where I supervised engineering for the Kaiser auto plant in Cordoba for two years. Almost immediately after our return from Argentina we were notified that the Ardley home was within the right of way of the new McArthur Freeway and we had to move.

What led us to the Piedmont Pines area above Montclair, a location I must have thought too pricey, is lost in memory. The fact is we found a home where we were to live for the next forty four years. Built two years before our purchase, it was at the end of a two-hundred-foot driveway with no possibility of construction beyond. It offered a view of the Bay, including the Golden Gate and Richmond-San Rafael bridges. Between us and the closest house out on Ascot there was nothing but a pathway through the trees leading to an old patio on our lot. Homes above and below were screened by trees and other growth. It was quiet and we all loved it.

Some time around 1950, there was activity next door. Trees were being yanked out ruthlessly with cables and bulldozers. A house followed and the Mew family moved in. What wonderful neighbors they were. George and Martha brought four children, Barry and three beautiful girls. We attended the weddings of all four. Now and then we attended the Chinese church in Berkeley. George and Martha moved to an apartment in 1994 and Grandmother and I were sorry to see them leave.

In 1968, a fire burned our home to the ground, taking all our possessions in the conflagration. We were taken in by a neighbor, Eleanor Moran, and learned what a caring friend can mean at a difficult time. We had dinners in elegant style in the formal dining room of her big old home, and we had a room and bath to ourselves. For years after we would stop by on our way home for a chat and coffee. Every couple of weeks we would call and tell her to join us for dinner on the waterfront. I believe it was on Thanksgiving Day in 1980 that Eleanor passed away from lung cancer, a victim of cigarettes. Such a wonderful friend. Such a terrible loss!

While our home was being rebuilt we rented a home on Castle Drive, and I recall it was there Lori and I built a television set and a hi-fi amplifier from kits. We were glad to be back to Ascot Drive at the end of September, 1968.

We rebuilt on the original foundations, but I redesigned the interior, giving us more open space. In addition, I added a five-foot extension to the dinning room and garage. The added garage space gave me room for a well equipped shop and a small darkroom. These two things were the most painful to give up when we moved, because I had built many pieces of furniture, music-center cabinets, and parts for the big stereo speakers that were in the cathedral ceiling. The very last project in the workshop was two hope chests for you, my granddaughters. They were a work of love and I hope you will use them for many years.

From the windows along the full length of the living room and the dining room, Grandmother and I could watch the weather out over the Bay. It was an always-changing scene. We could watch a storm, distant at first, but then shouldering its way through the Golden Gate, moving toward us until the Bay was a leaden gray and clouds had engulfed us with a burst of wind and splatter of rain. And the fog! Sandburg's short little poem describes it so well: "the fog comes in on little cat feet." We would watch little tendrils of that fog spill over the hills near Tamalpais like the cat's feet and run down in a sea of vapor until they flooded into the Bay. From there the fog followed an unvarying path to the Berkeley auto ferry pier, where, as the Bay filled, the mist marched up University Avenue until bay and city were lost beneath a soft blanket. "Sits quietly looking over harbor and city" until the sun burns it away, "and moves on." I had made a sketch of the Golden Gate Bridge half-enveloped in fog with Sandburg's poem penned beneath. That sketch was also lost in the 1968 fire.

Sunsets were another joy. Sometimes we just watched the last tip of light being extinguished as the sun slid below the hills, or the glorious panorama of brilliant colors form over the bay as they slowly faded with the coming of darkness. I miss it all!

At the end of 2000, we were slowing down. Your mothers were pushing us to sell Ascot and move to an apartment or senior residence where life would be easier. It is hard for me to describe how difficult this time was for us. Much that was collected over a lifetime of living was given away, donated, or sold for a fraction of the original price. And finally the books, photos, china and crystal, a few pieces of furniture, and other things we could not bear to part with were piled into a van and locked away in a cold, distant warehouse. With reluctance, we sold our wonderful home and moved into a two-bedroom apartment at Grand Lake Gardens Independent Living in July of 2001, just after my eighty-sixth birthday. Grandmother's eighty-sixth would be at the end of October.

I never thought inanimate objects could evoke so many memories. I can close my eyes and recall every detail of the home on Ascot Drive, the speakers in the ceiling, my workshop and darkroom, redoing the bathrooms and the rumpus room. I will never forget Grandmother's love of the big, open kitchen where she could stand before the sink and watch the morning sun light her collection of tiny colored-glass vases. I am reminded of the prisms suspended near the living room windows; I had found them in a war surplus store in Washington, D.C., while there in 1961. I had arranged five in a circle beneath a Plexiglas frame. In the late afternoon sun the beautiful spectrum of colors was displayed on the walls of the living room. It is difficult to describe the emotional intensity those colors imparted and it was always a symbol of an end of another day, to be watched as a gift from the sun. There are special memories of Grandmother and me in our bathrobes having our ritual Christmas breakfast before a blazing fireplace with presents on the floor around us. I confess to feeling a deep longing for all that has passed.

THE TERRIBLE CRASH

In June of 2003 I lost my driver's license because of failing eyesight (macular degeneration). The day I got that notification was a dark day for me. Grandmother took over the driving and, in spite of being out of practice, seemingly regained her old skills. I wonder now how hard it was for her.

On December 11, 2003, we had shopped at Safeway Grocery and were on the way to pick out a Christmas tree. As we exited the Safeway parking lot in Montclair we were hit by a huge truck and sent careening into a stone and glass storefront. The crash deployed air bags and tightened seat belts, no doubt saving us from fatal injury, but the impact of the bags caused traumatic bruising. Taken to Summit Hospital, I have no memory of the next two weeks, although I know now I was sedated, on oxygen most of the time, and eventually I had a stomach feeding tube installed, as I was unable to swallow. On Christmas day I was able to understand that Grandmother was back in the apartment, under twenty-four hour care. Not long after Christmas, I was taken by ambulance to convalescent care at Piedmont Gardens. On New Year's Eve, I was returned to the hospital with internal bleeding. I spent six hours listening to the rush of emergency cases before a room became available. I did not know yet that Grandmother had also returned to the hospital that same night with serious internal system failures.

I was wheeled down to visit Grandmother twice in the hospital before I went back to Piedmont Gardens for physical therapy. I was told Grandmother would soon join me there and a bed was prepared next to mine. Her release from the hospital was delayed, and I went back to the apartment on January twenty-seventh to begin my home convalescence. It wasn't until mid-February that Grandmother was released from the hospital to Piedmont Gardens. I was well enough to visit her every day there, and remember the day I said to her, "Butch, I want you to know I love you very much, and I want you to get well and come back to the apartment with me." She smiled that big beautiful smile and I reached down and kissed her, not aware that it would be the last time. Soon after, I had to admit there was no hope she would ever rejoin me. I could only stand there and watch the woman I had loved for sixty-four years slowly fade from my life forever. You cannot imagine the anguish I felt in those last days. On the third of March, 2004, she left us. Her ashes are buried beneath the tree she most loved up at Mace. I cannot stop the tears as I write this.

END OF THIS CHAPTER.

The sixty-four years of my marriage to your grandmother was a beautiful and important part of my life. Her love, devotion, and support were always there for me. I sometimes wonder what my life would have been had I not proposed to that beautiful young woman in 1938 as we sat on the steps of the Alameda house.

Grandmother and I had twenty-one years after the last consulting work of 1982 to spend all the time together doing a thousand things that would take a very long chapter to describe. Only one thing remains to be said, and that is a word about our sixtieth anniversary. I wanted to do something special to show Grandmother how much those sixty years had meant to me. I decided the best way to do this was to reaffirm the marriage vows we had made on January 9, 1940. We did this at the Montclair Presbyterian Church with friends and family present. The food, photos, and flowers done by our family made the occasion one I will never forget, and I am certain Grandmother never did either. (See illustration.)

My story has been a long time in telling. The writing of it began around 1972, thirty-five years ago! Sometimes it sat untouched for long periods, and I am not sure why. Your grandmother and I wanted you to see the different world in which we began our lives. Now you and I have come to the end of the story living in the same world together. I end *Tales from a Grandfather* with the wish that your life may be as wonderful and fulfilling as mine has been. May your hope chests be full of memories that you will share with those who follow you. All my love, Grandpa Bill.

Epilogue

I had a rush of emotions as I came to the end of the last chapter in *Tales from a Grandfather* on the fifth of October in 2005. I sat staring at the last few words until the screen saver erased them, and, finally, the power saver left only a black monitor and a jumble of thoughts rattling around in my head where a few floated to the surface for me to see.

First there was pride that I had stuck with this story for thirty-three years. Next was the satisfaction that I had provided you with a narrative of my life and times. Finally, I was happy to have accomplished what your grandmother wanted me to do back in 1972. Last, there is the feeling of losing a friend because the manuscript has been such a part of my life for a long time.

You may ask how I came to be an engineer, and I think it came about as a result of three experiences in my early life: the predawn sound of an engine coming to life and the sight of that big tractor, driven by my Dad, pulling a harvester on the way to a wheat field; my first view of a steam locomotive when Grandfather took me down to watch the morning train come in to town; and, a few years later, working in my Dad's garage and machine shop. It all culminated in a love of machinery and equipment I did not realize at the time. Ultimately, the years on the survey party during summer vacations were what led me to enroll in an engineering curriculum in college. Looking back, I cannot imagine any profession other than engineering. It has been a great forty-four years of excitement and adventure.

As is true with all of us, I have had help from others throughout my career and I want to thank them for all they have done. I particularly wish to offer my sincere thanks to my friends and associates from Kaiser Engineers. We have had a long ride together.

Now it is time to dedicate these stories to the three most important people in my life. First are my parents, Liberta C. and William B. Ball. They instilled in me a curiosity and desire to learn everything I could about this world and the universe. They never allowed me to go to class with unfinished homework. They often applied well-deserved discipline at the end of a willow switch or piece of kindling from the wood box on the front screen porch. Above all, they had the wisdom to allow me the freedom to explore the fields, woods, and river around my hometown, a privilege for which I will be forever grateful. We never thank our parents enough for what they do for us, but I hope mine were rewarded by my love for them.

The last dedication is to my wife, your grandmother. It was she who suggested these *Tales* in the first place, and she was critic and editor for most of them. It is hard for me to put my feelings into words as I remember those sixty-four years of our beautiful marriage. Just when I fell in love with the beautiful woman who was to be your grandmother I cannot be certain, but it was, no doubt, happening in 1936 as we celebrated the Cal/Stanford big game at Brookdale Lodge. That date lingers in my memory as second only to January 9, 1940, the year of our marriage, more completely described in Chapter 17.

I dedicate *Tales from a Grandfather* to the memory of Helen L. Ball, who was always there to offer me love, devotion, and support every day of our long lives together. I have a profound sense of loss and sadness that your grandmother is not here to celebrate the completion of these *Tales*. She would have been so happy.

I will prepare for you a collection of little stories, musings, and thoughts I have been writing. Maybe I will finish *Worm Holes*, a story I have been working on for some time. There is still much to do, and I like to think of it as Robert Frost says in the last line of his lovely little poem, *A Road Less Traveled*, "For I have miles to go before I sleep."

I leave you with the wish that your hope chests may be filled with memories of a wonderful life. All my love, Grandpa Bill.

60th Anniversary—Helen & Bill